"With lilting prose and sparkling insight, Armstrong draws us into the spiritual riches of medieval Christianity. He shows how the era managed to combine faith and reason, spirit and nature, health and healing, joy and discipline, and Word and sacrament in a way that all Christians, and especially evangelicals, acutely need today. Armstrong uses the insights of C. S. Lewis and other modern interpreters to shine a light on that long-past yet still remarkably relevant era. This book will serve equally well in college, seminary, and church education classrooms."

—**Grant Wacker**, Duke Divinity School

"Evangelicals have come a long way in the past twenty years in recovering the richness of the Christian past. There is still a long way to go, and this book takes a big stride in the right direction. In *Medieval Wisdom for Modern Christians*, Chris Armstrong offers a convincing rationale for why evangelical believers are quick to reject the Middle Ages but slow to appreciate the era's theological and spiritual riches. Using the wisdom of C. S. Lewis as a point of entry, Armstrong unpacks the material and sacramental world of the medieval church, demonstrating why such dated material is not only relevant but also much needed in the life of the evangelical church today. As Lewis knew well, the way to the future lies in the past, and Armstrong provides a fascinating glimpse into what will be gained from exploring medieval wisdom. This is a must-read for anyone who cares about the evangelical church's future."

—**Greg Peters**, Biola University; author of *The Story of Monasticism*

"Armstrong's approach to introducing twenty-first-century Christians to the rich resources of medieval and monastic wisdom is ingenious. He uses C. S. Lewis to invite us into a conversation with other contemporaries who have found that this oft-neglected period of Christian history provides the kind of *embodied* and *holistic* spiritual life that is needed as a remedy for today's gnostic, individualistic, and shallow spirituality. The reader who knows little about the medieval period will end up with an appetite whetted for more and with enough wisdom to begin practicing a deeper faith."

—**Dennis Okholm**, Azusa Pacific University; author of *Dangerous Passions, Deadly Sins: Learning from the Psychology of Ancient Monks*

"With a searching evaluation of his own evangelical leanings and inspired by the discerning medievalism of his spiritual mentor C. S. Lewis, Chris Armstrong takes us on a delightful tour through the insights of medieval Christians that have most profited him. With Armstrong's sparkling prose, the journey never turns arcane or becomes tiresome, and it leaves us with many treasures to ponder."

—**Robert B. Kruschwitz**, Institute for Faith and Learning,
Baylor University

"Accessible and engaging, *Medieval Wisdom for Modern Christians* is a wonderful introduction to our neglected Christian tradition for all those who feel something is missing in the modern church. It is also a real treat for fans of C. S. Lewis."

—**Devin Brown**, Asbury University; author of *A Life Observed: A Spiritual Biography of C. S. Lewis*

"Chris Armstrong knows what ails modern American Protestantism, and the right medicines, he says, are available on the pharmacy shelves of the Middle Ages. Here is an excellent introduction to medieval spirituality, philosophy, theology, and Christian practice, which offer strong medicines for serious conditions."

—**David Neff**, former editor in chief, *Christianity Today*
and *Christian History*

# MEDIEVAL WISDOM

## ——— *for* ———

# MODERN CHRISTIANS

FINDING AUTHENTIC FAITH

◆ IN A FORGOTTEN AGE ◆

WITH C. S. LEWIS

# CHRIS R. ARMSTRONG

**Brazos** Press

*a division of Baker Publishing Group*

www.BrazosPress.com

Published by Brazos Press
a division of Baker Publishing Group
P.O. Box 6287, Grand Rapids, MI 49516-6287
www.brazospress.com

Printed and bound by CPI Group (UK) Ltd, Croydon, CR0 4YY

Library of Congress Cataloging-in-Publication Data
Names: Armstrong, Chris R. (Christopher Robert), 1963– author.
Title: Medieval wisdom for modern Christians : finding authentic faith in a forgotten age with
   C. S. Lewis / Chris R. Armstrong.
Description: Grand Rapids : Brazos Press, 2016. | Includes bibliographical references and index.
Identifiers: LCCN 2015047192 | ISBN 9781587433788 (pbk. : alk. paper)
Subjects: LCSH: Church history—Middle Ages, 600-1500. | Christian literature.
Classification: LCC BR162.3 .A76 2016 | DDC 270.3—dc23
LC record available at http://lccn.loc.gov/2015047192

To my mother, Barbara Armstrong, and to my father, Stan Armstrong,
whose long-ago suppertime readings of stories from C. S. Lewis
and other medieval-smitten moderns started all of this.

To the Duke University Inklings Group of the late '90s
and early aughts—Andy and Quita Sauerwein,
Edwin and Jennifer Woodruff Tait, Neil and LaVonne Carlson,
Jennifer Trafton Peterson, Brian Averette,
and other occasional attendees—who read to each other
some of the same stories I had first heard read by my father,
as well as some we had written ourselves.

And to my wife, Sharon, and children,
Kate, Caleb, Grace, Ross, and John Allen:
may they each find wisdom in the writings
of Christ-following sages from other eras.

# Contents

# 1

# My Angle of Approach

I grew up in a home where my father, a theology professor, read to my two brothers and me the delightfully neomedieval stories of C. S. Lewis, J. R. R. Tolkien, George MacDonald, and others.[1] These were influences in shaping not only my imagination but also the faith I would find as a young adult. From the moment Christianity became my heart language, I searched its vocabulary and traditions for the angles of vision first opened to me in those early literary stirrings. Where I found these angles, they tended to help me move forward in my faith. Where I did not find them, I wondered why not.

Since then, I've never lost my fascination with either those modern authors or the medieval world they loved. Of course, they sometimes romanticized that world. But they also, as we'll see, took it quite seriously as a source of wisdom for living. During my doctoral program in American church history at Duke University, a band of friends formed an "Inklings" group. Together we read and discussed those same medieval-influenced authors, reaching for the older Christian wisdom from which they drew.

After Duke, I took a job editing *Christian History* magazine at Christianity Today. While there, I edited issues and wrote articles on Lewis and Tolkien, as well as G. K. Chesterton (author of two splendid biographies of important medieval Christians), Dorothy L. Sayers (translator of Dante and medieval French literature), and others. At the same time, I was able to continue my exploration—begun in graduate school—of such medieval thinkers as Benedict of Nursia (ca. 480–543/47), Bernard of Clairvaux (1090–1153), and the scholastic precursors of the scientific revolution. In those years, I began work on my first book, *Patron Saints for Postmoderns*,[2] in which I explore the medieval worlds and worldviews of Gregory the Great (540–604), Dante Alighieri (ca. 1265–1321), and Margery Kempe (ca. 1373–after 1438), among others. All of this began to prepare me to see beyond modern caricatures of the medieval church to the animating Christian spirit of that age.

But at the same time, I was becoming more and more acutely aware of certain realities of the church today—especially its evangelical Protestant forms—that make it hard for modern Christians truly to receive "medieval wisdom."

When in 2004 I flew from Chicagoland to Minnesota to interview for a church history position at Bethel Seminary, the interviewers asked what period I thought my evangelical students would most need to hear about. I did not yet entirely know why, but I blurted out "the Middle Ages."

## A One-Sided Story

I soon found ample evidence, both negative and positive, to back up that impulsive answer. In my first year at Bethel, the evangelical-authored text-book I chose to use with my classes proved embarrassingly incomplete and biased in its treatment of medieval faith. Even after I found better sources and began sharing the good as well as the bad and the ugly in my lectures on the period, some of my students seemed unable to surmount their preconceptions. Many ignored the warning attached to my standard essay question on the lessons we can learn from the medieval church ("Do not limit yourself to negative examples"). They listed only parodies and partial truths (the state ruled the church, money corrupted the church and prevented it from helping the people, the Bible was taken away from the people, the monastics failed to evangelize or engage the culture, etc.). Slowly, as I learned how to better teach the period, some of my students began to find rich resources in the disciplines of the monastics, the devotion of the mystics, the intellectual passion of the scholastics, and much more. Formerly suspicious of all things medieval, these students began to discover and value some of the wisdom this book points to.

Increasingly, though, I wondered about the hole in modern popular accounts of church history, particularly the glaring omission of the story of medieval faith except as a cautionary tale. Why did my students and friends so often seem to assume that the church apostatized after it gained cultural influence in the time of Constantine (fourth century) and returned to God only after the sixteenth-century Reformation (or perhaps even only after the evangelical revivals of the eighteenth century)? Why this dismissal of more than a millennium of church history—more than *half* of the time between Christ and today?

I don't deny that the terrain of the medieval church seems alien to most of us. Before us, relics peer out from within gilded boxes, and the devout approach them as conduits to divine power. Above us, saints hover supernaturally, and the earthbound plead for their intercession. At the high altar, the priest, with his back to the congregation, performs an elaborate sacred drama, elevating the bread and wine and speaking the Words of Institution while the devout await the ringing of the bell, gazing at those elements and seeing the literal body and blood of Christ. Within the confessional, the penitent kneels, receives absolution, and hears the works of satisfaction she must perform for her soul's sake. And in cathedrals, cloisters, and cow pastures, mitered bishops pronounce on doctrine, tonsured monks sing psalms, and ragged peasants supplicate Mary with weeping.

## Lenses of Relevance

It seems to me, however, that the chasm between us and our medieval forebears in the faith has to do less with any intrinsic oddness of the Christians of that time and more with certain philosophical and cultural presuppositions of our own. Though it may seem strange for a book about "medieval wisdom" to start with an assessment of the church today, this one will, for two reasons.

First, this is my scholarly center of gravity. I come to the wisdom of medieval faith not through long technical study of the church of the Middle Ages (though I have read many of the key primary works in translation, along with many helpful secondary sources) but through scholarship on American Christianity that, alongside a decade of teaching in an evangelical seminary and daily experience in many Western evangelical ecclesial settings, has given me an acute sense of some deep needs of these churches today.

Second, although the historical guild warns us against pressing historical periods to answer modern questions alien to their own realities, an approach to history that does not account for its modern relevance may quite literally be worse than useless.[3] Finding moral, intellectual, and spiritual value for our own lives is the whole *point* of doing history. There is no way to understand the value of the past for our present experience without understanding our own time well.

Of course I see the Middle Ages through modern lenses, but so do even the most careful of scholar-specialists. Indeed, the best of them do this not only unconsciously but also quite intentionally. They know that when we study a past period without connecting it to our own, we fall into mere antiquarianism—like the numismatist collecting rare coins for no purpose higher than the sheer pleasure of having them. G. K. Chesterton thought you could not be a proper medievalist until you cared deeply enough about today to apply medieval insights to your own life and thinking.[4] I think he's exactly right. To be an antiquarian—beguiling yourself with stories and collecting facts like butterflies but never asking what it all might mean for us today—is to fail to be a useful historian, no matter what era turns your crank.

So the only sensible reason to care about the past is that, through knowing it, you believe you can make a better present. The chief purpose of history is moral improvement. This means we must derive *lessons for today* from our study of history. But to do so, we must discern our own time, too.

## A Church in Need of New Life

The American church today is in turmoil. We have tried, by turns, rational apologetics, pop-culture inflected consumerist church programs, ecstatic charismatic experience, and postmodern experimentation. But none of these has proved lasting.

- The rationalism of modern apologetics has collapsed as the questions of the unchurched have turned away from doctrine, and the agonies of the churched have centered on spirituality and practice rather than belief.

- The beguiling concerts and spectacles of the church-growth technicians have fallen short of their promise, revealing the dismally shallow spirituality behind the curtain.[5]
- The experientialism of the charismatic movement has faltered in the quest to build lasting, faithful, discipled churches as worshipers have bounced from one high to the next.
- The postmodernism of the now-faded "emerging" movement never found a positive program for reform to accompany its often strident critique of current church culture.

Could it be that God is driving us out of these failed experiments and into the wilderness, traveling as pilgrims toward a more solid faith and a more faithful church? Turning to a more dire metaphor, could it be that the contemporary church lingers in a twilight between vitality and morbidity, sustained by a kind of spiritual life support? And if so, what is our prognosis?

I believe there is hope, for we are on the list for a life-giving transplant. It had better come soon, to be sure, but when it does, it promises to revive and strengthen us in ways unimaginable. This transplant, like most others, will involve the surgical implantation into the patient of living organs taken from a dead donor.

What living organs? The life-giving beliefs and practices of our own spiritual heritage. Which donor? Our mother, the church, in her first two thousand years. This is not traditional*ism*, which as Jaroslav Pelikan famously quipped is "the dead faith of the living." To transplant a dead organ will only kill the patient. Rather, it is tradition: "the living faith of the dead."[6] Weak and on our sickbeds, we await a transfusion of that life.

So far, surgeons such as D. H. Williams, Robert Louis Wilken, and Thomas Oden have found vital organs in the doctrinal formulations of the church's first six centuries, and they have rushed them to modern Christian hospitals. And individually, though not yet as *ecclesia*, a few here and there are beginning to receive these transplants and new life is flooding into them.

Other medics such as Richard Foster, Eugene Peterson, and the late Dallas Willard have turned to organs of spiritual practice. They provide from any and every Christian tradition a piecemeal infusion of intentional spirituality that, while still largely unformed and understudied, now sustains some. From the rich medieval tradition of spirituality in particular, these good doctors are leading modern Christians to rediscover ascetic practices, grow under spiritual directors, go on retreats at monasteries, and meditate after the manner of the *lectio divina*.

Yet many modern Protestants still believe that they can be faithful to their Reformation heritage only by rejecting the medieval heritage. They perceive medieval faith as not just catholic, but Roman Catholic (or in its Eastern forms, Eastern Orthodox) and thus hyper-sacramental, semi-Pelagian, institutional, nominal. For these folks, as for the Hollywood of *Pulp Fiction*, to "get medieval" is to do violence. It is to do violence both to the Reformation doctrinal heritage of salvation by faith and to the revivalist spiritual heritage of direct, unmediated access to God in Christ.

Those who succumb to these stereotypes do not know how badly they misconstrue the continental Reformation (and to a lesser degree American revivalism) and, especially, the medieval traditions from which they insist on cutting themselves off. God did not, after all, leave his church in the emperor Constantine's (272–337) day only to reappear with Martin Luther (1483–1546), John Wesley (1703–91), and Billy Graham (b. 1918).

## The Shorter Way

To begin to understand the barrier that stands between us and medieval wisdom, consider this vignette from the period that defined American evangelicalism more than any other: the Victorian era.

In 1850, Methodist laywoman Phoebe Worrall Palmer (1807–74) published a book called *The Way of Holiness*. In it, she said about the traditional Methodist teaching of sanctification: "Yes, brother, THERE IS A SHORTER WAY! O! I am sure this long waiting and struggling with the powers of darkness is not necessary. There is a shorter way."[7]

These words would turn out to be momentous for nineteenth-century American evangelicals. Already by that year a flood of church leaders, including several Methodist bishops, had for more than a decade been visiting Palmer's New York City parlor to attend her "Tuesday meetings for the promotion of holiness." And within a decade more, her "holiness movement" jumped denominational lines, initiating Presbyterians, Quakers, Baptists, and Episcopalians into this optimistic creed.

The essence of Palmer's message is this: No more would Christians have to pursue a fraught and painstaking path to holiness (reminiscent of the slow, agonizing road to conversion once trod by English and American Puritans). By simply gathering their resolve, making a single act of consecration, and "standing on the promises"—certain Scripture texts that seem to hold out entire sanctification as an attainable reality—they can enjoy total freedom from sin.

This message galvanized a generation and set a tone for evangelicalism that continues to ring out today. It may be fair to say that the teaching of a "shorter way to holiness," whether in Palmer's more Wesleyan formulation or in the Reformed-influenced "higher life" variations introduced later in the century, fueled the single most prominent and widespread movement among postbellum and Gilded Age evangelicals. It swept across the nation's West and South like a sanctified brushfire, birthed new denominations such as the Nazarenes and Christian & Missionary Alliance, fed the all-consuming fervor of temperance activism, and laid the groundwork for the Pentecostal movement of the following century.

Why? What made Palmer's "shorter way" such a natural fit for evangelicals in their century of growth and social prominence? And what does this have to do with the project to recover past wisdom in the church?

I'd like to suggest that the essence of this teaching, so essential to the formation of modern American evangelicalism, may be found in one word: "immediatism."

The first definition listed in *Merriam-Webster Unabridged* for "immediatism" is "immediate*ness*," which Webster's defines as "the quality that makes something seem important or interesting because it is or seems to be happening now."[8] I would relate this to what C. S. Lewis calls "chronological snobbery,"[9] or what one might simply call an obsession with novelty. Moreover, I think this quality can be recognized in the evangelical movement.

The second definition offered is "a policy or practice of gaining a desired end by immediate action." I would relate this to a syndrome of *pressurized pragmatism*, which Alasdair MacIntyre has identified as the chief cause of many American ills, militating as it does against careful reflection on accumulated wisdom.[10] I take the temperance movement as nineteenth-century-evangelicalism's Exhibit A, illustrating the sort of silver bullet solution to all social problems offered by many evangelical social causes of that day—and many today. Get people to stop drinking, and it will fix all our problems. Take these three simple steps and your church will grow.

The third definition of "immediatism" follows: "An epistemological theory that views the object of perception as directly knowable." This was the philosophical mother's milk of nineteenth-century evangelicals, emerging from eighteenth-century Scottish Common Sense Realism.[11] This immediatist epistemology allowed its devotees to bypass all mediating traditions and interpretations and go directly to the supposedly commonsense meaning of Scripture. The typical one-page faith statement used by evangelical organizations and churches today is a legacy of this intellectual immediatism, or "shorter way."

## Going Straight to the Throne

For my purposes I offer a fourth definition, and though it amounts to a new coinage, it works etymologically and fits hand in glove with the first three definitions. The immediatism of American evangelicals is also *a way to God without mediation.* I would relate this to both the "heart religion" modern evangelicals have inherited from the Pietists and the related impatience with all priestly and sacramental mediation bequeathed to us by the Puritans.

Among evangelicals, the first three senses of "immediatism"—love of novelty, pressurized pragmatism, and Common Sense epistemology—both support and are supported by immediatism in this fourth sense.

This fourth sense of immediatism is, I believe, the most potent and ingrained idea that stands between today's evangelical Christians and the wisdom of their medieval heritage—that is, our fancy that we can always, in every daily need and difficulty, go straight to the throne of God and receive both a direct and emotion-inflected sense of God's presence and clear, divine answers to our questions and problems. Or rather, our fancy that this unmediated, individual access is the *only* kind we need—to be set against all priestly, institutional, or material mediation. The revivalist heritage of modern evangelicals tells us that we can and indeed must access

God directly, coming to his throne without consulting any human, or any "human-made traditions" of liturgy, catechism, discipline, or doctrine.

If I am right about this, then an open exploration and application of truths and practices from the medieval period requires from modern evangelicals a new stance toward faith that goes against our deepest inclinations. To move toward medieval wisdom is to swim against a powerful immediatist undertow. For this direction is not the "shorter way" by any stretch. It is a way that requires (at least from our teachers) long and careful study, wise cultural adaptation, and (from each of us) habituation to new rhythms of worship and life. This book launches only in the most preliminary way the long study that would be required truly to bring us "medieval wisdom."

## A Nutshell History of Protestant Allergy to Mediation and the Modern Challenge

The belief that the average layperson has direct, individual access to God, with no other mediator beside Christ, can be found at evangelicalism's Protestant roots. Since the Reformation, Protestants have distrusted tradition as potentially leading people back into what Martin Luther called the "Babylonian Captivity of the Church."[12] Luther and the other Reformers sought to strip away a mass of rituals and requirements that had accumulated, as they imagined, like malignant barnacles on the ship of the church during Christianity's thousand-year "middle age." These traditions, it seemed to them, obscured the central truth of salvation by grace through faith—God reaching directly to the believer and achieving the work of salvation without human effort.

An irony here is that the theologian who looms over the whole medieval period—and on whose thinking, as Jaroslav Pelikan has said, all of medieval theology served as something like a set of footnotes[13]—Augustine of Hippo (354–430), taught unequivocally that salvation can come to us by no other means than God's unaided grace. This was still the official teaching "on the books" of the medieval church right up until the Reformation—though a group of "modern" theologians, to whom Luther was reacting, were trying to import categories of human effort into the picture of how salvation takes place.

Augustine, however, was wise enough to see that the individual believer cannot come to faith outside the community of the church. And he had been willing to make some strong claims for the role of the church in salvation. The Reformation may even be considered, as some have said, the triumph of Augustine's soteriology (his understanding of salvation) against Augustine's ecclesiology (his understanding of the church). Those Protestants, however, who think that the whole Western medieval church believed in "salvation by works" are following a long tradition of Protestant insult-hurling that ignores much medieval evidence to the contrary.

Luther was not himself a thoroughgoing immediatist. He maintained, for example, a strongly sacramental liturgy. When attacked in his thoughts by the devil, he did not content himself with hurling inkpots but rather stood on his baptism, insisting that that sacrament had separated him forever from the works of the enemy. But Luther is not the end of the story. The French moderate Reformer John Calvin (1509–64) anchored his famous *Institutes* in the believer's union with Christ, beginning the book from the standpoint of religious experience, and the more radical Swiss leader Ulrich Zwingli (1484–1531) pushed hard to protect this privilege of the believer against "Roman traditions," even nailing shut the organ and stripping the religious art from the walls of his Grossmünster church in Zurich.

This immediatist trend intensified in the post-Reformation Puritans, turning in a more affective direction. Theirs was "an emotionally vibrant and spiritually vigorous group in the tradition of Platonic idealism and Augustinian piety; their zeal came from an insatiable quest for the spiritual ideal of union with God despite their human imperfections."[14]

In that quest, the Puritans distrusted both sacerdotalism (*human* mediation of God to individuals) and sacramentalism (*material* mediation of God to individuals). They resisted all claims that in order to meet God people must use mediating objects such as statues, images, or vestments as well as physical actions such as rituals, gestures, or postures presided over by ecclesiasts (which they lumped together in the epithet "priestcraft").

The proto-evangelical "free church" Protestants—first the Anabaptists, then all their theological kin in the Anglo stream—further intensified this allergy to church hierarchy, extending it to state control and involvement. How dare any human authority tell Christians that they must do this or that to reach God! Each person stands before God on his or her own two feet, and God, in turn, stands ready to meet each person in every time and situation of life, without the poor helps of human tradition.

On the early nineteenth-century American frontier, a new generation of free, self-sufficient Protestants extended the immediatist quest, now fighting for freedom from *intellectual* elites (the educated ministry with their laborious and elite four-year degrees) and from all the forms of tradition over which they claimed to be the masters and gatekeepers.[15]

Along the way, heart religion became similarly intensified. We may trace a straight and unwavering line from the sixteenth-century Puritans' "Augustinian Strains of Piety,"[16] which led them to require a compelling and heartfelt conversion narrative from each new church member, to John Wesley's Aldersgate experience of having his heart "strangely warmed," to the ecstasies of the nineteenth-century camp meeting and the twentieth- and twenty-first-century charismatic worship service. What we are doing in stepping back into the Middle Ages with Lewis's guidance is attempting to challenge that "line of immediatism" in two ways.

First, from the seventeenth century to today, the inherited, communally affirmed religious authorities of Scripture and tradition have increasingly given way to a new structure of religious authority that is grounded in individual reason and experience. To desire to learn from the cloud of witnesses or "church triumphant"—those on whose shoulders we stand—is to shift authority back to the older style, weighting Scripture-read-through-tradition more heavily than the dictates of our own freely exercised reason and experience.

Second, from the seventeenth century to today, the primary way individuals have met God has shifted from a church-mediated mode to an individual, unmediated mode. Any full and useful appropriation of the past—that is, one not content to offer only doctrinal direction—will likely seek to return to some form of churchly mediation (whether of liturgical forms, priestly roles, or both) in an attempt to reverse this post-Enlightenment trajectory.

## The Look, Feel, and Results of Immediatism

What, then, does immediatism look like in evangelical Protestant (and many other) churches today, and how does that degrade our ability to gain benefit from the church of the past?

### The Narrative of (Individual) Desire

David Bebbington famously defines evangelicalism with a fourfold ty-pology: biblicist (the Bible as the ultimate authority on all matters of faith and practice), crucicentrist (the atonement secured for us by Jesus on the cross as the central reality of our faith), conversionist (a "born again" crisis experience as necessary and definitive for the faith of each believer), and activist (the tasks of evangelizing individuals and reforming churches and societies as imperatives for all believers).

I suppose that when we talk about evangelical immediatism, we are talk-ing about something like Bebbington's "conversionism," but that category by itself is inadequate to describe the habitus of unmediated communion so central to this movement. To understand the continued impact of im-mediatism in evangelical faith, we need to expand Bebbington's "conver-sionism" to include a focus on personal relationship with God in Christ, which is not only accessed (immediately, in several senses) through a crisis conversion experience but also experienced in a continuing way through a series of direct, transforming encounters with God.

Again, in order to fully take into account the impact of immediatism on evangelicalism, we would also have to understand that evangelical "bibli-cism" has taken on a similarly direct, unmediated character: through read-ing the Bible as individuals, apart (as the movement has falsely imagined) from any communal or traditional filters, we have clear and immediate access to the mind of God.[17]

We are shaped by the stories we tell ourselves. The ruling story of mod-ern evangelicalism is one of unmediated access to God. As the twentieth-century ambassador of Pentecostalism David du Plessis puts it, "God has no grandchildren." That is, no individual—and for that matter no genera-tion—may claim faith based on his or her forebears (which is, after all, in a sense, the claim of all tradition!). All must meet God for themselves.

### The Pragmatic Shape of Church

Now, how does this look in our churches?

Structurally, evangelical immediatism is inherently individualistic and impatient with organizational structures and constraints. It has therefore created a kind of "hole in the ecclesiological donut" where everything that inhabits the realm between the mystical communion of the "church invisible" and the immediate communion of the individual with God is negotiable and, ultimately, a matter of *adiaphora* (that is, these mediating forms are considered inessential for salvation).[18]

Yes, the local church has often played a strong role in the lives of evangelicals, but one might argue that its primary role is not to mediate but to celebrate and foster the individual's immediate communion with God.

In other words, as historian Bruce Hindmarsh argues, the evangelical movement has always represented "an unparalleled subordination of church order to evangelical piety."[19] Thus almost all inherited forms—such as the practical, ecclesiastical wisdom of the early and medieval church, for instance—have been held lightly, as negotiable. (This has been true notwithstanding the tradition-oriented tendency of evangelicalism's Anglican parent, which much of evangelicalism has inherited, to center Christian identity in the forms of corporate worship.[20])

This allergy to churchly mediation has given evangelical churches a decided lean toward democratic, participatory forms of worship and leadership. Congregationalism has been the movement's favored leadership form, and worship styles tend to follow whatever seems to relate most naturally and directly to the worshiper. This means preaching in plain language and singing in popular styles (famously, even tavern tunes!); if God meets people immediately where they are, then people should use in worship whatever contemporary popular-culture material already feels natural and "homey" to them.

So far, I have made two arguments: First, a narrative of direct encounter and relationship with God drives immediatism. Second, immediatism drives pragmatic, plastic ecclesiology (and ecclesiastical authority is a subspecies of mediation, so immediatism seems best served by nonhierarchical forms of organization).

## Recent Attempts to Reclaim Past Wisdom

Let's pause to consider how these immediatist values have already prevented the contemporary church from accessing the wisdom of the past. In recent interviews with Richard Foster, Dallas Willard, and others involved,[21] in the last few decades, in trying to woo modern Christians to ancient disciplines and understandings, I heard the same refrain repeatedly: that the "spiritual disciplines" movement seems to have stalled out. Why?

First, discipline requires, by definition, *submission*. Still marked by the antitraditionalism and pragmatism of their fundamentalist roots, evangelicals seem by and large unwilling to submit their spiritual growth to anything that looks like a mediating practice or tradition. True, many evangelicals have been opened to the riches of Christian spiritual tradition, but like their ecclesiology, these experiments seem to have been mostly an ad hoc adjunct to the central experience with God.[22]

As an example, in his many books on worship the late Robert Webber offers evangelicals a way to incorporate the liturgies of the historic church through a simple order: the Gathering, the Word, the Table, and the Dismissal. He also recommends a restored commitment to the sacraments, especially the Eucharist, as part of the weekly worship event. Such liturgical borrowings open up a greater role in worship for ritual gesture, symbol, and visual art, which point (as they always have) to spiritual realities beyond themselves. By reentering these historic practices, evangelicals can "capture the mystery and transcendence of God in a way that modern forms of Protestant worship do not," thereby emphasizing the unity of the church.[23] But these practices also require liturgical leadership, which looks suspiciously like sacerdotal mediation. And they tend to require material mediation, which looks like sacramentalism.

Second, the attempt at spiritual *ressourcement* led by Richard Foster, Dallas Willard, Eugene Peterson, and others, insists that words—preaching, instruction—are simply not enough. As Willard puts it in his 1990 *Spirit of the Disciplines*, "The gospel preached and the instruction and example given" to evangelical congregations "simply do not do justice to the *nature of human personality, as embodied, incarnate*." Willard contrasts this situation to "the secret of the standard, historically proven spiritual disciplines," which "*do* respect and count on the bodily nature of human personality. . . . They show us effectively *how* we can 'offer our bodies as living sacrifices, holy and acceptable unto God' and how our 'spiritual worship' (Rom. 12:1) really is inseparable from the offering up of our bodies in specific physical ways."[24] Customary evangelical modes of Christian living were simply not enough. They "did not even," as Willard says, "take life—our lives, the ordinary minutes and hours of our days—seriously in the process of redemption."[25] But this, of course, raises the red flag of sacramental mediation.

Some have overcome their nervousness about sacramentalism and "Romanism" enough to walk a ways down this more embodied road. However, Willard identifies a lack of holism between our biblical and theological understandings and our understanding of embodied spiritual practices.

The latter, he says, have essentially been ghettoized in the seminaries. Typically "spiritual formation" is given a place to call its own in the seminary, but it has never been welcomed or integrated in biblical studies or theology. The problem is that evangelical culture and especially evangelical higher education is still marked by that intellectual immediatism of nineteenth-century Common Sense Realism; it seeks the shortest, most immediate line between Scripture and practice. Faced with the tenuous and complex relationship between the Bible and early church practices, it hesitates to do the hard theological work necessary to make the connection. And that, in our colleges and seminaries, is the kiss of death.

Third and more specifically, since Kathleen Norris's *Cloister Walk* (1996), evangelicals have become fascinated with monasticism. They have sought to understand it and mine it for their own purposes, and have even sought oblate or other third-order status in existing monastic communities. Usually, however, even when founding their own "new monastic" communities (which are a horse of a much more activist, outward-focused color than ancient monasticism), they have stopped short of the kind of radical communal accountability that has always been Benedictine monasticism's beating heart.

I've seen this repeatedly in my students' encounters with the principle and notion of stability within the Benedictine tradition (that is, the demand in Benedict's Rule that the monk vow himself to a single community for his entire life). It is something they yearn for, but they balk at the commitment. Why? Certainly full monastic commitment clashes (as it always has) with commitments to family, jobs, and other realities of modern Western life. But this did not stop hundreds of thousands from committing to monasteries in the medieval millennium. For my students and other Christians today, another impediment to the monastic principle of stability arises: to commit to a single religious community is to admit that we so often need that community to mediate God to us. And our fundamental immediatism won't allow us to submit to that—we believe we can always go directly to the throne.

Fourth, the "emerging church," in search of Christian authenticity against acculturation of the church, has dabbled with the materials of tradition—from candles to labyrinths to the *lectio divina*. But with its postmodern sensitivity to power dynamics and fear of having the church associated with any form of power, sacerdotal, even sacramental, forms of mediation have remained well beyond the pale. Worship forms and spiritual forms that were once (in the early and medieval church) authoritative are now, in the hands of the emerging crowd, nothing but tools for romantic individualism to be wielded at will—even at whim.

## Where the Immediatists Are Right

At the risk of seeming to argue against my own case, I should admit that I have some sympathy for the anti-Catholic Reformers, Puritans, and frontier American evangelicals who turned their backs on old forms in search of the face of God. Their fear of elite religious control was born out of European and Protestant history. People in search of power, as some in the church hierarchy had been during the late medieval period, can easily exert their desired control through the forms of church life. Who can say that those democratizing evangelicals didn't see real abuses in the intellectual elites of their day as their Augustinian strain of piety melded with a free-range populism yearning to be free from the yoke of an "educated ministry"?

Who can say that the gatekeepers of tradition *today* are themselves immune to abusing their power? What may be lost when the elites take over and control the means of grace is this: immediate access to God in Christ by the Holy Spirit. Under the abuse of power, form becomes formalism, and tradition, "the living faith of the dead" (again, as Jaroslav Pelikan lamented) traditionalism, "the dead faith of the living." Whatever healthy *ressourcement* means, it cannot mean a return to the Babylonian captivity of the church.

On the positive side of the ledger, evangelicalism's single-minded immediatism has protected and promoted a powerful relational, emotional piety; a deep commitment to the practical injunctions of the gospel; a lively expectation of the return of Christ; a passion for evangelism and missions; a legacy of thoroughgoing social reform; and long practice in concerted, ecumenical effort. Any evangelical *ressourcement* must proceed without damaging these.

Immediatism is not as new as one might think. It is deep in the tradition of Christianity, with forms and flowers in the early and medieval church. Indeed, it is present in the Old Testament writers—Hosea, for example, through whom God told his people that his relationship with him is like a marriage. Paul was caught up to the "third heaven" (2 Cor. 12:2). The direct experience of God's power and presence is also present in the church's earliest years—days of instant healing and deliverance from demonic oppression.[26] It is present in the direct, experiential communion that fed Origen's (184/85–253/54) reinterpretation of the Song of Songs from a story about sex and human relations to a story about the communion of the individual soul with God. It is present in the powerful confessions and prayers of St. Augustine and his revolution of seeking God within his own consciousness. It is present in the entire glorious history of the Christian hospital, which accelerated rapidly in the thirteenth century as worshipers experienced Christ's suffering and compassion for them (quite directly and emotionally) at worship and in contemplation and sought to practice that same compassion for others. It is present in the transports and high reflections of the mystics and the monastics. It is present in Martin Luther's mystical image of the wedding ring of faith and the direct transfer of our sin to Christ and Christ's righteousness to us.

But in all of these times and episodes, immediatism was balanced with the mediation of church and sacrament. It is only in the increasingly individualistic, reason- and experience-driven heart religion of post-Enlightenment groups such as the Pietists, Moravians, Wesleyans, and Pentecostals that immediatism has, at first haltingly, begun asserting an independent right to define *all* aspects of our faith. The multifold harvest of that development includes many more negative legacies: a suspicion of academic inquiry; an impatient push to make black-and-white moral and social judgments and offer simplistic, immediatist social solutions; a retraction of Christian responsibility from the public to a new "private" (individual and familial) sphere; a domestication of God; a divisive sectarianism; and an overrealized eschatology.

In short, immediatism in its modern evangelical form courts presumption—even arrogance. It petulantly dismisses all the helps of church discipline, doctrine, worship, and leadership as "merely human." And in doing so, it defies most of our experience for most of our lives, which are full of the need for community, with its guidance, discipline, doctrine, and liturgy (whether explicit or implicit).[27] On reflection, honesty compels us to admit that if we are to have a hope of living and working "as unto the Lord," we need all of those mediations and more.

## The Ironies of Evangelical Immediatism

None of this proves that evangelical immediatism is wrong. But there is another problem with our immediatism: it implicates us in real difficulties about some of the traditions evangelicals hold dear.

First, immediatism finds indigestible the real story—Lewis would have called it the *mere Christian* understanding—of how the Bible became a canon of texts that communicates to us the self-revelation of God. The problem immediatism has with the historical Christian understanding of canonical revelation is one, we might say, of process. As is quite easy to verify from the historical sources, that canon comes down the ages to us today not by being dropped, wholesale and intact, from heaven to earth but through an extended, circuitous communal process—that is, through human mediation.

For me, as for almost the entire historic church, this long and contentious process does not call into question the Bible's status as revelation. This is because the church has always affirmed that the process of canon formation was guided and in a sense guaranteed by God. It certainly does, however, call into question the naive hermeneutic of those modern Christians who presume that a clear-eyed reading of those same mediated documents provides direct, unmediated access to the mind of God.[28]

The Bible is, as a set of human-mediated texts, complex, quirky, and many-layered—and therefore open to a wide array of interpretative approaches and understandings. It needs to be read and understood in and through human community, freshly for each context and historical moment. There are certainly many areas in which the voices of the canon speak, as it were, "singly," or in unison (in fact, I would join the historic church in affirming that *in all the areas required for our faith and flourishing* they speak in unison). But the canon cannot do so for us apart from a mediating communal process and context—that is, the Holy Spirit speaking through the church, both historically and in the modern moment. Its truths cannot be accessed with any sustained effectiveness immediately (without mediation) by the individual believer, reading his or her Bible alone in the closet by the light of a flashlight and individual reason, divorced from the community of the church.

Along with the doctrine of revelation, immediatism also causes problems for another historically held "mere Christian" doctrine, or more accurately, a precious and widely shared cluster of beliefs affirmed without hesitation by evangelicals but rarely examined to see whether it comports with our immediatism. This is the linked set of teachings that Christ is and always has been divine and that he is a coequal member of a "Trinity" with God the Father and God the Holy Spirit. As in the case of the Bible, evangelicals tend to treat these important doctrinal foundations of faith as if dropped directly from heaven—or at least from a clear-eyed, direct, and obvious reading of Scripture. But, to take just one (quite crucial) example, anyone familiar with the fourth-century Arian controversy and the series of councils that followed knows the truth: today's orthodox understanding of the Trinity and Christ's divinity, which we affirm in our creeds and faith statements, is *not* directly obvious from Scripture. It *did* travel a circuitous and tortuous human path of development—political, contested, and contentious—that was by all appearances historically contingent (though again, as the church believes, guided by God's Spirit).

So we are in a dilemma. How do we at the same time both foster the immediatism that is part of the modern church's heritage (especially of evangelical and other pietistic groups) and push back against its most arrogant claims? How may we, this side of the Enlightenment, acknowledge the necessity to our human condition of mediating forms at the same time that we recognize the tremendous gift of God that is his direct communication to our individual hearts and minds? How do we admit that we dwell neither in the glow of the seventh heaven nor in the rare flashes of direct illumination and that we need human, communal mediation, with its firm but still fallible checks and balances of liturgy, of church discipline, of doctrine?

Though we cannot ourselves (of course) become medieval in any direct sense, if we read the period honestly we will find something like the ordered minuet of immediate and mediated modes of faith—here a sober celebration of church and sacrament, there a joyful riot of ecstatic personal encounter with God.

The answer to the question is not either/or; it is both/and. But we have lost the "and" of tradition, and we've lost the "and" of mediation. Because we see through a glass darkly, we need to hear the whole community of the church, including the church triumphant that's gone on before. We need again to submit our worship to forms past and present, our theology to communities past and present, our practice to time-tested spiritual disciplines. And inasmuch as we can do so in the secular, pluralist space of modern Western culture, we need to find ways to mediate our arts and sciences and education through the Christian history of art, the Christian history of science, the Christian history of all human cultural activity that has gone before us (and in doing so we return, really, to our own recent past, since most universities in the United States were founded out of this Christian cultural impulse).

This is as T. S. Eliot argues in his essay about what it is to be a writer:[29] you can't hope to become a writer worth reading without the tradition. So too, although you can *start* to be Christian by the great and direct grace of God, you cannot hope to become a well-formed person of faith without modes of mediation to go *along with* the amazing direct encounters God has always, quite astoundingly, granted to those who seek him. To do otherwise is arrogance.[30]

## New Roads Opened by Past Wisdom

As we launch into this study, let me offer some aspects of medieval faith that I take to be both potentially powerful for us today in our moment of need and all too absent from our own habits of life and devotion—hidden from us by our hyperactive immediatism. I'll put these in the form of a series of questions that medieval Christians dwelled upon deeply, but that many today ignore altogether:

1. Why should we commit ourselves to the wants and needs of mortal life when eternity looms?
2. What meaning can the material world have to us as spiritual, not carnal, beings?
3. What does suffering mean and how is God present to us in it?
4. If we have faith, then how much more should we do works of mercy?
5. How does human reason reflect the *logos* through which the Father created the world?

These were not the incidental but rather the organizing questions of medieval Western Christianity.

Medieval answers to the question of the significance of temporal life in light of eternity were fraught. First came the medieval division of religion workers into the "religious" (those who live according to a rule, in a community dedicated in a special way to the purposes of God) and the "secular" (those, including parish clergy, who deal daily with the concerns of others caught up in the *saeculum*, the hurly-burly of this age). From the fourth-century desert fathers and mothers to the twelfth-century preaching friars to the late medieval (that is, fourteenth- and fifteenth-century) laypeople who imitated their disciplines, the brightly burning life of the ascetics captivated everyone who sought salvation. By the time Henry VIII (1491–1547) started dismantling the monastic superstructure of England in 1536, every town of any size in England had at least three or four sizable monasteries.

But from the high medieval period (1000–1300) through the Reformation, a rebirth of education and the arts swept Europeans into a new era of cultural engagement in arts, sciences, and practical social disciplines. The culture was reawakened to Gregory the Great's assertion that the active, earthly life and the contemplative life serve each other and that every aspect of our mortal, material life can serve as a conduit of divine communication and a forum for redemptive living. The preaching orders of the Franciscans, Dominicans, and Augustinians rapidly blanketed Europe, bringing not only the message of the gospel but also a reborn tradition of the liberal arts.

The question of creation's sacramental meaning spurred medievals both to a special attention to the ways God speaks to us in flowers and birds (following the time of Francis of Assisi [1181/82–1226]) and to the most stunning and luminous achievements of a millennium of religious art—icons, reliquaries, cathedrals, and canvases of spiritual power and aching beauty.

Animated by the perennial question of the meaning of suffering, medievals plunged into the passion of their Lord, finding in that mystery a profound sense of connection with a God who cares enough to suffer together with his creation and who urges us to imitate him in this—walking with others in their sufferings too.

The medieval solution to the problem of the place of good works in a system of grace set off a social explosion as rank upon rank of hospitals burst forth and spread over Europe, caring above all for the poor and sick who had no resources to keep themselves comfortable in their illnesses or to surround themselves with help and companionship in their dying days.

From the awareness of reason's sacred purpose emerged all of the grandeur of scholastic theology as well as the birth of the university, perhaps Europe's most powerful single institution apart from the church. This institution dedicated itself to the glorious celebration of creation's goodness, the fruitful exercise of what Dante called "the good of the intellect,"[31] and the intricate exploration of the way of salvation.

## The Crux: Creation and Incarnation

Is there a way to summarize the negative effects of our modern "immediatism gone to seed" and the medieval balm that could be applied to heal our self-inflicted wounds? Many ways, no doubt, but I keep coming back to the doctrines of the creation and the incarnation, particularly their eclipse in the modern scientific age and their potential recovery through clear-eyed and openhearted engagement with medieval wisdom.

I believe (and Lewis observed) that the scientific revolution and its sequels—such as the Enlightenment—began to sap the material world of its spiritual and moral significance, and that this diminishment has only continued and intensified through today. In 1954 Lewis argued that the closing of Jane Austen's heyday (1775–1817) marked a turning point in Western history,[32] whose catastrophic outcomes he had already limned in his argument "The Abolition of Man" (1943) and its novelistic outworking *That Hideous Strength* (1945). But whenever it happened, the modern disenchantment of the material universe has hidden from us the spiritual importance of both creation (God making all flesh) and incarnation (God becoming flesh).

Gregory the Great, spiritual father of the Middle Ages, whose writings filled the cupboards of the great monastic libraries,[33] insisted that while pastors or laypeople are engaged in the active life, *everything in their experience and in the world becomes a potential instrument of God's direct, special communication to them.* Chance meetings. Storms. Landscapes. Crafted objects. A thousand other things. God is always speaking to us, if we but have ears to hear and eyes to see. Gregory emphasized "God's involvement with creation and the sacramental presence of spiritual truths in the things of this world."[34]

This sense of God at work in the material world and in our own embodied, material, social, and cultural experience became part of the orthodox Christian understanding of the world for the whole period from Gregory to the Reformation—and, in many circles, both before and after this period. This was not pantheism, but rather the sense of both God's glory reflected in creation and God's grace working through ordinary things in creation.

Since the scientific revolution, philosophical materialism (as Lewis argues in his *Discarded Image*) has sapped our physical world of life and mystery, including the life of God and the mystery of redemption. As a result, humankind finds it a dull fact worthy of little interest that the supreme God over all the universe came in the flesh of a human being, entering into the world(s) he had made. All the rich resonances of incarnation and all the glories and intricacies of human life within creation were left for the irrelevant musings of oddball romantic poets such as Gerard Manley Hopkins. The world, of course, did not stop being charged with the grandeur of God. It did not stop flaming out like "shining from shook foil."[35] But only the poets and the mystics noticed anymore.

The medievals, on the other hand, saw God reflected and actively at work in every aspect of the created world. Theirs was "a world of built-in significance."[36] What would a medieval person looking up at the night sky have actually *seen*? To become that ancient night watcher, says Lewis, "you must conceive yourself looking up at a world lighted, warmed, and resonant with music."[37] The medieval cosmos was one of vibrancy and wonder. In his *Out of the Silent Planet*, Lewis's protagonist, Ransom, peers out of the window of a spaceship to see not the black void of space but a pulsing, glowing matrix of glory. This is how the medievals saw their universe, as a place where "each sphere . . . is a conscious and intellectual being, moved by 'intellectual love' of God."[38]

Medieval poets and artists dwelled on the particularities of the material world because those particularities made them feel the fitness and rightness of all things. It was the strength of that medieval worldview, says Lewis in his *English Literature of the Sixteenth Century*, to think always and at the same time in both the universal and the particular. Medievals oscillated in their thinking and talking between boots and angels, pigs and prophecy, with stunning rapidity and naturalness.[39]

Lewis found himself living in a modern age of philosophical materialism, in which everything was simply atoms. In this newer and poorer world, all the spiritual meaning that medievals had seen looking up into the night sky had vanished, leaving a Newtonian machine-universe in its place. Yet Lewis would not go gentle into that "good" night: "I have made no serious effort to hide the fact that the old Model delights me as I believe it delighted our ancestors. Few constructions of the imagination seem to me to have combined splendour, sobriety, and coherence in the same degree."[40] To which the response of many modern commentators is "How medieval!"

That is, how quaint. How backward. How wrong.

Does such mystical understanding of the cosmos reduce God to some sort of magician, meddling in material stuff to gain cheap effects among his human audience? Does it encourage rank "superstition," which is a modern term for attributing to spiritual origins anything we still don't understand? That's certainly the understanding of many moderns faced with the "discarded image" of the Middle Ages.

## Why Can't We Hear the Medievals on Creation and Incarnation?

A crucial reason we cannot hear what medievals *actually* said about the world and God's relationship to it is that we assume, from our privileged modern scientific vantage point, that they were impenetrably ignorant about the world. To take just one example: everyone knows that medieval people believed the world is flat, right? But this supposed "fact" is actually a complete fabrication, as we will see in chapter 4.

I would argue, and Lewis makes a similar argument in his *Discarded Image*, that if we are to return to the nourishing truths of the Middle Ages, rooted as they are in a very different understanding of the material world than we hold today, then we will need to tear away some significant polemical barriers erected by supposedly enlightened moderns (such as the flat-earth myth). Only by doing so can we begin to shuck off *our own* impenetrable materialist ignorance and intractable scientific superstition. Only then can we begin to take seriously the scriptural stories of creation and incarnation as clues that the material world is not just a random collocation of atoms. We scientific moderns, who "know better," will have to allow the possibility that all this material *stuff* is, first, the handiwork of God, and, second, still used by God to comfort, confront, discipline, and delight us. Further, we will have to open ourselves to the truth that what we do with our own stuff—our bodies, families, goods, economic work, neighborhoods, food—*does* matter to God.

In other words, Christianity is not a *merely spiritual* religion. Today many say, "I am spiritual, but I am not religious," meaning something like, "I have spiritual thoughts and feelings, but I don't have to act on them in organized, physical, communal worship in church or in concrete, biblical ethical action in the world to know that I'm in touch with God." A medieval Christian would have laughed.

Our modern tendency to spiritualize faith out of all earthly recognition is not just an evasion of the unchurched. It has rooted itself deep in Christian culture. To many, faith simply does not touch the physical. This extends even to the Person of Christ: the single important thing about him is that he was divine—his humanity doesn't matter much. We have perhaps not become, as some argue, body-denying gnostics (although there is a family resemblance). We are far too fond of our creature comforts to condemn our bodies as evil as the gnostics did. Rather, we just now assume that those comforts are spiritually neutral. This leaves us heedless of our bodies' significance as the one and only "place" in which we meet God.

## Harvest of a Disembodied Faith

We do not live outside our experience of embodiedness and relatedness with other bodies. We do not live apart from sex. All we know how to do anymore is to put up barriers and proscriptions: "NO sex before marriage." "NO homosexual activity or feelings." "NO abortion." We are at a loss to find wisdom in Scripture or Christian tradition for how to do sex well (though the medieval church is admittedly not the best place to look for that wisdom either!). And we certainly do not know how to use the rich imagery of marriage and sexuality to talk about our own relationship with God, as Bernard of Clairvaux (and Origen long before him) did. What's more, we do not know how to see the motherly—as well as the fatherly—dimension of God, as Julian of Norwich (1342–ca. 1416) did.

We do not live apart from the pleasures of the table. All we do anymore is to put up barriers and proscriptions: "NO overeating." "NO laziness and lack of exercise." We do not know how to find scriptural or traditional warrants for the good, positive use of food. And we certainly don't use the rich imagery of convivial feasting to talk about our relationship with God both in heaven and here on earth, as did Margery Kempe and many others in the Middle Ages who wrote and talked about the marriage supper of the Lamb or savoring the wine of the Eucharist as a created good—even with its potential for intoxication.

We do not live apart from emotion—strong emotion. The most our church cultures know how to do is to try to channel that emotion to God, sometimes quietly in private devotion or sitting in solemn reverence in the sanctuary and sometimes more expressively in charismatic worship. We don't know what to do with it in our relationships other than to counsel sober good sense and careful reining-in of the "passions."

And of course, that's wise. The passions are dynamite. But if God wants to work in our everyday emotional lives—our relationships and pleasures and temptations and sins—well, we don't know anything about that. Sounds dangerous. Better keep emotion carefully hemmed in to church services and prayer closets. We certainly don't know about the outrageous everyday joy of Francis of Assisi and his merry band. I think of Francis's friend Friar Masseo; the *Little Flowers of Saint Francis* says that he was "filled with such grace of the yearned-for virtue of humility, and of the light of God, that . . . he was ever blithe of heart. And many times he made a joyous sound like the cooing of a dove. 'Coo, coo, coo.'"[41] Or consider the Cistercian Aelred of Rievaulx (1110–67), who took surpassing joy in the fellowship of his order, so that he said, "Without friends there is absolutely no pleasure in life."[42]

Because we think these things—sex, food, and emotion—have to do only with biological matters of reproduction and sustenance, or with unfortunate physical tendencies that cloud our judgment and confuse our ability to see truth, and that they have no spiritual significance, we live our lives with God as a giant game of pretend. We pretend that the only part of us that matters is our "spiritual" part (whatever that is, really). We pretend we can sustain a relationship with him by attending only to that part. We pretend that a vertical relationship is enough and that our horizontal relationships with spouses, children, parents, and coworkers will simply sort themselves out if we spend enough time reaching out to God inside our heads and hearts—as if "alone" is the only place God can be met.

And because of all this, we cannot take seriously the power of disciplines such as celibacy (temporary or lifelong), fasting (brief or protracted), or stability within one community. Since the body is not a place where spirituality gets done, mortifying the body is not part of our spirituality. Fasting is no gift to God, for the material world has no significance. Keeping the heart for God by abstaining from sex is no important spiritual discipline, for God does not care about what we do with our bodies in the intimacy of our bedrooms (as long as we follow a few rules). Keeping fidelity to one community is no way to serve God, because the social dimension lacks spiritual significance. God is a God of the spiritual things, not of the material things. God is a God who seems to have come, in Jesus, as a spiritual being, not truly as a material (which is to say fully human) being. So that bodily realm has no spiritual significance for us. It is not evil, as the gnostics held. It is simply irrelevant.

Because this is in fact not true—rather, it is devastatingly false—divorce rates are the same for Christians as for non-Christians. We have no lower rate of obesity than do non-Christians (perhaps worse, as a study some time ago of Southern Baptists suggested, because eating is the one vice left to a group that has historically been hedged in with the "NO" signs). We do not make art worth looking at. We do not write poems worth reading. We do not build churches worth walking into or worshiping in. We do not give council to married people worth hearing. We do not understand how to pass on our faith to our children, who are the "fruit of our loins" (to use the colorful, and very earthy, biblical image; Acts 2:30 KJV).

On the other hand, we do not take seriously the ascetic disciplines that address our pressing, spiritually engaged bodies in ways that turn them always back to our Lord. And, it should be said, we have forgotten the art of dying well (*ars moriendi*) that was so well understood and lavishly explained in the late Middle Ages especially. If our bodily lives lack spiritual significance, then so too do our bodily deaths. And again, because we downgrade our horizontal relatedness in the quest for vertical relatedness, we find the idea of mystical communion and fellowship with "saints" who have gone on before us both irrelevant and indeed irreverent.

If we think our material existence is irrelevant, then of course we do not study how to live bodily "as unto God." On the one hand, our devotion is not "full boisterous" and we do not engage in "dalliance" with our Lord, as was the case with the medieval lay mystic Margery Kempe.[43] In our worship, we abstain from incense, art, vestments, kneeling, prostrating ourselves, crossing ourselves, and all that other "medieval" stuff. Such things are reminiscent (say many modern Protestants) of those idolatrous, superstitious Catholics who muddy the pure and proper spiritual life with a slew of unbiblical activities. After all, to do such things in the name of religion is to be dragged back down into our embodiedness, into the material world that, as we scientific moderns know, has no spiritual significance.

As we've seen, this super-spiritualizing tendency sprouted up as long ago as the Reformation, growing to strength in the vineyard of Reformed piety rooted in the thought of Ulrich Zwingli. This piety distrusted all religious exercises or activities that engaged or pointed to the "outer," physical life. Only the inner and spiritual was to be trusted, not only in worship and devotion but also in the ethic of daily life: "The outer, whether it meant Church-as-institution, the sacrament or ascetic practices was automatically reduced to the role of being no more than an expression (always suspect and dangerous at that) of the inner, or else was condemned outright as materialistic and idolatrous."[44]

This reflection on the spiritual significance of material creation is a taste of the ending as we begin. This book leads to and culminates in what I have found to be the wisest piece of medieval wisdom: creation and incarnation are not rote doctrines to be learned, committed to memory, and ignored in our daily practice, but rather are practical linchpins of what it means to lead a good human life in the light of the gospel.

# 2

# C. S. Lewis—A Modern Medieval Man

Every journey needs its guide. No less this time-traveling exploration. Since 1950, Billy Graham has been the foremost evangelist and "statesman" for conservative Protestants of revivalist heritage. But their foremost intellectual has been, without possible competition, C. S. Lewis.

Old-school evangelicals once tended to say of Lewis, "He smokes, he drinks, and yet he is a Christian!" In today's more culturally accommodated church, such habits are more easily forgiven, even embraced (not always to our benefit). But there is still an aspect of Lewis that modern Protestants just don't know what to do with: his thoroughgoing, if selective, medievalism. Lewis, like many in his close circle (e.g., Charles Williams, J. R. R. Tolkien, Dorothy L. Sayers) and many of his influences (e.g., George MacDonald, G. K. Chesterton), was a medievalist. Some in this circle of imaginative writers were medievalists professionally (Lewis, Tolkien, Sayers, and arguably Williams, though he did not hold a medievalist doctorate); some were not (MacDonald, Chesterton). But each found in the medieval world a potent antidote to the malaises of the modern.

This is indeed a head-scratcher for American fans of Lewis: What has NYC to do with Camelot? What has 9/11 to do with the Quest for the Holy Grail?

We may love the neomedieval tales of these authors: Lewis's Narnian Chronicles and Ransom Trilogy with their medieval cosmology and morality, Williams's spiritual thrillers with their Dantean theology of love and personal sacrifice, Tolkien's *Hobbit* and Lord of the Rings Trilogy with their heroic chivalry and deep affection for tradition, Sayers's mystery novels and morality plays with their orthodox theological underpinnings, MacDonald's gothic novels and fantasies for adults and children with their deeply human understanding of sin and suffering, and Chesterton's quirky novels and Father Brown short stories with their clear-eyed Christian responses to modern philosophical materialism.

But those are "just stories," after all, aren't they? Really, fantasies about a lost time, right? To set out to learn from people who don't just insist on reveling in the imaginative world of the Middle Ages but who actually believe it holds the keys to a saner, more faithful life today, well, can people who seriously think in "medieval ways" about modern problems really help us?

Before entering the medieval lists against modernity with Lewis,[1] let's peek into the complementary medievalism of two of his friends. In his affection for medieval wisdom, C. S. Lewis was by no means alone in his era. Charles Williams—a central member of the "Inklings" literary circle to which Lewis, J. R. R. Tolkien, and others belonged—wrote both essays and imaginative literature with a deeply Christian message. And Dorothy Sayers—detective novelist, playwright, and essayist—corresponded with both Lewis and Williams and developed her own powerful Christian apologetic, which she expressed in both nonfiction and fiction.

These three literary Brits shared more than a lively Christian faith, the writing of imaginative literature, and a strong mutual regard. Together they launched a holy war on their era's scientific materialism and the spiritual declension that accompanied it. Each lifted up in their writings a rich, world-embracing Christian vision against the gray deadness of modern secular[izing] society. For each, this was a life-and-death battle, with the future of the Western world hanging in the balance. They saw their age's new creed of hard-nosed scientific pragmatism draining the world of spirit and meaning, which, as Lewis put it, threatened to abolish humanity itself.

In that precarious moment of Western history, on the war-torn front of secularization, Lewis, Williams, and Sayers took cues from the venerable four-star general of twentieth-century Christian literary antimodernism, journalist and amateur medievalist G. K. Chesterton. Although they never came to share Chesterton's Roman Catholic faith, Lewis, Williams, and Sayers took a very Chestertonian approach to their own antimodern campaign: they turned for help to the faith-filled energy of the medieval worldview.

Each of the three was a professional medievalist with an Oxford University connection. Lewis was an Oxford (and later Cambridge) professor of medieval and renaissance literature whose imaginative works marinated in the medieval. Williams was an autodidactic editor at Oxford University Press and sometime lecturer on Milton (1608–74) who dwelled long and lovingly on medieval themes in his poetry, plays, and novels. And Sayers did her graduate work at Oxford in medieval French and found time between writing detective novels to translate Dante and other medieval authors.

None of these three followed Chesterton slavishly in their medievalism. That jovial Catholic had looked to such figures as Francis of Assisi and Thomas Aquinas (1225–74), as well as a medieval guild-based economic vision of homesteading and small crafts. But Lewis, Williams, and Sayers found their inspiration in a medieval source that Chesterton left largely unmined. All specialists in literature, they sat together at the feet of the great thirteenth-century Italian poet Dante Alighieri.

## The Living Cosmos

Interestingly, while the three Oxonians joined in loving Dante, they could hardly have been more varied in their devotion. Each found in the great Florentine poet a distinctive tonic for the ills of modernity.

It was Dante's vivid rendering of the medieval cosmology—the "discarded image" of a prescientific age—that captivated Lewis. In the spiritualized planetary spheres of Dante's Ptolemaic universe, Lewis found a vividly sacramental sense of the aliveness of all things, to be treasured in the face of much that was deadening in modernity. Lewis fell in love with the living cosmos and the individuality of the planets themselves, rooted in pagan mythology but thoroughly Christianized by medieval authors. "The characters of the planets, as conceived by medieval astrology," he says, "seem to me to have a permanent value as spiritual symbols."[2]

Michael Ward argues that the medieval planets (including the sun) make up the hidden pattern of Lewis's Chronicles of Narnia.[3] Carefully peeling back the layers of Lewis's lifelong fascination with this older cosmology, Ward shows that even in his childhood, he was attracted imaginatively to the medieval idea that the planets are themselves living beings—something like angels or guardians of the heavenly realms. Lewis recorded in *Surprised by Joy* that when he was ten years old, "the idea of other planets exercised upon me then a peculiar, heady attraction."[4]

It was, however, Dante's great three-part poem, *The Divine Comedy* or *Commedia* (whose culmination at the end of the *Paradiso* Lewis considered, borrowing T. S. Eliot's words, "the highest point that poetry has ever reached"[5]) that plunged Lewis into full-blown infatuation with the Ptolemaic universe. Lewis treasured Dante as the only poet to have infused the medieval model of the heavens with "high religious ardour." Adds Ward: "Dante is no longer alone in this latter respect, because Lewis has joined him."[6] Lewis did so in the hidden structure of the Narnian Chronicles, in the living, throbbing cosmos of the Space Trilogy, and in his erudite but accessible lectures on the medieval worldview, published as *The Discarded Image*.

## Romantic Theology

For Charles Williams it was Dante's lifelong obsession with the girl Beatrice that drew him to recover an older "Affirmative Way" of faith—the ancient Christian spiritual road of the "affirmation of images," in which earthly things lead us on to spiritual realities. He found this way embodied compellingly in the story of how the aristocratic girl Bice Portinari (Beatrice) became Dante's muse and spiritual guide. Williams drew from this *exemplum* a rich theological picture of how God works a kind of divine alchemy through human relationships, turning the mundane material of romantic love into the heavenly gold of salvation. Williams worked out this theme in his masterly exegesis of Dante's work, *The Figure of Beatrice*. He then used this Dantean theme, along with his idea of "co-inherence" (the human possibility of indwelling each other to the point of redemptively sharing each other's sufferings), to forge a romantic theology.

But Williams also painted sin in all its hues—his stories contain some of the most penetrating and harrowing portrayals of human sinfulness in modern literature. And in this, too, he was formed by reading Dante. The Florentine poet, like all medievals, was deeply imbued in the theology of Augustine of Hippo, and Dante's *Purgatorio* and *Inferno* show the shades of sin and levels of depravity as so many variations on the theme of disordered love. Williams's "supernatural thrillers" and his *Figure of Beatrice* explore the many wrong turnings and sordid alleys of this Dantean/Augustinian disorder.

## The Drama of the Soul's Choice

For Dorothy Sayers, it was Dante's striking and forceful rendering of humanity's condition that made her imagination rise and her pen flow over as she forged an ancient-future moral vision in the wartime shambles of European life. The brilliant Sayers was an accomplished novelist, translator, and literary critic who was among the first class of female students at Oxford to receive a master's degree. Her area of scholarly specialty was modern (that is, postclassical) languages—to be precise, medieval French. When she first encountered Dante, she had already translated key texts in that area. Then she read Williams's *Figure of Beatrice* and, in a London bomb shelter with German V-1 rockets screaming down over the city around her, started into the *Commedia* itself. The poem stirred her deeply.

Sayers loved Dante's storytelling skill, the earthiness and vividness of his spirituality, and the way he wove together the fine details of everything from astronomy to Thomist theology. She made the translation of Dante her last great lifework. But for Sayers, Dante's value went beyond his literary mastery. His moral worldview presented an antidote to modern maladies: she saw wartime Europe descending into passivity, blame-shifting, and an alarming susceptibility to propaganda. And there stood the *Commedia*, towering over world literature as "the drama of the soul's choice"[7]—a gripping, multilayered narrative poem whose very theme is moral responsibility. For Sayers, the *Commedia* was a tract for our times.

This book could have taken any one, or all, of this circle of literary lay theologians as guides. Early on, I tried to bring them all to the table, but Lewis alone takes a lifetime to know. And in the works of this man, gifted with such omnivorous intellectual proclivities, close fellowship with

like-minded colleagues, and prodigious memory, are preserved many of
the themes of his friends as well. So, to Lewis we turn.

## The Intuitive Medievalism of C. S. Lewis

Lewis's academic career was always multifaceted, including study and
writing in classics, philosophy, literature, and literary criticism (his most
substantial scholarly book is on sixteenth-century English literature).
But the center that held all the rest together—from his early *Allegory of
Love* to his late *Discarded Image*—was the Middle Ages. By 1935, Lewis
was already identifying himself as most fundamentally a medievalist.
In that year, in a letter to an old college friend whose acquaintance he
wanted to renew, Lewis provides a quick update on his life. He reports
on his father's death, his brother's retirement from the army, and his
own incipient baldness and well-established Christian faith. Then he
identifies himself vocationally in this way: "Professionally I am chiefly
a medievalist."[8]

But Lewis's interest in the medieval was more than professional—I
would argue that it was "intuitive." That term might mean several things
about Lewis's interaction with medieval culture, literature, and faith. One
possible meaning is that Lewis loved the medieval from an early age. This,
I think, can be demonstrated easily. For example, at age eighteen he wrote
to Arthur Greeves,

> When I was reading [Beowulf] I tried to imagine myself as an old Saxon
> thane sitting in my hall of a winter's night, with the wolves & storm outside
> and the old fellow singing his story. In this way you get the atmosphere of
> terror that runs through it—the horror of the old barbarous days when the
> land was all forests and when you thought that a demon might come to
> your house any night & carry you off. The description of Grendel stalking
> up from his "fen and fastness" thrilled me.[9]

One might also argue for an intuitiveness in Lewis's medievalism by showing its ubiquitous presence in his writings or showing that it conditioned
almost every part of his thought and life. As for Lewis's writings, when
he wrote imaginative stories, they were often (though not always) suffused
with the medieval: in his imagery, atmosphere, characters, places, and ideas,

medieval material poured out from his imagination, a faculty that, as Lewis learned from Victorian romanticism, is deeper than reason.[10]

As for his thought and life, to say Lewis's medievalism was intuitive could also point to his adoption of *philosophy* as much more than an interesting intellectual pursuit—an estimation of that ancient art shared both by the classical thinkers he learned as a teenager and by the medieval thinkers he came to love later. One day early in his Oxford career, while lunching with fellow don Owen Barfield and a student named Bede Griffiths, Lewis happened to refer to philosophy as a "subject." Right away, Barfield snapped back, "It wasn't a *subject* to Plato. It was a way."[11] Lewis had to admit that Barfield was right: the pagan philosophers' contemplative quest was anything but coldly intellectual. Intellectual, yes. But characterized by desire, yearning, even passion—a passion for meaning, a passion to see God.

Lewis's medievalism was very much like this. The medieval worldview was never an inert object of study—a "subject." It was a "way"—a road traveled to get to meaning. In one of Lewis's favorite images, he sets out to "look along the sunbeam" of the medieval mind to see what it illumines rather than to look at the sunbeam and see nothing but the dust motes floating in it. To use the technical terms Lewis borrowed to describe this difference, he *enjoyed* medieval values for the ways they helped him see the world but did not *contemplate* them as objects in and of themselves.[12]

I think that medievalism was important for Lewis not only as a source of understanding of the truth of things but also as a primary way that his "chest"—the seat of his affections and thus his moral reasoning—received its formation. He was medieval not only in his mind but also in his heart. This can be seen not only in his youthful encounters with *sehnsucht* (joy) while reading medieval Norse myths and in his abiding affection for the poetic vision of Dante but also in his love for the way medieval people viewed the world and their place in it.

### Beginnings: Finding Tradition as Truth-Source

From his earliest years, Lewis found the greatest pleasure in both reading and writing. His father's house contained many books, which he read avidly, finding in some of them those earliest experiences of *sehnsucht*. By age eight he was trying his hand at authorship, writing and illustrating stories with his brother Warnie (Warren).

Then from ages sixteen to eighteen, Lewis studied with the former headmaster of an Irish college, William T. Kirkpatrick, who observed that Lewis read more classics than any other boy he had taught. Lewis's training in the classics under Kirkpatrick prepared Lewis to find in "old books" not only aesthetic pleasures but also meaning for living, and in this he was attuned more to the medieval than the modern era, as we'll see. In *The Discarded Image*, he speaks of "the overwhelmingly bookish . . . character of medieval culture"[13]—a character that Lewis shared, as I will explore in the next chapter.

What kind of books does Lewis tell us medievals loved? Perhaps disappointingly, given his own proclivities for the genre, Lewis insists that romances (tales of adventure such as the Arthurian cycle) were not the most typical, representative medieval form. Rather, even among the poets, it was books systematizing knowledge that formed medievals' favorite class of reading material: "At his most characteristic," says Lewis, "medieval man was not a dreamer nor a wanderer. He was an organiser, a codifier, a builder of systems. . . . There was nothing which medieval people liked better, or did better, than sorting out and tidying up."[14]

Though many may feel Lewis is at his most "medieval" when he imitates Dantean allegory in romantic tales such as his Narnia Chronicles or *The Great Divorce*, he was in tune with habits of medieval thought as much in his philosophical and ethical thought (and therefore his Christian apologetics) as in his literary scholarship and his imaginative writings. Lewis shared the systematic bent of the scholastics, who exhausted all their resources of ingenuity in the attempt to cover every conceivable doctrinal and ethical question and to unify all the disparate strands of the church fathers' thought. Perhaps it is in such works, then, as his *English Literature in the Sixteenth Century*, which is based on voluminous reading and intensely systematizing thinking, that Lewis is actually most "medieval."

### Lewis and Scholasticism

But what did Lewis really think of scholasticism? In a word, he defended it. I will dig into this more in chapter 4, but in the aforementioned *English Literature in the Sixteenth Century* for the Oxford History of English Literature series, Lewis censures the humanists for their anti-medievalism, which included a liberal dose of anti-scholasticism. Lewis accuses the humanists of undertaking "a war against ideas," and this charge strongly implies that he himself found in scholasticism some worthy intellectual substance. Moreover, he names the result of their attack a "new ignorance," surely indicating the loss not of useless speculation but of valuable knowledge. Indeed, Lewis offers such a forceful and complete rehabilitation of the scholastics and such a thoroughgoing scolding of their enemies that, as Dennis Danielson says, he fell into the trap of "countering caricature with caricature, oversimplification with oversimplification," as when he used of the humanists such "jeering epithets" as "Philistine" and "obscurantist."[15]

One suspects that what led Lewis to such incautious polemical overstatement was that he had embraced the medieval not only intellectually but also affectively; thus, like a knight defending his lady's honor, he leaped to his feet, swinging his keen blade at her enemy with broad strokes both energetic and (at times) indiscriminate.

This heartfelt commitment may well have emerged from the distinctive mode in which Lewis approached history—that is, as a sort of genial docent who studies and imaginatively indwells the mind-set of each period, complete with its "thoughts, feelings, circumstances and characters,"[16] so that he can paint them vividly in his own writings, ushering his readers into an intimate experience of the alien worlds of the past. Out of Lewis's "continuous immersion in historical writings and themes" emerged not just a skillful scholar of the Middle Ages but also an "experiencer" and a "re-enacter" of that age.[17] He was indeed, as he argues in his Cambridge address, a "specimen" who identified at the deepest level with the period of his expertise.

But what about the substance of that period's theology? A good example here is Lewis's advocacy for natural law (to which I will return in chap. 5). Gilbert Meilaender notes "how deeply Aristotelian are the roots of Lewis's understanding of morality." This he bases on Lewis's understanding of character formation, moral education, and the training of the emotions. All of this is captured in the image Lewis uses in his *Abolition of Man*, of the "chest." "The head," he insists, "rules the belly through the chest." Or: "Reason disciplines appetite only with the aid of trained emotions."[18]

Lewis makes explicit that this is an "older" morality: "For the wise men of old . . . the cardinal problem had been how to conform the soul to reality, and the solution had been knowledge, self-discipline, and virtue."[19] Natural law is of course both a classical and a medieval idea. But since

Lewis's particular formulation of morality is distinctly Christian (he insists that we need moral training to overcome the distortions of sin), one may take it to be closer to the moral thought of Augustine and Aquinas than to strictly classical morality.[20]

Having become convinced of the objective reality of natural law, Lewis set out to teach it to others. Certainly he did this in both *The Abolition of Man* and *Mere Christianity*, as well as in other, shorter essays. He also taught morality by telling stories. This is consistent with his Aristotelian understanding that morality is best communicated by demonstration and imitation. But it also drew from the medieval tradition of didactic fiction.

The best and most extended example of this in Lewis's imaginative writings are his Narnia stories. Though we always knew that Lewis used story to teach morality, we now discover that he did this in a particularly medieval way: by subtly weaving into the stories, as epitomes of various virtues, the planets of the Ptolemaic cosmos, with all their ancient pagan and medieval Christian resonances.[21] In this and many other ways, Lewis follows the man who was perhaps his true literary master—Dante.[22]

### Pagan Sources, "Happy Syncretism"

This brings us to one more way Lewis reflects the medievals' bookish, systematizing bent—exemplified in both the scholastics and Dante. As they created their compendia of knowledge for their readers, medievals syncretized gleefully. That is, they cared little whether great truths had first been discovered and expressed by Christians or by ancient pagans. Christianity always provided the framework for truth. But within that framework, one might fit all the best thought of the pagans, as Christian thinkers had been doing ever since Justin Martyr (100–165) and Clement of Alexandria (ca. 150–ca. 215). To take one of many examples, modern science emerged out of the medieval encounter between Christian theology and the thought of Aristotle.

Lewis, too, felt more affinity to a thoroughgoing pagan person, pursuing virtue by pagan lights, than to a "post-Christian" modern, and he returned again and again throughout his writing life to the wisdom of the ancients. The possibility that the Chronicles of Narnia may, if we believe Michael Ward, hang on an elaborate secret scaffolding of pagan planetary mythology, or that *The Abolition of Man* and *Mere Christianity* ransack Aristotelian virtue ethics and natural law theory for their ethical understanding, or that Lewis's favorite of his own novels—*Till We Have Faces*—is a reworked pagan myth did not, for Lewis, contradict his Christianity. Like medievals from Boethius (ca. 480–524) and the Beowulf author to Dante, Lewis was a happy syncretist, at least in the medieval sense of "plundering the Egyptians" for usable material while maintaining a firm Christian intellectual framework.

### Lewis's Devotional Medievalism

Lewis's was not simply an intellectual medievalism. One of the places where his medievalism touched his heart most deeply was in his Christian conversion and subsequent devotional practice.

Though at times low church in his worship, Lewis increasingly, as he grew older, turned to the early and medieval catholic traditions revived and preserved in high-church Anglicanism. Starting in 1940, he confessed his sins every Friday to a "spiritual director," a high-church Anglican priest named Father Walter Adams. Having completed his first confession, he said "that the experience was like a tonic to his soul."[23]

Lyle Dorsett says that Adams taught Lewis to love "liturgy, the 1662 Prayer Book, the Daily Office, and praying through the Psalter each month." Adams "helped Lewis learn that the Eucharist is more than a memorial and symbol," until he found himself able to "experience Real Presence in the Blessed Sacrament."[24] Beyond this, Lewis in his later years used the church calendar to identify with Christ and embraced the sacramental view of marriage and the veneration of the cross in Good Friday services.

This devotional medievalism came out not only in Lewis's own practice and beliefs but also in his spiritual advice to others. In the course of giving advice for spiritual growth to "Sarah Tate" (not her real name) in 1949, Lewis recommends other "old books I expect I've mentioned before: e.g. The *Imitation*, Hilton's *Scale of Perfection*, . . . *Theologia Germanica* . . . Lady Julian, *Revelations of Divine Love*."[25]

Lewis's personal copy of the late fourteenth-century *Theologia*, which addresses the struggle in the believer between God's will and self-will, bears frequent annotations. In his own works, Lewis cites the *Theologia* on the proper relation between Christianity and secular learning (along with Augustine, Aquinas, and Milton). *The Problem of Pain* quotes twice from the *Theologia*, and Lewis scholar David Downing suggests that the portrayal of Ransom in *Perelandra* as the "piebald man," burned by the sun on one side of his body and pallid white on the other because of his journey to Venus, which reflects the inner struggle of natural self and spiritual self, can perhaps be traced to "the conflict between what the *Theologia Germanica* calls 'God-hood' and 'I-hood.'"[26]

Lewis also deeply appreciated the mysticism of such medieval saints as Bernard of Clairvaux and Francis of Assisi. He refers to the Cistercian as "one of the 'great spiritual writers' of the Middle Ages." In *Allegory of Love*, Lewis cites Gilson's *La Theologie Mystique de St. Bernard*, and Downing argues that Lewis's use, in his essay "Transposition," of metaphors from everyday life to describe spiritual realities was likely sparked by his encounter with Bernard's imagery of the soul's spiritual marriage with Christ.[27] Lewis's copies of Gilson's book and Bruno S. James's biography of Bernard are both carefully annotated.

As for Francis, Lewis insisted to his friend Arthur Greeves that the Assisian was one of the "shining examples of human holiness."[28] He loved the friar's "gentle spirit and profound love of nature" and was so taken with Francis's habitual moniker for his own physical body, "Brother Ass," that he sometimes used it as a sign-off in his own letters.[29]

Even Thomas Aquinas—whom Lewis appreciated for his theological thought, citing him "over a dozen times in *The Allegory of Love* and *The Discarded Image* alone"—became for the Oxford don a devotional paradigm. On this point Downing adduces *Letters to Malcolm*, in which Lewis "observes that the great ideal in prayer is to speak to God as he really is from the depths of ourselves as we really are, without pretentions or evasions."[30] "The most blessed result of prayer," says Lewis, "would be to rise thinking, 'But I never knew before, I never dreamed . . .'" Then he muses, "I suppose it was at such a moment that Thomas Aquinas said of all his own theology, 'It reminds me of straw.'"[31]

Among the mystics, Julian was one of Lewis's particular favorites. Downing notes:

> Julian's visions made a deep impression on Lewis, and he refers to her in half a dozen of his books. In a letter written in 1940 to his friend Sister Penelope, he spends more than a page talking about Julian's vision of holding the whole universe in the palm of her hand and of Christ's reassurances

that "All shall be well." . . . Lewis concluded his sermon "Miracles" with Julian's vision of the hazelnut and referred to it again in *The Four Loves* as a vivid image to help Christians understand how far beneath the majesty of God are even the most magnificent things in his created order. Lewis quoted Julian on Christ's reassurance that "All shall be well" in *The Great Divorce*, *The Problem of Pain* and again in his essay "Psalms," collected in *Christian Reflections*. Clearly, Julian is the sort of person Lewis had in mind when he described mysticism (in the same paragraph where he discusses the hazelnut vision) as "wonderful foretastes of the fruition of God vouchsafed to some in their earthly life."[32]

Also well known is Lewis's appreciation for the doctrine of purgatory. In *Letters to Malcolm* he writes, "I believe in Purgatory," though he qualifies this by agreeing that the Reformers had been right to oppose "'the Romish doctrine concerning Purgatory' as [it] had then become." Lewis loved instead the portrayal of purgatory found in Newman's poem *The Dream of Gerontius*, in which "the saved soul, at the very foot of the throne, begs to be taken away and cleansed. It cannot bear for a moment longer 'with its darkness to affront that light.'"[33] He once wrote to his friend Sister Penelope, "Look me up in Purgatory."[34] Lewis clearly absorbed much of medieval Western practice in his own devotional life, drawing the line only at such Catholic practices as saying the "Hail Mary" and praying the rosary.

Early on, as he struggled toward conversion, Lewis also appreciated both the asceticism and the aesthetics of the Middle Ages. The spiritual aesthetic of Dante's *Commedia* continued to influence his thought and writings to the end of his life, as well as the grandeur of the scholastic theology from which Dante drew. In a 1930 letter to his friend Arthur Greeves, he describes the *Paradiso* as "feeling more important than any poetry I have ever read." He found in Dante's crowning cantica a "blend of complexity and beauty . . . very like Catholic theology—wheel within wheel, but wheels of glory, and the One radiat[ing] through the Many."[35]

Lewis's love of concrete and common things—trees, mountains, weather—was not just aesthetic but sacramental: he wrote "every created thing is, in its degree, an image of God, and the ordinate and faithful appreciation of that thing a clue which, truly followed, will lead back to Him."[36] He lamented the sapping of the medieval spirit from the world, and then from humanity, resulting in the abolition not only of the spiritual dimensions of the material world but also of the very spirits of human beings.

"We can observe," Lewis writes, in the preface of another author's book,

> a single one-way progression. At the outset the universe appears packed with will, intelligence, life and positive qualities; every tree is a nymph and every planet a god. Man himself is akin to the gods. The advance of knowledge gradually empties this rich and genial universe: first of its gods, then of its colours, smells, sounds and tastes, finally of solidity itself as solidity was originally imagined. As these items are taken from the world, they are transferred to the subjective side of the account. . . . The Subject becomes gorged, inflated, at the expense of the Object. But the matter does not rest there. The same method which has emptied the world now proceeds to empty ourselves. The masters of the method soon announce that we were just as mistaken . . . when we attributed "souls," or "selves" or "minds" to human organisms, as when we attributed Dryads to the trees.[37]

This process of reduction of the world and reduction of ourselves, says Lewis, "has led us from the living universe where man meets the gods to the final void where almost-nobody discovers his mistakes about almost-nothing." One scholar imagines how Lewis's heart must have ached, having reconstructed "the heavens of medieval man, filled with life, light, and music," to now live as one born out of time, in "the final void of the modern space age."[38]

Let us, then, follow this genial docent back through the mists of time, to the medieval era of Christian faith. Few guides could serve us better than the eccentric genius who, in many ways, resonated more with that period than his own. C. S. Lewis's affection for the medieval era and the ways he absorbed its lessons will also help us to understand and benefit from medieval Christians' love affair with tradition and theological inquiry, their grounded and detailed moral code and the compassionate ministry it underwrote, their sacramental understanding of creation, their emotion as they approached the divine, their sense of how the incarnation lifted up their own humanity, and the ways they disciplined that humanity to keep their hearts fixed on God.

# 3

## Getting Rooted

### *Tradition as Source of Truth*

It's spring, and something is stirring under the white steeple of Wheaton College's Billy Graham Center. A motley group—young and clean-cut, goateed and pierced, white-haired and bespectacled—fills the center's Barrows Auditorium and join their voices to sing of "the saints who nobly fought of old" and "mystic sweet communion with those whose rest is won." A speaker walks an attentive group through the prayers in the fifth-century Gelasian Sacramentary, recommending them as templates for worship in Protestant churches today. Another recommends the pastoral strengths of the medieval fourfold hermeneutic. Another gleefully passes on the news that Liberty University has observed the ancient liturgical season of Lent. The "t" word (yes, "tradition") echoes in the halls.[1]

Just what is going on here, in this veritable shrine to pragmatic evangelistic methods and no-nonsense, back-to-the-Bible Protestantism? Have the Catholics taken over? No, this is the sixteenth annual Wheaton Theology Conference, held April 12–14, 2007. Its theme is "The Ancient Faith for the Church's Future."

In 1978, conference instigator Robert Webber began his groundbreaking *Common Roots: A Call to Evangelical Maturity* by throwing down the gauntlet: "My argument is that the era of the early church (AD 100–500), and particularly the second century, contains insights which evangelicals need to recover."[2] Twenty-four years later, he could rejoice in the pages of his *Younger Evangelicals* that "the younger evangelical[s] . . . want to immerse themselves in the past and form a culture that is connected to the past, a culture that remembers its tradition as it moves into the future."[3] Webber observes that evangelicals have entered the new millennium with a new surge into the past.

As I sat in sessions and listened to hallway and cafeteria conversations during that spring week in 2007, it became clear to me that the message Webber brought to the church in his more than forty books was attracting not only more people than ever but also more committed, careful study. All signs pointed to the maturing of the ancient-future church.

This conference was no uncritical engagement. Appropriate cautions were voiced against romanticizing the tradition uncritically, against grabbing ancient beliefs and practices "cafeteria style" out of context, and against slapping them down in the twenty-first century without the necessary hard work of understanding what they meant to those who originally held them. These wise reflections arose from the classic academic virtue of careful, critical thinking. Indeed, this evangelical reengagement with history has clearly been setting down roots in evangelical higher education. In 2001, Daryl Charles, a professor at Taylor University, testified, "As one who teaches at a broadly evangelical liberal arts university, I have witnessed a growing hunger among young adults whose backgrounds are largely nondenominational or free-church to think historically, critically, and ecumenically. While this is not true of all undergraduates, it is true of significant numbers."[4] Seven years later, D. H. Williams added:

> Who would have thought, a decade ago, that one of the most vibrant and serious fields of Christian study at the beginning of the twenty-first century would be the ancient church fathers? There has been an opening of new avenues, especially among free-church Protestants, by the almost overnight popularity of bishops and monks, martyrs and apologists, philosophers and historians who first fashioned a Christian culture 1500 years ago.[5]

One subset of these "classical disciplines" has proved particularly grip-ping for those seeking the spiritual balance Richard Foster and Dallas Willard describe: practices historically associated with monasticism (and to these we will return at the end of this book). In *The New Faithful* (2004),[6] journalist Colleen Carroll notes the public love affair with things monastic that surged with the 1996 publication of Benedictine oblate Kathleen Norris's *The Cloister Walk*. Among evangelicals, the trend has extended to retreats at Catholic monasteries, recovery of Celtic spirituality, and observance of the divine hours.

Not surprisingly, given its biblical focus, the slow, meditative, monastic prayer technique called the *lectio divina* has captivated many evangelicals, who have taken up the practice guided by such books as the three-volume *Divine Hours* by Phyllis Tickle, *The Rhythm of God's Grace: Uncovering Morning and Evening Hours of Prayer* by Mennonite professor Arthur Boers, and a book for youth, *Divine Intervention: Encountering God through the Ancient Practice of Lectio Divina*, by Minneapolis emerging-church leader Tony Jones.

The broader appeal of monastic practices has been explored in the past few years in *Monk Habits for Everyday People: Benedictine Spirituality for Protestants* (2007) by evangelical Anglican theologian Dennis Okholm, *The Attentive Life: Discerning God's Presence in All Things* (2008) by Billy Graham associate Leighton Ford, and *The Story of Monasticism: Retrieving an Ancient Tradition for Contemporary Spirituality* (2015) by Biola medievalist Greg Peters, among other appreciative works by evangelical scholars.

## The Evangelical Protestant Identity Crisis

The evangelical Protestant reengagement with tradition, though still perhaps a little trickle and not a great torrent, originated in the decade of the 1970s. Arguably, that decade marked the beginning—or at least intensification—of an evangelical identity crisis from which we have not yet emerged. An evangelical "growth spurt," which became a media focus especially after the 1977 election of the "born-again" president Jimmy Carter, "left the movement with multiple crises of identity."[7]

I began experiencing those crises myself when, in 1985, I gave my life to Christ in a Canadian charismatic setting. My church was one of those modern suburban megachurches with an auditorium-like sanctuary that someone had decorated to look like a suburban living room, complete with plush carpeting and rubber plants. On Sunday mornings, I would walk in and feel the palpable presence of the all-powerful and all-loving Lord. On Saturday nights, at cell-group prayer meetings, I was mentored by wise "fathers and mothers in the Lord." On Monday nights, I participated in the music ministry of a dynamic youth group.

Yet through the years, although this wonderful church formed me in the "joy of the Lord" that is my strength, I still felt like we were missing something. Our faith, as a stalwart outpost of the kingdom in a threatening world, seemed somehow precarious. We stood, as we faced that world, on a foundation made up of the words of our favorite Bible passages (our "canon within the canon"), the sermons of our pastors, and a roster of approved visiting evangelists. There was no sense at all of the whole mystical, historical massiveness of a church that had been around for two thousand years, no sense that our foundation actually stretched down and back through time, resting on such giants in the faith as John Wesley, Martin Luther, Bernard of Clairvaux, and Ignatius of Antioch (though I did not then know any of these well).

I now see that my early sense of the insecurity of the church stemmed from what J. I. Packer identifies as evangelicalism's "stunted ecclesiology," rooted in our alienation from our own past. Without a healthy engagement with our past, including historical definitions of "church," we are being true neither to Scripture nor to our theological identity as church![8]

The recent interest in tradition, especially among young evangelicals, suggests that evangelicalism is still struggling with an identity crisis. This generation seems uneasy and alienated in the environment of mall-like church buildings, high-energy and entertainment-oriented worship, and boomer ministry strategies and structures modeled on the business world. Increasingly they ask just how these culturally camouflaged churches can help them rise above the values of the consumerist world around them, enabling them to make a difference for Christ.

So what to do? Easy, says this emerging "ancient-future" youth movement. Stop endlessly debating and advertising Christianity, and just *embody* it. Live it faithfully, in community with others (especially others beyond the white suburban world of so many megachurch ministries). Embrace symbols and sacraments. Dialogue with the "other two" historic confessions. Recognize that the road to the church's future is through its past. And break out the candles and incense. Pray the *lectio divina*. Tap all the riches of Christian tradition that you can find.

## C. S. Lewis States the Modern Problem

The situation evangelicals find themselves in, needing to defend tradition in the Christian church as a good thing, dates back to C. S. Lewis's day and before. In his famous lecture to the Cambridge University audience assembled to witness his installation as the Chair of Medieval and Renaissance Literature at that university, Lewis describes his own mid-twentieth-century European setting as one of cultural darkness and amnesia and himself as a kind of dinosaur—one of the few left in that dark age of wars and rumors of wars. He described himself as a specimen who still spoke the native language of the old Christian Western tradition as a native, and who could thus be a precious resource for a society and a culture that had drifted far from its moorings in the Great Tradition of Christianized Greek thought.[9]

Lewis found this change diabolical, and he made this clear by putting it in the mouth of the senior demon in *The Screwtape Letters*: "Only the learned read old books and we have now so dealt with the learned that they are of all men the least likely to acquire wisdom by doing so." The infernal realm accomplished this, Screwtape continues, by making "the Historical Point of View" into a scholarly dogma. Those infected by historicism never ask whether the things they read in ancient sources are true. Instead, they perform all sorts of tortuous text-critical tests on them, to find out

> who influenced the ancient writer, and how far the statement is consistent with what he said in other books, and what phase in the writer's development, or in the general history of thought, it illustrates, and how it affected later writers, and how often it has been misunderstood (specially by the learned man's own colleagues) and what the general course of criticism on it has been for the last ten years, and what is the "present state of the question."

In other words, the scholar is immunized against seeing in old texts anything that "could possibly modify your thoughts or your behavior."

The result is the tragic loss of the wisdom accumulated over countless centuries:

> Since we cannot deceive the whole human race all the time, *it is most important thus to cut every generation off from all others*; for where learning makes a free commerce between the ages there is always the danger that the characteristic errors of one may be corrected by the characteristic truths of another. But thanks be to Our Father and the Historical Point of View, great scholars are now as little nourished by the past as the most ignorant mechanic who holds that "history is bunk."[10]

I suspect that there has never been a culture more inclined than our modern Western (and *how much more so* our postmodern American) to ride out like the lone cowboy, remaking ourselves and cutting ourselves off from all that came before. Lewis was seeing that already in the mid-twentieth century, and we are living with the relativistic, fragmented, weak, amoral, confused fruit of that movement, which began in the eighteenth-century Enlightenment and was shaped by the historicism that rose to prominence in the nineteenth century.

### Lewis the Traditioner

For an idea of how Lewis viewed the power of tradition, it is helpful to look to his preface in Sister Penelope's translation of Athanasius of Alexandria's (ca. 296/98–373) *De Incarnatione*, retitled "On Reading Old Books" in later anthologies, or (even more) to his "*De Descriptione Temporum*" address at Cambridge in the fall of 1954. In both of these texts, we find him lamenting that in abandoning tradition the modern world dealt itself a grievous wound, which only his Christian faith kept him from seeing as inevitably fatal.

Lewis was perhaps the best-prepared person of his generation for the task of appreciating and passing on the wisdom of past generations to those yet to come. We have seen how, as a boy, he found the greatest pleasure in reading the "old books" he found in his lawyer father's house, and how he found in some of them early experiences of what he would call *sehnsucht* or joy. Later, in his teenage years, devouring the classics with William Kirkpatrick, he found in those same old books a more than aesthetic appeal; now, a sense that they contained meaning for living. This willingness to be taught wisdom by the ancients is, again, more a medieval than a modern trait. In fact, it is a trait of the Christian church, which, as a "people of the book," grounded itself for more than a millennium in the apostolic teachings handed down in narrative form from generation to generation.

Books were Lewis's native element. That so many of the books he read were ancient or medieval is certainly important, but that they were books, and that Lewis loved them and sought in them wisdom for living, shows him to be intuitively at one with medievalism. In other words, Lewis came early to that bedrock medieval presupposition: our best authorities for truth are the ancient, written authorities.

### "Why—Damn It—It's Medieval!"

It is true that as a young man Lewis turned consciously against this insight, building instead a teetering modern "new look" philosophical edifice. But the respect for tradition was always present in the background, and it didn't take long to reemerge in the oddest of ways.

It happened at Oxford when his friends Cecil Harwood and Owen Barfield converted—not to orthodox Christianity but to the mystical philosophy (anthroposophy) of Rudolf Steiner. As Lewis saw their new creed at the time:

> Here, apparently, were all the abominations; none more abominable than those which had once attracted me. Here were gods, spirits, after-life, and pre-existence, initiates, occult knowledge, meditation. "Why—damn it—it's medieval," I exclaimed; for I still had all the chronological snobbery of my period and used the names of earlier periods as terms of abuse. Here was everything which the New Look had been designed to exclude; everything that might lead one off the main road into those dark places where men wallow on the floor and scream that they are being dragged down into Hell. Of course it was all arrant nonsense. There was no danger of my being taken in.[11]

Of course Lewis sets us up with this statement. Very soon after this episode, Lewis *was* "taken in" by many things that were "medieval." In fact, he found himself on a path that wound up not only in traditional, orthodox Christianity but also in the Cambridge Chair of Medieval and Renaissance Literature. And one of the chief aspects of Lewis's movement from idealism to theism to Christianity was his increased sense of the permanent verity and validity of truths and traditions of the past, as well as the fact that in many ways these older understandings had not been improved upon, especially in the areas of religion and ethics. And this was a medieval insight. Discussing how medieval authors, despite the rarity of books, often presented or repeated things quite familiar to their audience, Lewis says, "One gets the impression that medieval people, like Professor Tolkien's Hobbits, enjoyed books which told them what they already knew."[12] In ancient and medieval worship, this principle is called "anamnesis"—it is the bringing of important things to memory again and again by communal recitation in order to work them deeply into our hearts.

In the ensuing "Great War" with Barfield, Barfield's responses to Lewis's "violent" arguments against Steiner's teachings

> made short work of what I have called my "chronological snobbery," the uncritical acceptance of the intellectual climate common to our own age and the assumption that whatever has gone out of date is on that account discredited. You must find why it went out of date. Was it ever refuted (and if so by whom, where, and how conclusively) or did it merely die away as fashions do? If the latter, this tells us nothing about its truth or falsehood. From seeing this, one passes to the realization that our own age is also "a period," and certainly has, like all periods, its own characteristic illusions. They are likeliest to lurk in those widespread assumptions which are so ingrained in the age that no one dares to attack or feels it necessary to defend them.[13]

### "Good Philosophy" and the Moral Law

This understanding of the limitations and blind spots of his age—and of the necessity to turn to other ages for wisdom that will heal those blind spots—shows up in many other places in Lewis's writings. In fact, it forms the core of his argument for the necessity of education, even in wartime.[14]

Meanwhile, Lewis's own early career seemed destined to be in academic philosophy. In 1925 he became a teacher of English literature at Magdalen College, Oxford, with some temporary duties teaching philosophy, where, according to Lewis scholar James Patrick, "the most important philosopher was the great idealist John Alexander Smith, who . . . displayed a polite skepticism toward anyone who would propose in 1920 to reject the cumulative moral wisdom of over two thousand years on behalf of any conceivable new theory."[15]

Patrick goes on to explain how thoroughly this notion of the natural moral law suffused the medieval period:

> Aristotle had assumed it, and Plato. Cicero had spoken of it when he called it the law that is not written down. When St. Paul wrote that even the Gentiles knew that certain kinds of behavior were wrong, he was appealing to natural law. This same idea informed the thought of St. Augustine in the fourth century and St. Thomas in the thirteenth, and influenced Anglicanism at its origin through Richard Hooker's [scholastically framed] Laws of Ecclesiastical Polity.[16]

In other words, Lewis believed that "natural law is a metaphysical reality," as the whole Western medieval tradition, from one end to the other, had assumed. "In the last essay he wrote for publication, Lewis said of natural law, 'I hold this conception to be basic to all civilization.'"[17]

## Lewis on Recovering the Tradition

In his Cambridge lecture "*De Descriptione Temporum*," Lewis insists that we needn't think of history as nostalgia or a slavish following of past wisdom. He reminds his listeners of the freeing effect experienced by those in therapy who surface and deal with forgotten elements from their individual pasts. Similarly, he argues, "I think no class of men are less enslaved to the past than historians. It is the unhistorical who are usually without knowing it enslaved to a very recent past."[18] In his sermon "Learning in War-Time," Lewis continues in this vein of thought:

> Most of all, perhaps, we need intimate knowledge of the past . . . because we . . . need something to set against the present, to remind us that the basic assumptions have been quite different in different periods. . . . A man who has lived in many places is not likely to be deceived by the local errors of his native village; the scholar has lived in many times and is therefore in some degree immune from the great cataract of nonsense that pours from the press and the microphone of his own age.[19]

As Christians and citizens we *must*, Lewis insists, acquaint ourselves with the "old books." This is so because, sadly, at the points in their Christian experiences where people *most* need a firm and reliable sense of Christian doctrine (including standards of worship and conduct), they are *least* inclined to reach for the testimony of "the tradition" handed down through the ages. This was true in Lewis's day as it is now: "Wherever you find a little study circle of Christian laity," Lewis observed, "you can be almost certain that they are studying not St. Luke or St. Paul or St. Augustine or Thomas Aquinas or Hooker or Butler, but M. Berdyaev or M. Maritain or M. Niebuhr or Miss Sayers or even myself."[20]

This, says Lewis in his introduction to *St. Athanasius on the Incarnation*, is backward. The older books are flat-out more valuable.

> A new book is still on its trial and the amateur is not in a position to judge it. It has to be tested against the great body of Christian thought down the ages, and all its hidden implications (often unsuspected by the author himself) have to be brought to light. . . . The only safety is to have a standard of plain, central Christianity ("mere Christianity" as Baxter called it) which puts the controversies of the moment in their proper perspective. Such a standard [which I would say is very close to the early Church's "rule of faith"] can be acquired only from the old books.[21]

Our modern biases, on the other hand, create a sort of blindness, which is only fed and increased if we read nothing but modern books. We must, says Lewis, "keep the clean sea breeze of the centuries blowing through our minds, and this can be done only by reading old books."[22]

And what does one discover about the Great Tradition of Christianity as one reads old Christian books (among them Athanasius's *On the Incarnation*)? One crucial correction offered by acquaintance with our own Christian tradition is that Christianity doesn't mean everything and nothing at all. The faith handed down through the centuries was "no insipid interdenominational transparency, but something positive, self-consistent, and inexhaustible."[23]

### Lewis and Athanasius

Then Lewis turns to Athanasius, and he finds in Athanasius's role as staunch defender of trinitarian orthodoxy (of, that is, the Great Tradition) a positive tonic for modern heresies:

> He stood for the Trinitarian doctrine, "whole and undefiled," when it looked as if all the civilized world was slipping back from Christianity into the

religion of Arius—into one of those "sensible" synthetic religions which are so strongly recommended to-day and which, then as now, included among their devotees many highly cultivated clergymen. It is his glory that he did not move with the times; it is his reward that he now remains when those times, as all times do, have moved away.[24]

Lewis certainly practiced the sensitivity to tradition that he preached: he read every page of Sister Penelope's translation at least twice, *after* he wrote the book's introduction, and at the top of every page he summarized the main points.

Lewis valued Athanasius's *De Incarnatione* as the work of a uniquely courageous and solid Christian living in a better time. "We cannot," he admits, "appropriate all [Athanasius's] confidence to-day. We cannot point to the high virtue of Christian living and the gay, almost mocking courage of Christian martyrdom, as a proof of our doctrines with quite that assurance which Athanasius takes as a matter of course. But whoever may be to blame for that it is not Athanasius."[25]

Athanasius and the Arian controversy that defined his life's work stand at the crux of perhaps one of the best cases that can be made for tradition today. Most Christians assume the traditional doctrine of the Trinity and assume it is plainly present in the Bible. But it is not. There is plenty of Bible evidence that points in other directions. The Gospel of Mark, for example, seems to show a very human Jesus who is a servant of the Father but is in no way equal to him. Most early Christians therefore held to some form of a loose "subordinationism": Jesus is divine, certainly, but not "as divine" as the Father. It took more than a century, both before and after the Council of Nicaea in 325, and (as we've said) the courage of Athanasius, who was exiled five times for his troubles, to straighten out the record and reflect the full scriptural witness in a robust doctrine of the Trinity. Without the tradition protected and handed down, sometimes under extreme duress, by teachers such as Athanasius, we would be living not by the message of the gospel but by a potpourri of heterodox opinions.

Lewis was not content just to stand on the sidelines of modern discussions about Christian theology and lob in the occasional reminder of tradition. Again and again in his essays, stories, and letters, he insists that apart from tradition we are adrift in the errors of our own age. Indeed, soon after his 1931 conversion, this compulsion became a full-blown vocation for the Oxford don and lay theologian. He became a public intellectual—a conduit to past wisdom for an amnesiac age. It was a vocation he shared with one of his favorite writers, who was also one of the most influential thought leaders in the medieval period—a man who wrote as the Roman Empire was crumbling around him and attempted to preserve Christian as well as Greek philosophical truth for a time in danger of losing its inherited wisdom.

### Lewis the Boethian

In 1962, *The Christian Century* magazine asked Lewis the question, "What books did most to shape your vocational attitude and your philosophy of life?" Of the ten books this great medievalist listed in response, only one is medieval: Boethius's *Consolation of Philosophy*. But Lewis's debt was not limited to the holding of certain Boethian ideas. Like any good schoolchild, Lewis would have paid careful attention to the wording of the question the *Century* set for him. They asked him not "Whose ideas do you admire the most?" or "Who influenced your literary style?" Rather, they asked about the shaping of his vocation and philosophy of life. Those are deep sorts of influence indeed.

Boethius was a Christian philosopher who drew from classical wells and found no contradiction in doing so. Precedents abounded in the early church, from Justin Martyr to Clement of Alexandria to Origen to Augustine. And in that openness to wisdom *wherever it was found*, but understood and corrected through the lenses of the Christian faith, he prefigured the attitude of the High (1000–1300; Anselm through Dante) and late (1300–1500; Wycliffe through Luther) Middle Ages. This, despite his own position at the cusp of a period of near-loss of the classical sources—what is typically known in the literature as the "Dark Ages," or simply early Middle Ages (500s–1000; Benedict through the Carolingian Empire), though the self-designated Holy Roman emperor Charlemagne (742/47–814) did try, in a limited and derivative way, to revive classical learning.

If you know about Lewis, the following description of Boethius should sound familiar:

- He was perhaps the best-educated man of his generation—and that generation found itself already gathering speed as it rolled down into a valley of forgetfulness and ignorance, heedless of the rich traditions that had nurtured its parents and grandparents.

- He became to that dark generation a public intellectual and educator of huge popular impact—an impact that continued after his death.
- He wrote accessible theological works of an orthodox sort—content to pass on to those less erudite than he the wisdom of tradition.

For Boethius, however, that tradition most certainly included the best of the pagan philosophers; he wove their wisdom into his writings; and indeed, he revered Plato (ca. 428–348/47 BC), Aristotle (384–322 BC), and their ilk so highly that some questioned his commitment to the Christian faith.

Nonetheless, many devout Christians who came after him called his name blessed (even "sainted") and tried (with varying degrees of success) to repeat his arguments and make use of his literary techniques.

Boethius was sensitive to people's existential troubles and emotional states; in fact, when passing on the wisdom of the ancients, he started with human experience. He was foremost a moral philosopher, not only in his treatises but also in his imaginative work.

In short, Boethius, like C. S. Lewis, was a public intellectual. The public intellectual stands at a time of radical cultural change. Certainly this was true of Boethius, to the degree that he has been interpreted as the "last educated man" warning against an encroaching barbarism. This image is made vivid, of course, by the nature of his end. This cultured philosopher was first imprisoned by barbarians—the Ostrogothic king Theodoric (454–526) and, as Lewis puts it, his "huge, fair-skinned, beer-drinking, boasting thanes"—until "presently they twisted ropes round his head till his eyes dropped out and finished him off with a bludgeon."[26] What a tempting symbol of the death of the old Roman culture and the dawning of the Dark Ages. Yet Boethius's death did not terminate the influence of that classical culture—not by a long shot. The blood of this martyr was the seed of Christian culture, bearing the fruit of tradition long after his death.

### Standing in the Gap

Lewis valued Boethius highly as a historian and traditioner, bringing the light of one age's wisdom into the darkness of another's depravity and forgetfulness. He refers to Boethius as "that divine popularizer,"[27] which indicates the "translative" function served by public intellectuals. To speak intelligibly to a diverse company, "patrician and plebian, bourgeoisie and proletariat, rich and poor, educated and semi-educated, specialist and nonspecialist,"[28] the public intellectual must use a language they all understand—the vernacular. Aside from the *Consolation*, the work of Boethius that most shaped the Middle Ages was his labor translating the wisdom of the ancient Greeks, which he read in their original language, into the vernacular of his day, Latin. And Lewis of course both was master of many languages and could "translate" the most complex philosophical ideas not just into clear radio addresses for the masses but also into the imaginative, concrete world of children's books.

It is hard to think of a more apt description, in fact, of C. S. Lewis. As much as did Boethius, Lewis wanted to stand in the gap of cataclysmic cultural loss, to bring "the tradition" back to the people. He told his Cambridge audience, "I myself belong far more to that Old Western order than to yours. . . . I read as a native texts that you must read as foreigners. . . . That way, where I fail as a critic, I may yet be useful as a specimen."[29] In other words, Lewis didn't just study the medieval and renaissance period as a "subject" (in his role as a scholar and professor), and he didn't just teach it as a "subject." He was medieval in that he treated both philosophy and medievalism as a "way" to be absorbed imaginatively as well as intellectually.

His attention to the medieval "atmosphere" or "mood" is not to be undervalued in Lewis's thought. It is akin to the "model" of his *Discarded Image*: a "way of seeing." As a historian Lewis sought to indwell, to recreate the experience of, other eras. To keep alive an experience, a way of seeing, as Boethius did, was for Lewis perhaps the same thing as keeping a living tradition alive and thus preserving the wisdom of that tradition for future generations. This, at least, seems to be part of the burden of what Lewis is saying in Screwtape Letter 27.

And for this, Lewis loved Boethius. It is clear from Lewis's answer to *The Christian Century* that he felt a kind of vocational kinship to Boethius. His epithet for Boethius—"divine popularizer"—is a heroic epithet in which he hoped to participate (almost mystically) himself. This was a man who saw books as friends and relished their reading (as many do) in the fellowship of others, with a lively discussion over cakes and ales. To be in continuity with the elders of days of yore is to be in their fellowship and to "hear" them, and Boethius's primary work was making the elders heard in his age—a Dark Age, desperate for wisdom and sustenance, as Lewis felt his own, too, was dark and needy. It may not be an exaggeration to say, echoing Frederick Buechner's definition of vocation, that for Lewis "the place where his deep gladness met the world's deep need"[30] was the modern abandonment of tradition.

### Recovering Tradition through Imagination

Nowhere did Lewis exercise this vocation more clearly than in his imaginative writing. He saw literature's purpose as "delighting and informing." It could be argued that he placed a heavy (didactic) emphasis on the latter. But what he did in his stories was to re-narrate the stories of our traditions, allowing his readers to indwell truths of the past, "enjoying" them (that is, seeing the world by their light) and not just "contemplating" them (that is, knowing them analytically and propositionally).[31] This was his practical application of a principle he enunciates as follows: "reason is the natural organ of truth; but imagination is the organ of meaning."[32] Lewis, like the allegorist Boethius, knew that if we are to pass the meaning of our faith from generation to generation, an excellent way to do so is through story. And Lewis succeeded in doing just that, passing the meaning of faith to other generations by means of his stories.

Humans pass their wisdom from generation to generation through a traditioning process—that is the meaning of the word "tradition": handing down to posterity that which is most vital to the living of life—through stories told around the campfire as much as through manuals studied in libraries and schools. Storytelling is the knowledge of intimacy rather than convention (analysis). And effective narrative, to be indwelt, must form us (affectively) by giving us materials for our imaginations to dwell on, chew on, and be nourished by—materials that address our ancient desires, as Tolkien says in *On Fairy-Stories*.[33]

This is Michael Ward's argument in *Planet Narnia*: that what Lewis is doing by secretly weaving the Ptolemaic and medieval planets—the planets as virtues—into his Chronicles is *seeding the imaginative material of those virtues into the story* so that we would fall in love with those virtues. He is doing what his friend Tolkien claimed to be doing with the characters in his stories, who are (in a sense, like every human being) living allegories "embodying in a particular tale and clothed in the garments of time and place, universal truth and everlasting life."[34] And in turn, this is just what the Christian tradition does in its liturgies and sacramental forms.

In his delightful *Companion to Narnia*, Paul F. Ford characterizes Lewis's theology of prayer as grounded in desire. Ford finds the raw materials of this theology in Augustine of Hippo's famous letter of response to the North African woman Proba, who had written to the great theologian about her prayer life (Augustine's letter may be considered an antecedent, Ford suggests, to Lewis's own *Letters to Malcolm: Chiefly on Prayer*). In Augustine's words (cited by Ford):

> "Why [God] should ask us to pray, when he knows what we need before we ask him, may perplex us if we do not realize that our Lord and God does not want to know what we want (for he cannot fail to know it) but wants us rather to exercise our desire through our prayers, so that we may be able to receive what he is preparing to give us. His gift is very great indeed, but our capacity is too small and limited to receive it. That is why we are told: *Enlarge your desires, do not bear the yoke with unbelievers.*"[35]

Ford is right—this is very Lewisian indeed—and I will turn again to this matter of the desires as part of the discussion of affective devotion in chapter 8. If you'd like to check into this now, read Lewis's sermon "The Weight of Glory," in which he argues (in Augustinian tone) that Christians' desires are not too strong but too weak.

Having become convinced of the objective reality and perennial pan-cultural presence of the basic morality also taught in traditional Christianity, Lewis set out to teach it to others. Certainly he did this in both *The Abolition of Man* and *Mere Christianity*, as well as in other, shorter essays. But he also taught morality by telling stories. This was consistent with his Aristotelian understanding that virtues are best developed by demonstration and imitation. But didactic fiction was also a venerable medieval tradition.

Lewis follows Boethius in this practice as well. We have in Boethius's *Consolation* a consummate didactic fiction, which if not fully allegorical at least borders on the allegorical, and which bridges Lewis's first scholarly love, classical philosophy, to his second scholarly love, medieval literature.

## Medievals and Tradition: Delighting in the Church Triumphant

In *The Discarded Image* (a compendium of lectures he gave at Cambridge), Lewis shows us that medievals implicitly trusted historical texts as the repositories of God's truth. As we've seen, Lewis understood "the overwhelmingly bookish . . . character of medieval culture." He elaborates upon this in "The Medieval Situation," the first chapter of *The Discarded Image*: "When we speak of the Middle Ages as the ages of authority we are usually thinking about the authority of the Church. But they were the age not only of her authority, but of authorities. . . . Every writer, if he possibly can, bases himself on an earlier writer . . . preferably a Latin one." Lewis distinguishes this impulse both from the "savage" (primitive) community, in which "you absorb your culture . . . from the immemorial pattern of behavior," and from the modern West, in which "most knowledge depends, in the last resort, on observation" (that is, the empiricism of the scientific method). Unlike these ages, "the Middle Ages depended predominantly on books"—despite lower literacy rates than much of the modern world enjoys.[36]

For the medieval person, tradition was not past but present. And it was not merely intellectual, like some card file of truths that one drags out in an argument. Tradition was a matter of the heart. "Historically," writes Lewis, "medieval man stood at the foot of a stairway; looking up, he felt delight." Delight, and the warmth of companionship: "The saints looked down on one's spiritual life, the kings, sages, and warriors on one's secular life, the great lovers of old on one's own amours, to foster, encourage, and instruct. There were friends, ancestors, patrons in every age. One had one's place, however modest, in a great succession; one need be neither proud nor lonely."[37]

In other words, the medieval person actively belonged to a family that stretched far back in time. That family was constantly recognized. It was recognized through the cult of the saints, through prayer for intercession to those same saints, and prayer for those who were in purgatory (a belief that itself developed out of the ancient Christian practice of praying for the dead at every service). That family also shines out in the pair of terms medievals used for the church. Both referred to the same church, but there were two parts of the body of Christ: the church militant (those still on earth, fighting the good fight) and the church triumphant (in heaven, who

are cheering for those still on earth). For medievals, the church triumphant was still very much a part of the church militant (and vice versa),
and we have access to them as mentors, guides, intercessors. So what we
have is not just a legacy of doctrine—a legacy of intellect—but also a
legacy of love.

### Tradition as Communal Discernment of Scripture

One barrier that still stands in the way of broader acceptance of tradition among free-church Protestants is a misunderstanding of the Reformation that says that medieval Christians treated tradition as a source
of authority separate from (and potentially, in some cases, superior to)
Scripture.[38] The notion would have been ludicrous to medievals. Scripture
and tradition were never separated in the early church. The church had
met together in councils repeatedly to discern the meanings of Scripture.
The resulting creeds (elaborated out of long-repeated local church creeds
that developed out of the heart of worship) became part of tradition as
protections against wildfire teachings such as Arianism, docetism, and
monophysitism. In fact, tradition was the careful, communal deliberation
on Scripture.

Now it is also true that the New Testament canon itself, whose now-
accepted list of books did not appear until AD 367 in an Easter letter of
Athanasius, emerged out of a process of communal discernment led, as the
church believed, by the Holy Spirit. Which books and letters, they asked,
when read in the congregations, evidenced spiritual power and truth by
supporting and edifying the congregants and building up the church? It
was only in the late medieval period, when tradition became a crutch and
a tool of power on the part of some of those at the top of the church, that
Christian thinkers such as John Wycliffe (ca. 1331–84) and Jan Hus (ca.
1369–1415) seriously doubted the seamlessness of Scripture and tradition
and their necessity to each other.

From the time of the earliest church—from Irenaeus battling the heretics—it is only the tradition, the narrative rule of faith, and the proto-
creeds and creeds passed down that allowed Christians to hold together in
their minds the true meanings of the narrated Scriptures so that they could
indwell those truths and be formed by them in their affections and habitual
actions. Where the heretics went wrong, as the post-Nicene Cappadocians

insisted, was (in Lewis's terms) in "contemplating" that which is to be "enjoyed"—that is, making into a merely intellectual matter that which must be absorbed through the heart and lived in action. Those who refused to live the gospel discipline, who merely played with the text, privileging their own individual interpretations, *they* were the heretics. The Scriptures should not even be given to them to read; the Scriptures do not belong to them because they read the Scriptures without reference to the Christian community, with its traditional linkages back to the apostolic witness. This logic was followed throughout the Middle Ages, Jaroslav Pelikan tells us, as "the definition of Christian doctrine was set by the authority of tradition."[39]

### Tradition as Inclusive of All God's Truth

In *The Discarded Image*, Lewis shows us that medieval Christians implicitly trusted historical texts as the repositories of God's truth. He also shows that they saw truth not just in Scripture and explicitly Christian tradition but also in the words of the pagan philosophers and the works of Greco-Roman culture (indeed, far more the Greco-Roman than the Germanic authorities).[40]

This was true from Clement of Alexandria and Justin Martyr through Boethius, Thomas Aquinas, and Dante. Though the pagan philosophers had not known Christ in his incarnate form, they too, along with all people, had been given access to the *logos*, the wisdom of the Second Person of the Trinity.

In other words, medieval poets, jurists, moral teachers, romance writers, and theologians, who all created compendia of knowledge for their readers, were often gleefully syncretistic. Not that they didn't care whether the deepest truth of things was to be understood in Christian, Platonic, Stoic, or pagan terms. Christianity always provided the framework, the "norming norm," for truth. But within that framework one might fit all the best thought of the pagans, as Christian thinkers had been doing ever since Paul spoke to the Greeks at Mars Hill about their "unknown god" (Acts 17:23), using the words of their own poets: "In him we live and move and have our being" (Acts 17:28).

What else would we expect from the early spread of "the way" to the gentiles? Who else were the gentiles in the Roman Empire but those educated in the spiritual metaphysics of Plato, the robust moralism of the Stoics, and the epic adventures of Homer (ca. eighth century BC)? These writers provided the air the gentiles breathed, the water in which they swam. Naturally, they sought to understand the best in their own culture by a Christian light.

Certainly, aspects of pagan teaching did not mesh with the gospel, and these were quietly dropped. Few Christians, for example, attempted to salvage the materialism and hedonism of the Epicureans. But the philosophical quest for Truth, Goodness, and Beauty, along with the classical virtues of Prudence, Justice, Temperance, and Courage, were found good. Yes, they needed to be seen in the light of the theological virtues of Faith, Hope, and Love, but that was no reason to deny their practical wisdom. From this principled and careful "Christianization of Hellenism"[41] came modern science. As such devout men as Roger Bacon (ca. 1214–92), Albertus Magnus (before 1200–80), and Thomas Aquinas processed Aristotle's natural philosophy through the Bible and Christian tradition, they laid the foundation for science as we know it.

Modern American evangelical critics of this Greek cast to early and medieval Christian thought would do well to consider the many ways—both helpful and harmful—in which their own faith has become "Americanized." Enculturation is not an avoidable phenomenon. Every time Christianity enters a new culture, it both revises and revitalizes it; and every time, there are blessings to be had along with the banes. This is Lamin Sanneh's principle of the unparalleled "translatability" of Christianity.[42]

## Lewis and the Wisdom of the Pagans

All of this points us back to that other area of Lewis's intuitive medievalism that I introduced in chapter 2. A devout and public Christian, Lewis always felt more affinity for an honest pagan than for a godless modern who has dismissed all religion and virtue equally as "fantasy," and, like Boethius, he drank deeply from ancient wells. In a letter to Dom Bede Griffiths, Lewis shows that he had indeed absorbed this distinctively medieval esteem for the past, including the pagan past: "It is only since I have become a Christian that I have learned really to value the elements of truth in Paganism and Idealism. I *wished* to value them in the old days; now I really do. Don't suppose that I ever thought myself that certain elements of pantheism were incompatible with Christianity or with Catholicism."[43]

Lewis tells us how thoroughgoing this medieval Christian appreciation for the classical pagan sources was, especially from the scholastic period onward: "From the twelfth to the seventeenth century Europe seems to have taken an unfailing delight in classical mythology. If the numbers and the gusto of pictures and poems were to be the criterion of belief, we should judge that those ages were pagan, which we know to be untrue."[44] Lewis's time with Kirkpatrick certainly prepared him to be an intuitive medievalist, particularly in his syncretic use of classical material.

It is hard to overstate how important this insight was to Lewis. As Michael Ward observes, he had been told as a boy that "Christianity was 100 per cent correct and every other religion, including the pagan myths of ancient Greece and Rome, was 100 per cent wrong."[45] But because he had already encountered the wisdom of the philosophers, he found that this insistence on the opposition of Christianity to paganism drove him away from, rather than toward, the Christian faith. As it turned out, he abandoned his childhood faith "largely under the influence of classical education."[46] It was to this experience that Lewis owed his "firm conviction that the only possible basis for Christian apologetics is a proper respect for Paganism."[47] This is a key connection with Boethius, who was a Christian who believed in the wisdom of classical philosophy and set out to translate all of Aristotle for his day (Greek to Latin). Lewis, likewise, set himself a "translative" task in his own age.

### Recovering the Pagan Past

Lewis felt a knowledge of pagan classical authors was the essential prerequisite, and much of the substance, of an understanding of the Middle Ages. He said as much in a letter to his American friend Sister Madeleva when she asked him for a strategy to familiarize herself with the field.[48] Michael Ward summarizes Lewis's attitude well: "If paganism could be shown to have something in common with Christianity, 'so much the better for paganism,' not 'so much the worse for Christianity.'"[49] Classical wisdom had always been fair game for Christian teachers. Why cut ourselves off from it now?

I've said that Lewis warned his Cambridge audience that it was living in a new Dark Ages. What light, exactly, did he feel was being lost in his day? Not "just" tales and songs, myths and poems, but the very wisdom that, following Barfield, he felt was inextricably embodied in that lost literature. What wisdom? The Christian gospel? Well, yes, that. But more deeply, the particular complex, perceptive, philosophically sophisticated, and morally robust appropriation of the gospel to the pagan mind that Boethius epitomized. After all, Lewis says, "Christians and Pagans had much more in common with each other than either has with a post-Christian. The gap between those who worship different gods is not so wide as that between those who worship and those who do not."[50]

In fact, this point about paganism is an important one that occurs throughout Lewis's writings and joins him even more firmly to Boethius. In response to those who argue that the modern world is lapsing into paganism, Lewis responds, in essence, "If only we would!," for there is wisdom in pagan culture that we need (a "consolation" of philosophy). But alas, in this new Dark Ages, "the post-Christian is cut off from the Christian past and therefore doubly from the Pagan past."[51]

Much ink has been spilled on the question of why Boethius—imprisoned, exiled, his goods scattered, and awaiting execution—turned not to the consolation of *religion* but rather to the consolation of *philosophy*. Certainly there are Christian elements in his book that none of his pagan sources would have recognized, such as his recommendation of prayer and his portrayal of God in personal terms. First, I want to say that modern scholarship has shown with no reasonable doubt that Boethius was a Christian, of an orthodox and a committed sort. Second, Lewis, who taught philosophy before he taught literature and who read the classics voraciously before coming to Christianity, joined Boethius in feeling the power of such consolation. This can be seen in Lewis's words to Bede Griffiths about learning "really to value the elements of truth" in paganism. In a 1944 address to the Socratic Club at Oxford, he makes the point more emphatically:

> Theology, while saying that a special illumination has been vouchsafed to
> Christians and (earlier) to Jews, also says that there is some divine illumina-
> tion vouchsafed to *all* men. The Divine light, we are told, "lighteneth every
> man." We should, therefore, expect to find in the imagination of great Pagan

teachers and myth makers some glimpse of that theme which we believe to be the very plot of the whole cosmic story—the theme of incarnation, death, and rebirth.[52]

### Lewis the Boethian and the New Dark Ages

The nature of the modern darkness in Lewis's eyes is well known: materialism, utilitarianism, and subjectivism all conspired to destroy the wisdom that had made it all the way from the ancients to the time of Jane Austen and Sir Walter Scott. Now, especially in the face of cataclysmic world wars, even Oxford's students were wondering to themselves, *Why study philosophy?* In his address "Learning in War-Time," Lewis gives the answer: "Good philosophy must exist, if for no other reason, because bad philosophy needs to be answered." And where is that good philosophy to be found? "Most of all . . . we need intimate knowledge of the past."[53] In short, Lewis saw himself as the educator, the popularizer, the traditioner who could become the Boethius for this new Dark Age.

Of course he recognized, and understood that Boethius also recognized, that there are limits to all merely human philosophy. But its power could be great nonetheless. In his essay "Christianity and Culture," Lewis reflects:

> Culture is a storehouse of the best (sub-Christian) values. These values are in themselves of the soul, not the spirit. But God created the soul. Its values may be expected, therefore, to contain some reflection or antepast of the spiritual values. They will save no man. They resemble the regenerate life only as affection resembles charity, or honour resembles virtue, or the moon the sun. But though "like is not the same," it is better than unlike. Imitation may pass into initiation. . . . There is another way in which it [that is, culture, especially literature] may predispose to conversion. The difficulty of converting an uneducated man nowadays lies in his complacency. Popularized science, the conventions or "unconventions" of his immediate circle, party programmes, etc., enclose him in a tiny windowless universe which he mistakes for the only possible universe. There are no distant horizons, no mysteries. He thinks everything has been settled.[54]

A tiny windowless universe. I am reminded of G. K. Chesterton's definition of insanity: "The clean and well-lit prison of one idea."[55] Our modern room is well lit by the bare bulb of science. But of what lies beyond, we see nothing. Like the children in the *Silver Chair*, trapped underground with the witch, we cannot even reason from the lightbulb to the sun of heaven. For that, we would need to open the windows of culture. Lewis continues: "A cultured person, on the other hand, is almost compelled to be aware that reality is very odd and that the ultimate truth, whatever it may be, *must* have the characteristics of strangeness—*must* be something that would seem remote and fantastic to the uncultured. Thus some obstacles to faith have been removed already."[56]

### The Philosophical Path to Faith

What better description can we find than this of Boethius's *Consolation*? Boethius the character starts the book grieving hysterically in the small, blind room of his own bad fortune. Slowly, gently, Lady Philosophy opens the windows, allowing Boethius to see that his happiness cannot and *must* not rest in the things on earth that fortune both gives and takes away. This is a Platonic insight as well as a Christian one—a classical philosophical foretaste of an important truth given fully only in the Christian gospel. Lady Philosophy is bringing Boethius to a "pre-evangelistic" realization by which, as Lewis says of culture in general, "obstacles" to faith may be removed.

Boethius's realization is a close cousin to the "argument from desire" so often used by Lewis (even as the framework for his artful story about his own conversion). It does—it must—start with the existential: the miserable reality of our own sense of the wrongness of the world and our own inability to find happiness in it. Lady Philosophy slowly leads Boethius to conclude that if one's happiness rests only in earthly fortune, then that happiness can never be secure.

Lewis ends his essay about Christianity and culture with the assertion that "culture has a distinct part to play in bringing certain souls to Christ."[57] Without doubt, he would have said that one of these "certain souls" was himself. Perhaps Boethius's *Consolation* even had a role in that philosophical journey, which is told in outline in *Surprised by Joy* and in great detail in *The Pilgrim's Regress*. But whether it did or not, this vocational understanding that Lewis had of himself as a Boethian public intellectual, traditioner, and conduit of culture was surely made even more powerful by the fact that he shared Boethius's faith and, like Boethius, adeptly wove that faith into a garment of writings that seem purely cultural, philosophical, and poetical.

One senses that Lewis would have been a genial presence at the Wheaton ancient-future conference, with Boethius, perhaps, right there at his side. These two consummate, traditionally informed, Christian public intellectuals would have told the assembled audience, eager to reach back to earlier wisdom, that this is a right and a good thing to do—and that it in no way contradicts their faith.

# 4

## Getting Thoughtful

### *The Medieval Passion for Theological Knowledge*

In the charismatic church where I came to Christ as a young man, we couldn't wait for Sunday. Week after week we experienced rich, life-changing ministry in worship and prayer. Night after night, the altar was jammed with eager worshipers seeking a "touch from the Lord." And it seemed like God was always there to meet us. After the service, we would leave the building with our hearts bursting with gratitude and joy. We even joked that it might not be safe to drive in that condition! And it didn't take much prodding for us to evangelize: Who wouldn't want to share such riches?

I will always be grateful for those days. Some folks accuse charismatics of not giving God or Christ his due. "There's so much 'me' language in their songs," they grump. And sure, our worship could become self-indulgent. But we used the first person so much in church not because we lacked reverence but because we lived in constant awe that the God of the cosmos condescended to save and to love even *us*.

More than this, we loved church because we knew that it changed us. Of course there was still plenty of imperfection in our lives, but along with the love-fest came real, personal transformation: Sins confessed. Grace experienced. Old wounds healed. Broken relationships restored. Release from addictions. God not only loved us—he made us better people.

## The Evangelical Abdication of Truth; or, Two Out of Three Is Really, Really Bad

But here's the thing. As the Greek philosophers knew, humans cannot live on Beauty and Goodness alone. There is a third realm necessary for human flourishing: the realm of Truth. And in that area, the charismatic church of my twenties was standing on thin ice. Many of our key teachings came from self-taught celebrities whose preaching skewed heavily to the topical and away from the exegetical. By dint of stringing together out-of-context Bible verses with some homespun wisdom, these teachers took us down some garden paths: the prosperity gospel, blame-the-victim faith healing, demon-in-every-doorknob spiritual warfare.[1] We fell over ourselves to get to all that wonderful Beauty and Goodness, leaving Truth in the ditch.

I've seen the same syndrome in a lot of churches, noncharismatic and charismatic alike. In the rush to *apply* the gospel, to change ourselves and change the world, we bypass truth-seeking. After all, we've found "the answer." Why do we need to spend our precious time in a reasoned exploration of truth? We're pragmatic, can-do Americans. We go straight from experience to application, with a minimum of reflection in between. (This too is part of the syndrome of "immediatism" I describe in chap. 1 of this book.)

What C. S. Lewis and the medievals help us know is that we cannot content ourselves with seeking (only) the experience of encountering God in worship—in the awesome "beauty of his holiness"—or even (only) the amendment of our own character, or the reform of society, as important as each of these things is in the Christian life. For ultimately a life can become—and remain—Beautiful and Good only if we also live it in the light of Truth. And since Christians know God as the source of truth, we must turn to God as the first and most proper subject for reasoned inquiry. Which is to say, none of us—even the simplest and most untutored—can abdicate our responsibility (and privilege) as theologians.

Now, grasping the intricacies of theology is mainly the job of theologians, professors, and pastors—those who serve the church through the gift of teaching. But all Christians are theologians in other ways. First and most simply, *to pray* is to do theology, as the Eastern Orthodox tradition has always insisted.[2] Second, we do theology when we listen carefully to our pastors and teachers and read Scripture in the light of the tradition they pass on to us.

If we don't seek and have truth in our "inmost parts," then we experience confusion or self-contradiction, and that affects everything else in our lives. At its root, the Western tradition has treated philosophy as a way of life, not an intellectual game. (Again, the early Christians had a word for those who do theology in the mode of abstraction: "heretic.") So my entreaty to modern Christians in this chapter is to blow the dust off the theological tomes that are our communal heritage, for the pursuit of wisdom and truth is about *life*, and so it should be pursued passionately, with all our hearts as well as all our minds. Along with Anselm of Canterbury (1033–1109), we too must be about "faith seeking understanding." And we could find much worse guides in our seeking than such medieval theologians as Anselm, Bernard of Clairvaux, and Thomas Aquinas. Their passion for theology was a passion for God.

Simplistic theology is not dangerous just because it can lead to heresy. When we refuse to "think with God" as Christians, we fail to understand not just God but also the world God has given us. God has fashioned us and our world in supremely intricate, beautiful, and rational ways. He is a God of reason, and he gives us reason to understand our world. When we fail in that understanding, we become captive to the fads and fancies of our culture. We fall prey to the seductive fantasies of Hollywood, the touted pleasures of Madison Avenue, and the strident slogans of Washington. Because we fail to see ourselves and our world in the light of God's truth—that is, because we fail to do good theology—we hurt ourselves in so many sad and unnecessary ways.

Beauty and Goodness cannot last without Truth. And the kinds of Truth we need to learn are truths not just about God but also about the intricate and rationally structured world God made. In this chapter, we will learn how medieval theologians brought together faith and reason, love and logic, religion and science, and Word and world in a breathtaking synthesis that delved deep into the Bible for wisdom about our life with God and also birthed such cultural institutions as the university, the research laboratory, and the hospital. The great engine driving early and medieval

Christians' search for theological truth about God and the world was not idle or sterile intellectual curiosity but rather the desire to know how to live in the light of the Creator God's love for his creation.

## C. S. Lewis the Philosopher and the Medieval Passion for Theology

C. S. Lewis was not a professional philosopher (though that was his first love and career intention), but by both his education and his native earnest curiosity, he was well prepared to pursue philosophical study as not a game of abstractions but the key to life. From his early reading in classics, through his "greats" philosophy study at Oxford, and on into his first teaching job there (in philosophy), Lewis chose to "follow the guidance of reason and perform numerous spiritual exercises . . . in a genuine attempt to live according to what he thought was true; as he said, 'I [was] trying to find out truth.'"[3]

After his conversion, Lewis followed up this traditional training and personal discipline with intensive reading in the church fathers and medieval theologians and spiritual writers. A self-described "dinosaur,"[4] Lewis the Christian came to see in logical positivism and other modern trends in philosophy the kind of inhuman abstraction that speaks as if we do not have personalities or imagination. He tried to help his audiences think both rigorously and imaginatively along with the best ancient and medieval thinkers. Out of his appreciation for scholastic theology and the spiritual theology of people like Julian of Norwich, Walter Hilton (1340/45–1396), and Thomas á Kempis (1380–1471), he sought not only to bring the ancient and medieval tradition of Christian thought alive again for his contemporaries but also, importantly, to help them rediscover what it is like to *think within that tradition.*

As we've seen, in *Surprised by Joy* Lewis describes this holistic understanding of philosophy as hard-won in his own life. Recall from chapter 2 the story he tells in which Barfield supposedly had to remind Lewis that philosophy was not a subject but a *way.* What this means is that the pagan philosophers' contemplative quest—which would be taken up by Christian philosophers of the second century and passed down through the medieval era and into the modern—was anything but coldly intellectual. Intellectual, yes. But also both eminently practical (meant to be lived out) and characterized by desire, yearning, even passion—a passion for meaning, a passion to see God, focused on the *telos* of living a better life.

Lewis wrote this anecdote, as he wrote the whole memoir that contained it, to show how his own movement from atheism to Christianity was mediated through this dawning awareness of the Great Tradition, which helped him to overcome his own attempts to set aside his imagination and indeed his heart (which had long since been captivated by the quest for "joy") and apply only severe logic to the big questions of life. It's not surprising that Lewis would frame this rejoinder from Barfield as something of a revelation to him. Barfield himself, however, found this characterization by Lewis of his young atheist self as "pure applesauce." His brilliant friend, Barfield insisted, was "constitutionally incapable of treating philosophy as a merely academic exercise." Indeed, ever since Barfield met Lewis, Barfield found that Lewis "could not help trying to live by what he thought."[5] This seriousness about philosophy as a way of life appeared in the Oxford don's academic life from the beginning. In the first classes he taught at Oxford during a one-year philosophy position at University College in his twenties, Lewis taught on "moral good."[6]

### The Quest for the Holy Philosophy

It should be no surprise, then, that this young professor's path to faith was a philosophical one: "I gave up Christianity at about fourteen. Came back to it when getting on for thirty. Not an emotional conversion: almost purely philosophical."[7] When asked to make his conversion story public, he replied, "The details of my own conversion were so technically philosophical on one side, and so intimate on the other that they just can't be used in the way you suggest."[8]

Yet he tried to detail that quest, twice. *Surprised by Joy* is the second attempt, and the more successful for most readers, precisely because it does not dwell on the "details." But in *The Pilgrim's Regress*, Lewis's first attempt to narrate his conversion (in an allegorical mode), we encounter the sort of philosophical quest once typical of honest men and women of education, especially in the late ancient and medieval years of Christianity's maturing. On the book's first page, Lewis quotes Plato, perhaps the greatest of the classical philosophers, followed by Boethius, Plato's greatest late-ancient translator and interpreter:

> This every soul seeketh and for the sake of this doth all her actions, having an inkling[9] that it is; but *what* it is she cannot sufficiently discern, and she knoweth not her way, and concerning this she hath no constant assurance as she hath of other things. (Plato)

> Whose souls, albeit in a cloudy memory, yet seek back their good, but, like drunk men, know not the road home. (Boethius)[10]

Lewis carried out this philosophical journey in a manner both sympathetic to and influenced by his readings as a medievalist. As we have seen, in response to a question from the American publication *The Christian Century*, Lewis listed Boethius's *Consolation of Philosophy* as one of the ten books that most influenced his philosophy of life. He found its philosophical argument a doorway, or "philosophical preliminary," into faith.[11] The *Consolation* was one of the most retranslated and reprinted books of the entire medieval era. "To acquire a taste for it," Lewis says, "is almost to become naturalised in the Middle Ages."[12]

So Lewis sought wisdom through philosophy, in ways characteristic of medieval people,[13] and that wisdom led him on a path to Christianity. And he never stopped being a philosopher, even in writing his famous children's books. Professor Digory's exclamation in *The Last Battle* comes to mind: "It's all in Plato, all in Plato: bless me, what do they teach them at these schools!"[14]

A letter from Lewis to his friend Arthur Greeves gives an early glimpse of what would become Lewis's eager pursuit of medieval sources of theological knowledge. Here, in the year before his conversion (1930), we find Lewis articulating the beauty of Catholic theology as he describes his own first reading of Dante's *Paradiso*. He and Owen Barfield had taken a holiday week intended for intellectual fellowship, and each day they read both Aristotle's *Ethics* and Dante's *Paradiso*. Lewis wrote to Greeves that the *Paradiso* felt to him "more *important* than any poetry I have ever read. . . . Its blend of complexity and beauty is very like Catholic theology—wheel within wheel, but wheels of glory, and the One radiated through the Many."[15]

## *"Sorting Out and Tidying Up"*

Lewis's appreciation for medieval theology took both an aesthetic and a logical form. He was a master rhetorician, the terror (or inspirational leader, depending on whom you asked) of the Oxford "Socratic Club," an apologist and a public intellectual as well as a literary figure with solid skills in many forms of fiction, poetry, and essay writing. Yet Lewis was alert to the tendency of rhetoricians to get carried away with their own rhetoric. He did not devalue reason and truth just because he excelled in imagination and pursued meaning.

We see this priority for truth in Lewis's critique of the renaissance humanists. In putting forward their own "modern" moral and literary agendas, the humanists caricatured medieval scholastics as hairsplitters who used atrocious Latin to argue obscure and irrelevant theological minutiae.[16] Were these fair characterizations of the scholastics and their philosophical arguments? Anything but, says Lewis:

> These are not the terms in which a new philosophy attacks an old one: they are, unmistakably, the terms in which at all times the merely literary man . . . attacks philosophy itself. No humanist is now remembered as a philosopher. They jeer and do not refute. The schoolman [that is, the medieval scholastic] advanced, and supported, propositions about things: the humanist replied that his words were inelegant.

In conclusion, Lewis argues, "The war between the humanists and the schoolmen was not a war between ideas: it was, on the humanists' side, a war against ideas. It is a manifestation of the humanistic tendency to make eloquence the sole test of learning."[17]

Having labeled the humanists "Philistines" and their movement "obscurantist," Lewis concludes that their "New Learning" had also, sadly, created a "New Ignorance." And, he warned, *this was just what was going on is his own time.*[18] The erstwhile "passion for theology" had been beaten back once upon a time by renaissance humanists, and it was being beaten back again in the modern era.

The complexity of medieval scholastic theology did not bother Lewis; rather, as we see in his comments on Dante, he found it beautiful in its convoluted pursuit of difficult truths. What we see in Lewis's harsh judgment on the humanists conveys a sense of the value of the medieval pursuit of truth—the organizing, codifying, building of systems, "sorting out and tidying up" that Lewis described appreciatively to his Cambridge students. Lewis wished we could have something like the medievals' bookish, "intense love of system" again.[19]

## Out of the Medieval Darkness: The *Real* Story of Medieval Theology

The intellectual movement we're looking at here is still much misunderstood. The Enlightenment caricature lives on: the scholastics were pointy-headed, impractical fellows, happy to waste their time debating the number of angels that can dance on the head of a pin. But if we can get beyond the caricature, we will find that scholasticism's actual goals and achievements still have surprising currency today. If we're willing to engage the scholastics, we'll find ourselves both challenged and enriched by the ways they managed to hold together (not without tension and controversy) faith and reason, love and logic, religion and science, Word and world.

### *Medieval Faith in Reason? Surely Not!*

Many modern Protestant Christians still assume medieval people were ignorant haters of scientific knowledge who believed in a flat earth and were sitting around waiting for the Enlightenment to happen so they could finally crawl out of the darkness and into the clear light of reason.[20] In order to get back to the genius of medieval theology,[21] we first need to overcome the stereotype that medieval people were, well, stupid. In fact, nothing could be further from the truth.

One source of such nonsense today is a misbegotten (and still best-selling) book by William Manchester called *A World Lit Only by Fire*. Manchester was a historian, but he didn't let a staggering lack of knowledge of the medieval period hinder him from filling the book's pages with the Enlightenment polemical agenda hinted at in his title. This resulted (and I'm just scratching the surface here) in lurid and titillating exposés of the period's supposed barbarous sexual habits and a straight-faced argument that everyone in the Middle Ages believed the world was flat. Historian of science (and editor of the eight-volume *Cambridge History of Science*) David Lindberg says, "Nonsense."[22]

Manchester's story goes that before Columbus, Europeans believed nearly unanimously in a flat earth—a belief allegedly drawn from certain biblical statements and enforced by the medieval church. This myth, according to Lindberg, seems to have had an eighteenth-century origin. For their own reasons, the philosophes of the Enlightenment era, and many academics since then, developed and perpetuated the stereotype of medieval ignorance. But that doesn't make these stereotypes true. In fact, American author Washington Irving flagrantly fabricated evidence for the flat-earth belief in his four-volume history of Columbus. It was then picked up and widely disseminated in twentieth-century America by the anti-Christian president of Cornell University, Andrew Dickson White (1832–1918), and others.[23]

The truth is that it's almost impossible to find an educated person after Aristotle (d. 322 BC) who doubted that the earth is a sphere. In the Middle Ages, you couldn't emerge from any kind of higher education, whether in a cathedral school or in a university, without being perfectly clear about the earth's sphericity and even its approximate circumference.

### God's Image in Us

Quite contrary to the smear campaign of Manchester, White, and the philosophes, medievals understood human rational capacity to be the very image of God—his greatest gift to us. Discovering how best to employ it was, they thought, an important part of our stewardship as those given dominion over creation. This positive understanding of reason had continued undiminished since the earliest years of the church. As Jaroslav Pelikan puts it, "When the Christian gospel came into the world, it succeeded in converting the most rational of men, the Greek philosophers, to its message; this was proof that the gospel was not to be dismissed as irrationality and 'insanity.'"[24]

Historically, the church has always taught that we are made in the image of God, and it usually saw this "imageness" as primarily residing in human rationality. If I had understood this pro-reason Christian heritage as a young adult, it would have saved me some misery. I spent years struggling over the question of whether the disciplines of the mind, such as are practiced in the university, can be of any service whatsoever to the church. Medievalist David Bell summarizes the resounding answer to this question that the majority of medieval thinkers gave, following the early church fathers:

If we are images of God, and if God is eternal, it follows that we cannot be images of God in our physical and corruptible flesh since flesh is not eternal. But if our flesh is not eternal, what is? The answer is obvious: our soul. The soul, however, was believed to have more than one part. The lower part served to animate the body and enabled it to move around. That is something we share with the animals. But the higher part enabled us to think rationally and comprehend abstractions, and that is something we share only with the angels and God. The church therefore maintained that human beings are images of God in the higher, rational part of the soul, and that reason is the greatest natural gift we have.[25]

Because medieval Christians valued reason highly, seeing it as the image of God in humankind, they concluded that such an amazing gift must be given for a purpose. In Bell's words, "It is not to be squandered or neglected, but used appropriately in the service of the Giver."[26] And so they set out to understand God, themselves, and their world in rational terms. More than this: since reason was our surpassing gift from God, the medievals used it as one would any treasured instrument (think of a Stradivarius violin): with great passion, care, and discipline.

But this is not the end of the story about how medieval thinkers viewed and used reason. Since certain aspects of God seemed beyond reason—the Trinity, the incarnation, and the resurrection are just three—tension and controversy also arose. From the second century through the medieval period, and more urgently once the scholastic movement began in the twelfth century, faithful Christians argued about *how much* of a role reason should be given.

One thing became clear early on. Good theology could not be done with reason *alone*, in the realm of pure abstraction and logic-chopping. Put in positive terms, this meant that reason and faith, logic and love, must be held together. To separate them was to court heresy, as the church fathers had insisted.[27]

### The Rise and Genius[28] of the Scholastics

There are four polar pairs that Christians today often separate but that the medievals tried valiantly (if not always successfully) to keep together. To get *faith* and *reason* out of balance is to veer into either obscurantist fideism ("faith-ism") or some intellectual substitute for Christian faith.

To get *logic* and *love* out of balance is to focus on either self-righteous argumentation or fuzzy-headed sentimentalism. To get *religion* and *science* out of balance is to descend into anti-intellectualism or a modernist "demythologized" faith. And to get *Word* and *world* out of balance courts cultural irrelevance or cultural captivity. The synthesis of the medieval scholastics, as we'll see, represents the most breathtaking—and fruitful—attempt in history to keep each of these complementary pairs together.

"Scholasticism" simply means "theology done in the schools." The schools in question were "the monastic and cathedral schools of the eleventh and twelfth centuries—Bec, Laon, Chartres, Saint Victor, Notre Dame de Paris—and the universities of the thirteenth and fourteenth centuries—Paris and Oxford and the long line of their younger sisters."[29] Essentially, medieval scholasticism was the birth matrix of systematic theology, which is the attempt to apply logical categories and arguments to the materials of Scripture and Christian tradition.

While space does not allow even a summary of medieval theology, we may point to some thematic elements:

- the church fathers' characteristic appreciation for Greek philosophy as a sort of "schoolmaster" potentially leading people to the higher truths of the gospel
- Augustine's immense influence right through the Reformation
- the tenth- to eleventh-century expansion of Charlemagne's cathedral schools and the great monastic schools, which gave birth to the university in the twelfth century
- the university's fruitful confluence of theology and the liberal arts[30]
- the twelfth-century renaissance's new emphasis on empirical science and its concomitant technological advances (the magnetic compass, eyeglasses, windmills, mechanical clocks)[31]
- the thirteenth-century shift from Platonic mysticism to a more "scientific" and world-affirming Aristotelian theological method

At the center of these later developments were the scholastics, who appropriated the methods and modes of discourse of the sciences for their own theological purposes. Anselm of Canterbury wrote treatises on the existence of God and the nature of the atonement of Christ, as well as a set of impassioned devotional poems and prayers. Peter Abelard (1079–1142) proved the need for "dialectics" (logic) in theology by pulling together contradicting statements from many church fathers into one book, *Sic et Non* (when he wasn't penning impassioned love letters to his sweetheart, the cloistered Heloise d'Argenteuil [1090–1164], or writing woeful memoirs bemoaning his unluckiness in love and life). And of course there is Thomas Aquinas, on whom more will be said shortly.

### Aristotle's Rediscovery and the (Re)Birth of the Sciences

Before the rediscovery of the body of Aristotle's works in the thirteenth century, the prime philosophical influence on Christian thinkers in the West was Plato, via Augustine. Plato had essentially been a mystic, and his philosophy had been based on the principle that ideas such as the True, the Beautiful, and the Good have real existence apart from the visible world. In fact, he believed that the passing forms of this visible world, which we know through our senses, are not a real source of knowledge. Only our reason, which leads us to know these changeless, universal patterns called "ideas," gives true knowledge. This position is also known as "realism" and is held by such early scholastics as Anselm—again, as he and others of his time had inherited it through Augustine.

Aristotle, on the other hand, was far less mystical than Plato. To him, the visible world is real. Ideas are not presupposed structures that exist somewhere "out there." They exist as an integral part of the phenomena of the visible world. Therefore, the world is the prime object of knowledge for Aristotle. He is, in other words, a scientist. In fact, a large part of Aristotle's writings that were rediscovered in thirteenth-century Europe deal with physics and biology. His philosophical position, known as "moderate realism," came to be the accepted position of most scholastics from Abelard on.

The central issue of the scholastic philosophy was the nature of universals—that is, of broad, descriptive categories of things—for example, "humanness," "justice," "trees." Three different approaches emerged.

The first was that of the *extreme realists*. These philosophers included just about everyone in Europe up to the time of the scholastics, including early scholastics like Anselm. The extreme realists followed Plato in saying that *universal categories have their own reality*—that is, they exist apart from and antecedent to individual objects. For example, the genus "man" (humanity) both existed before and determined the existence of individual humans.[32]

Increasingly in the time of the scholastics, from Abelard on, this view was challenged by that of the *moderate realists*. Moderate realism followed Aristotle in saying that *universals exist only in connection with individual objects*. You can see how this is a view favorable to the development of science. Suddenly, it became important to come down from Plato's philosophical ivory tower and actually study the particulars of things, in order to discover the universals that are contained in them.

A third view arose at the end of the scholastic period. This was the position of the *nominalists*, who said that *universals in fact have no reality*—they are only abstract names (think of the English word "nominal," which means "in name only") for resemblances of individuals, existing only in the human mind. This view was partially responsible for breaking up the scholastic synthesis between faith and science.

The new breed of Aristotelian moderate realists, with their increased attention to data gathering and analysis (based on the belief that the things of the world, including the data of tradition and Scripture, really can lead us to universal truths), sparked a new style of study: How do you go about discovering truth in any given area of inquiry, including theology? You amass data (natural, traditional, scriptural), and then you apply scientific and philosophical reason, not just mystical contemplation of universals. In this way, every topic of theology—from the nature of God and the interpretation of God's laws to topics like the Trinity and the sacraments—becomes subject to detailed, rational study under the assumption that the particulars of that study will lead to truth.[33]

## THE PRINCE OF THE SCHOOLMEN: THOMAS AQUINAS

The greatest synthesizer of Aristotle and Augustine and the greatest of the scholastics was Thomas Aquinas.

A Dominican from the age of nineteen, this large, quiet man was known for a time as the "dumb ox." There is in fact a biography of him by G. K. Chesterton under that title. Aquinas taught, in his later years, mainly in Paris, and his two great books are the *Summa Contra Gentiles*, a textbook for missionaries defending Christianity against the Muslims, and *Summa Theologiae*, which is still the basis of much modern theology, especially Roman Catholic theology.

Like Anselm and Abelard, Aquinas was no dried-out intellectual. A powerfully warm, spiritual, pious man, he did indeed pioneer an advanced Christian philosophy, using a scholastic method, but he was far from relying on that method as the sole means of reaching God.

Aquinas started with the premise that faith completes reason and reason upholds faith. He was convinced that for all reasonable people he could establish beyond reasonable doubt that God exists, is eternal, and has certain other attributes. This he attempted to establish in his "five proofs" of the existence of God, calling God the First Cause, the Prime Mover, and so forth. Through such proofs, a non-Christian could be led, Aquinas said, to the "vestibule of faith."[34]

However, he also argues that "Scriptural revelation . . . contains things which are necessary to salvation and which could never be found out by reason alone."[35] These include the incarnation and the resurrection, which Aquinas felt are revealed only in Scripture and accepted only by faith.

With Aristotle, Aquinas believed that a person could get real knowledge by studying the natural world and thinking things through. Yet, going beyond Aristotle, he also saw faith in biblical revelation as a road to truth.

Then Aquinas asserted that because God is the origin of both nature and revelation, both reason and faith are from God and cannot be in conflict with each other. In other words, all truth is God's truth, and there is nothing to be feared from any amount of scientific study of the world or of human culture.

Aquinas was the great apologist to the intellectuals of his day. His achievement was stating the relationship between reason and faith so that those who accepted Aristotle's naturalistic philosophy could feel that they might consistently remain Christians. Moreover, this openness to Aristotle within the camp of Christian theology poured the foundation for the scientific revolution of the sixteenth and seventeenth centuries.

### The Scholastic Legacy among the Common People

All good things must come to an end. It was the profound skepticism of "nominalists" such as John Duns Scotus (1266–1308) and William of Ockham (1280–1349) that finally killed the grand synthesizing experiment of scholastic theology. These thinkers challenged the reality of universals and thus the reliability of traditional categories for theological thinking.

Essentially, the nominalists "gave up hope of reconciling the wisdom of man with the wisdom of God."[36] To them, as to Paul, the cross and all that was involved in it were foolishness when judged by the wisdom of the Greeks, and man through his wisdom had not known God.

But the labors of the scholastics continued to affect the laity profoundly through the vibrant preaching and educational efforts of the friars (e.g., Dominicans, Franciscans), right through the period of the Reformation. (Today's worldwide network of Jesuit colleges is just one part of that legacy.) The last indignity (and final coffin nail) suffered by the old scholastic tradition came in the time of the Enlightenment, when the unpaid bills of the institutional church came due. By the time of the French Revolution (1789), the use of reason in elite theology had come to be associated with the abuse of power and wealth by the church, which in turn was creating intolerable conditions for average people—that is, those of lower class than the aristocrats, who were the power brokers in the church and state. So Aquinas's work went into a centuries-long period of relative disuse (although it continued to be taught within the Dominican order) until its rediscovery in the Roman Catholic "neo-Thomist" movement of the nineteenth and twentieth centuries.

But did anyone really notice? Did scholasticism ever really do much for the common people? Wasn't it a pastime for highly educated elites? Had it at all helped the masses, many of whom were illiterate? As we've seen in Lewis's defense of the movement, ever since the sixteenth-century humanists got hold of scholasticism and gave it a good schoolyard thrashing, scholasticism has gotten a bad rap as obscurantist and elitist. But the scholastic doctors were in fact trying to make more intelligent and effective the loyalty to the Christian faith that had become, in some areas, only nominal through the mass conversions of the earlier medieval centuries.

Indeed, by emphasizing the importance of reason in theology, the doctors were actually beginning a *democratization* of the faith, which bore fruit in the Reformation. Their use of reason in theology made knowledge of God accessible, not merely to the cloistered monk with his constant Scripture reading and intense mystical exercises but also to anyone able and willing to think.

Certainly, few before the late medieval period had the literacy and training necessary to engage in much study. But in time scholasticism, the university, and an army of preaching, teaching friars would join to bring the faith alive to many people who had never seen the inside of a monastery. Out of this popularization of scholastic theology came preaching and writing that strengthened the faith of many more who had never seen a university.[37]

## The Medieval Balance: Faith Seeking Understanding

Having looked first at the evangelical problem with truth and then at the medieval scholastics' way of understanding and teaching truth, I now turn to the central story line of medieval theology: its unique attempt to hold faith and reason together.

When I say that medieval thinkers held reason and faith in a delicate balance, I am thinking of their ability to use reasoned understanding and argument not to erase mystery but to carefully couch and protect it. The modern tendency has been to put our trust in reason's supposed ability to fix all human problems and solve all conundrums. The postmodern tendency, on the contrary, is to point to the man behind the curtain or the emperor who has no clothes: to assume that anybody who claims to have figured things out via reason is actually making a power grab, disguising baser motives.

The fundamental insight of postmodernism is hard to argue with; people do in fact often claim to be following the direct dictates of reason when in fact their motives have little to do with reasoned understanding. What's more, this behavior isn't even intentional much of the time![38] But when we go back to a brilliant premodern Christian thinker such as Augustine, we find a different process. Instead of claiming that "reason solves all," Augustine frequently looks up from an argument he's just presented (say, on the nature of the Trinity or the incarnation) and says, in effect, "I didn't say you had to *like* it." That is, "I *know* this is paradoxical, contradictory, and intellectually unsatisfying. But it's the best we've got. Take it or leave it." Augustine is suspicious of people who think they've got all the answers neatly laid out: the oversimplifiers, the charlatans. Among these were the Manichaeans, whom he once thought wise.[39]

The roots of this crucial admission of mystery lie in the early church's struggle with the weeds in its theological garden: the heresies. Again, what's so interesting here is not *that* they struggled against heretics but rather *what* they accused them of.

Take, for example, the second-century defender of Christianity, Irenaeus (d. 202). One of the heretical groups he fights in his compendium
*Against Heresies* he calls the "Valentinians." He accuses these people of
not only teaching novel doctrines not found in the apostolic witness but
also twisting the parables, prophetic sayings, and apostolic teachings of
Scripture and thereby "dismember[ing] and destroy[ing] the truth." They
were like vandals who took apart a mosaic made of precious jewels that
represented a king and rearranged them into a poorly configured image
of a fox.[40]

### Against Intellectual Gamesmanship

Early orthodox churchmen argued that the worst thing about heretics
was that this sort of Scripture-mangling was mere intellectual gamesman-
ship. The heretics were not committed to the faith with their hearts and
lives. Instead of submitting themselves to personal moral transformation
in the midst of the community, they set up rational proofs as if they
could float free from true faith. Fourth-century father Gregory Nazianzen (329–90) outlines the problem in his theological orations—a series of
speeches against the Arians (those who taught that Christ was less than
fully divine).

Gregory attacks the Arians' misuse of Scripture. Rather than focus on
particular errors, he charges his opponents with nursing an ungodly "tone
of mind" that delights in "strifes about words, which tend to no profit."
They interpreted Scripture in an irreverent, jocular mode, making them
"a matter of pleasant gossip, like any other thing, after the races, or the
theater, or a concert, or a dinner, or still lower employments."[41]

These were not just words spoken in the heat of battle. Whatever Arius's
own motives in that time after Emperor Constantine, when Christianity
had become fashionable rather than persecuted, many lay Christians did
indeed amuse themselves as theological amateurs. Nazianzen's friend
Gregory of Nyssa (ca. 335–ca. 395) describes the situation in this way:

> Men of yesterday and the day before, mere mechanics, off-hand dogmatists
> in theology, servants, too, and slaves that have been flogged, runaways from
> servile work, are solemn with us, and philosophize about things incompre-
> hensible. Ask about pence, and the tradesman will discuss the generate and
> ingenerate; inquire the price of bread, and he will say, "Greater is the Father,

and the Son is subject"; say that a bath would suit you, and he defines, "the Son is out of nothing."[42]

The problem with these sorts of intellectual games, say both Gregorys and other fathers, is that those who play them leave no room for the mysteries and paradoxes at the heart of the orthodox faith. Forgetting the limits of their own human reason and the wonder and majesty of God's person, they reduce God to a pale image and Christ to a mere man.

As we've seen, this overreliance on reason to the detriment of the real paradox and mystery preserved in the scriptural record was taken to be a hallmark of heresy in general. So when the early bishops got together and intensely studied the problem of the relationship between the divine and human natures of Christ—a very difficult question that caused a lot of strife in the post-Constantinian church—they formulated a careful statement called the Definition of Chalcedon (451), which leaves a great deal of room for mystery.

Instead of trying to force the mystery of the two natures of Christ into a single logical box, their definition suggests boundaries that rule out some rationalizations that the logic-choppers might use. Called "the four fences of Chalcedon," these boundaries read as follows: "one and the same Christ, Son, Lord, only begotten, to be acknowledged in two natures, *without confusion, without change, without division, without separation.*"[43] What these four fences—the "withouts"—leave room for and protect is an irreducible paradoxical tension that says a thing (Jesus) can be both 100 percent one thing (divine) and 100 percent another thing (human). Of course, in the realms of mathematics, logic, or physics, this statement is impossible. But in the interest of preserving what seemed to them to be the clear witness of Scripture, the Chalcedonian bishops insisted on it.

### Two Medieval Explanations Designed to Preserve Paradox and Mystery

While the essence of heresy is to resolve a biblical paradox in one direction or the other in order to satisfy the human need for a consistent rational explanation of things, the early church used reason not to resolve or dismiss paradox and mystery but rather to protect it, as I've shown in the examples of Gregory Nazianzen, Gregory of Nyssa, and the Chalcedonian Definition.

Now I'd like to move on to the medieval period for two more examples of the use of reason to protect, rather than resolve or dismiss, the paradox and mystery at the very heart of Christian theology—that is, the incarnation.

### TRANSUBSTANTIATION

The first example is the doctrine of transubstantiation, promulgated at the Fourth Lateran Council in 1215. This explanation of how the Eucharist "works" extends the Chalcedonian Definition that one person (Christ) can indeed be both 100 percent God and 100 percent man, to a nuanced piece of (Aristotelian) scientific reasoning on how the same sort of "this and also that" reality can be true of the eucharistic elements. In other words, transubstantiation tries to explain, in terms accessible to scientific reason, how Jesus's words at the Last Supper instituting the Eucharist—"This is my body; this is my blood"—can possibly be true.

At issue here is not Christ and his two natures but the food elements of the Eucharist and *their* two natures. Essentially, the church has believed since its earliest centuries that the bread and wine are at the same time 100 percent bread and wine and 100 percent body and blood of Christ. This ancient doctrine of the Real Presence of Christ is based on the assumption that, at the Last Supper, Christ really means it when he says, "This is my body; this is my blood." One might guess that if you've believed one miracle (the perfect coexistence of the divine and human natures within Christ), it sets you up to believe another (the perfect coexistence of both of those natures within the bread and wine).

Transubstantiation is an attempt to explain this in more rational, scientific terms, without destroying the paradox. It says that the "accidents" of color, taste, feel, and smell of the bread and wine are preserved while the "essence" of the elements becomes the real body and blood of Christ. For many who disagree with transubstantiation, this explanation seems an unwarranted application of Aristotelian science to the mystery of the doctrine of the Real Presence. But we need to understand what's going on.

When this piece of Aristotelian explanation about accidents and essence is applied to the Eucharist, it is applied not to *erase* the mystery that the bread and wine is also the body and blood of Christ (a statement that, again, comes from the lips of Christ) but to *protect* it, while also trying to give some satisfaction to our God-given reason. And that indicates the role that reason plays in theology in the medieval period—it seeks not to explain away the paradoxes of the faith but rather indeed to protect those paradoxes and mysteries as much as possible.

As in so many other areas of medieval faith, this blend of reason, paradox, and mystery is not just "a Catholic thing." It is a Protestant legacy too. Particularly concerning this matter of the Eucharist, the desire both to preserve the mystery of the Real Presence of Christ in the elements *and* to have some sort of reasonable explanation for how that can happen is also found in the doctrines of the three root Protestant traditions (Lutheran, Reformed, and Anglican), each in its own way.

### ATONEMENT

The second example of this reason-protecting-mystery dynamic comes from the teachings of Anselm of Canterbury and Peter Abelard, both of whom we've already met; it is their reasoned explanations of the bloody scandal that was the crucifixion. Why on earth would God have to redeem his human creatures in such a bizarre and painful way? If you're a thoughtful Christian—or a thoughtful non-Christian considering the claims of the Christian faith—then you've likely wondered this yourself. Again, Anselm and Abelard used forms of reasoned explanation that made good sense in their cultural contexts to explain this paradox: God (the immortal and eternal) died.

This is perhaps not just "a paradox," but the greatest paradox imaginable: the divine being who is the only being who fully "owns" his own being, not owing it to any parent or creator, entered the stream of time, lived for a time, and then ceased, as all time-bound creatures do, to exist (at least, on earth and in time, as a creature). Anselm and Abelard, brilliant dialecticians, both refused to use reason to flatten this paradox, heretic-like, in one direction (Jesus was not really human, and thus God did not really die) or the other (Jesus was not really God, and thus God did not really die). Instead, each used cultural materials to protect that central mystery while offering reasonable explanations for why God the Second Person of the Trinity found it necessary to die on the cross—by which the ultimate Being submitted, however temporarily, to death, just like a sinful human.

### *Anselm's Explanation*

Anselm created his elegant argument in his masterful, and still influential, *Cur Deus Homo*. In the mode of reverent "faith seeking understanding," he asks a question that a lot of bright people, Christian and non-Christian alike, continue to ask today: "Why did God have to go through all this rigmarole—the incarnation, the crucifixion, and the resurrection—to accomplish humanity's salvation? Couldn't God have achieved our redemption in a less implausibly messy way?" On the face of things, it seems more than a bit bizarre that God himself, after a typically bloody, painful birth in a dirty, cold stable and then a difficult, sporadically persecuted life, should finally be tried as a criminal and nailed to a cross to die, doesn't it?

Certainly many non-Christians throughout history have laughed at this claim. It is the scandal, the *skandalon*; it is, as Paul says, "foolishness to the Greeks." Anselm does not make the story rationally consistent by cutting off some part of the revelation, by doing the sort of thing the early heretics did in getting rid of the tension between God's perfect divinity and his abject death. Anselm doesn't solve the conundrum by saying, "Well, God didn't *really* die because he never had a really human body, only the appearance of one," which is an explanation that some had tried to give early on (the Docetist heresy). Nor does Anselm veer to the other possible explanation, "Well, somebody did die, but it was someone who was less than God: the very special man Jesus" (the Arian heresy).

Instead, Anselm reasons from the structures of social understanding around him; he seeks in those cultural materials an explanation that will satisfy his hearers without destroying the mystery. The explanation he hits upon is that God's honor, like that of a feudal king, has been offended and diminished by the (original) sin of his human subjects and that this terrible transgression must be addressed through some act of "satisfaction" that restores the honor of the king. Anselm's carefully worked-out formulation does not resolve the mystery in one direction (Docetism) or the other (Arianism) but rather retains it and explains it through the reasonable cultural metaphor of "satisfaction," working out the mystery in elegantly logical language so that people of his age can understand it.

### Abelard's Explanation

Now around the same time Peter Abelard, who also valued reason very highly and also desired to protect the mystery, looked at the scriptural accounts and at the cultural (God-world) material around him to provide another explanation for the mystery of the atonement. Abelard's era witnessed the rise of individualism and a new focus on the subjective. A brilliant theologian, Abelard was interested in people's "inner terrain," and he was the first thinker since Augustine (way back in the fifth century) to recover and exploit the genre of internal spiritual biography that the great North African had pioneered centuries before.[44]

And so when he comes to explain the atonement, Abelard says in essence, "Well, it's not a feudal social model that's most helpful to retain the mystery—rather, it's a personal, relational model." Again, as with Anselm's "satisfaction" explanation, God *did* die (the mystery is preserved). But Abelard thinks he did so not to gain redress for his wounded honor but rather to demonstrate his great love *and to create in us an answering love* so that we would rush to him as the prodigal son rushed to his father, receiving his redemptive embrace.

Neither of these men's explanations of the atonement does violence to the central mystery, which is that the undying, fully divine God died. The biblical paradox is not disposed of. Just as the Chalcedonian Definition uses reason to retain the paradox of the two natures of Christ and the doctrine of transubstantiation uses reason to retain the paradox of bread and wine that is also Christ, Anselm and Abelard use reason to retain the paradox of the God-man who dies.[45]

The tradition is strong because it hands down not an unreasonable faith but a faith that at certain points carries us beyond reason. The existence of God can be reasonably proven, even as the final mystery of things that are unexplainable in human terms can be preserved—a Savior who is both God and man, a God who dies, and so forth. Aquinas erects on this bedrock commitment a dazzling scientific and philosophical edifice of theology, and he does so as a Dominican friar, from within a deeply devotional and monastic culture.[46]

But one more thing needs to be said about the faith in reason among Christians of the ancient and medieval periods. This faith was, most significantly, a confidence that humans may progress in our theological understanding. Ancient and medieval theologians knew that the founding texts of the Christian religion comprise not clearly enunciated laws requiring a "strict construction" by all future worshipers but rather accounts of a life—the life of Jesus—told from many perspectives by many observers. Therefore, they found it self-evident that the faith is susceptible to reasoned interpretation and that, by careful reflection within the community of the faithful, the church may understand God better over time.[47]

In *Mere Christianity*, C. S. Lewis defines faith as "the art of holding on to things your reason has once accepted, in spite of your changing moods."[48] The question for our own time is this: Are we going to believe the ignorant modern story that the Middle Ages corrupted the church beyond recognition, so that God became absent from his church in that time? Are we thus going to lose the heritage of what reason did accomplish when yoked to faith during this period? Are we going to miss the tremendous "controlled power" that emerged when people of faith treated reason not as an autonomous power apart from God, not as the individual possession of each human being who then goes and does whatever he or she pleases, but as a precious gift to be used in the midst of the community of faith and in submission to its common tradition?

## Monks versus Scholars: A Modern Misinterpretation

Here's a cardinal truth about reading history: just because you hear a story again and again doesn't mean it's true. In fact, it may indicate that a legend has taken on the aura of truth and is no longer being examined. That's something like what I think happens in the common "monasticism versus scholasticism" narrative you will often come across in modern attempts to explain medieval thought.

This popular, though incorrect, narrative takes the politicized struggle between two strong personalities—Bernard of Clairvaux and Peter Abelard—and derives from it a thesis about the relationship between monastic and scholastic thinking: namely, that the world of medieval theology was divided into obscurantist, fideist monastics who were afraid of using reason and dialectic and wanted to protect mystery, and intelligent, rational scholastics who didn't care which sacred cows they slaughtered en route to a more "systematic" theology. In this story, Bernard of Clairvaux leads the charge against logic as the arch-monastic, and Abelard stands as the champion of logic and systematization.

Space prevents me from making a full case against this portrayal here, and in any case it is beyond my competence, but the argument seems to rest on a shaky foundation. When one reads a scholar who really knows Abelard well (e.g., David N. Bell[49]) or who really knows Bernard well (e.g., John Sommerfeldt[50]), one discovers that Abelard wanted very much to preserve the central mysteries of the faith—though at times he used inju-dicious language to do so[51]—and that Bernard was no mystery-besotted obscurantist but rather a master dialectician who preserved a place for the Christian life of the mind.

It is certainly true that not every theological thinker was so taken by the new "scientific" approach of scholasticism, and that many of the skeptics were monastics. Scholastic theology was not the only game in the Middle Ages. Benedictine monasticism, born in the seventh century and harnessed to the educational task under Charlemagne in the ninth, created some of the root conditions for scholasticism and a continuing parallel stream of Christian thought throughout the scholastic period—a stream sometimes in significant tension with scholasticism.

So when Abelard pushed the claims of dialectic within theology, Cistercian monk Bernard of Clairvaux, himself a great intellect and quite capable of slinging syllogisms with the best of them, objected that the hot-headed young scholastic was endangering the piety of the church, and Bernard pursued Abelard relentlessly through the political machinery of the church hierarchy.

But the division and antagonism between these two theological ap-proaches was never anywhere near so complete as the modern scholastics-versus-monastics narrative would have it. So where does that bifurcated picture come from? As is usual with bad history, it comes from "pre-sentism"—that is, the imposition of modern realities and concerns.

First, the warfare story fits nicely into the centuries-long modern tension between academics and religious functionaries that still conditions the dialogue between faith and reason in many American universities.[52] This struggle resulted in the nearly unbroken popular sway of Andrew Dickson White's now-discredited turn-of-the-century thesis about the essential conflict in history between science and theology. Second, it works well with the tension between the world of "academic theology"—abstracted from the church, whose concern to appear modern and scientific resulted in a de-supernaturalized "liberal" version of theology—and the conserva-tive, especially "evangelical," body of church folk who inherently suspect any imposition of reason on matters of faith as alien and hostile (and so the common evangelical saying about those who have gone off to "cem-etery"—that is, seminary—to learn theology). How convenient to have a story about medieval theology that so nicely illustrates and confirms these modern situations in university and church.

What I find representative of medieval thinking is not a war between reason and faith (certainly no epic battle, though perhaps a few sporadic skirmishes) but the grand synthesis of, for example, Aquinas. Aquinas recognized the tensile strength of the Christian faith handed down from the early fathers. The tradition is strong because it hands down not an unreasonable faith but a faith that is both reasonable (its God, for example, can be proved to exist), and at certain points beyond reason (its God is trinity and is incarnated in history as a human being). Aquinas erects on this bedrock commitment a dazzling scientific and philosophical edifice of theology, and he does so (again) as a Dominican friar, from within a deeply devotional and monastic culture, not as a dried-out academic. In his very person he puts the lie to the stereotypical "faith versus reason" narrative.

# 5

## Getting Moral

### *The Ethical Fabric of Medieval Faith*

I had finished the first year of my seminary master's program when my evangelical pastor back home pulled me into his office: "How can I address the character issues in my congregation without seeming legalistic? Anything I say on morality seems to pull against the gospel message of grace." The question was heartfelt. But after a full year in a church history program, I was at a loss for an answer.

The history of Protestantism, in particular, seemed unhelpful.

I did know that Luther and his heirs had been accused of teaching that we can't expect any real moral change. Luther taught "imputed righteousness": being covered by the blood of Christ, making up for our complete inability to be good.

I knew that in the generations after the great Reformer, critics said this teaching led to "antinomianism," a fifty-dollar word for moral lawlessness. And early Protestants of Lutheran ilk did follow their master Luther in holding the "spiritual disciplines" in high suspicion. Even as late as the twentieth century, Dietrich Bonhoeffer (1906–45) identified in his Lutheran church this same suspicion of any Christian effort toward righteousness—he called it "cheap grace"—and responded by convening a quasi-monastic experience at his underground seminary.

I also knew that a century after Luther, in the 1600s, the Puritans and Pietists sought to reform state-church Christianity, charging that the lifestyles and actions of too many churchgoers belied their professions of fidelity to Christ. They reengaged some ancient modes of spiritual discipline and invented some new ones—journaling, for instance, and the contemplation of "emblems," images that allegorically render passages of Scripture.

Furthermore, I knew that in the 1700s John Wesley and his helpers pioneered small groups, which increased accountability and discipline among laypeople.

But none of this seemed to offer a ready-made solution to my pastor's problem. He was right. This conundrum of how to train believers in moral good while also teaching a radical message of grace still plagues evangelical Protestantism. Protestants have fallen so in love with the message of grace and have so spiritualized their faith that questions of morality—at least the morality of public, communal life—have receded from view. As the late Dallas Willard described many modern believers, we are "not only saved by grace [but] paralyzed by it."[1]

## The "Sanctification Gap"

Not only has public morality receded but private morality has as well. This may seem counterintuitive: all evangelicals can seem to talk about sometimes is sexual morality. But this is a topic more "preached at" than taught: *We* don't do this sort of thing (abortion, homosexuality, etc.). *You* do. Therefore *you* are wrong and sinful and must come to the truth. There is little in the way of teaching how we can become better, more virtuous people in our sexual lives.

In short, we have here what evangelical scholar-journalist Carl F. H. Henry calls *The Uneasy Conscience of Modern Fundamentalism*[2] and what historian Richard Lovelace identifies as a "sanctification gap" among evangelicals.[3] The news from the front has been grim—for decades.

In 2005, sociologist Christian Smith surveyed teenagers who had been brought up in Christian (including evangelical) homes in America. Smith discovered that their religion consisted of a vague sense that if they were just nice to people, a kindly grandfather God would certainly not keep them out of heaven. He calls this version of faith "moralistic therapeutic deism."[4] But its "moralism" is little more than a watered-down version of the Golden Rule.

That same year, theologian and social activist Ron Sider wrote *The Scandal of the Evangelical Conscience*, drawing on survey data that shows evangelical Christians are no more morally upright than anyone else; they manifest the same hedonism, materialism, racism, and so forth as their secular neighbors. His conclusion: evangelicals suffer a complete disconnect between their belief and their practice.[5]

Two years later, in the fall of 2007, Bill Hybels, pastor of the thirty-two-year-old Willow Creek Community Church, in South Barrington, Illinois, admitted that though his seminal megachurch attracted plenty of people to the faith through their "seeker-sensitive" model, they had utterly failed to help congregants mature in their character.[6]

One may point the finger, in part, at America. This seems to be a difficult place to practice a distinctively Christian ethical life. A gaggle of pundits and pollsters, building on Christopher Lasch's *Culture of Narcissism* in the 1970s and Robert Bellah's *Habits of the Heart* in the 1980s, argue that, from "Gen X" to "Gen Y" to the "Millennials," each new generation is slipping deeper into an inward-turned, selfish, and morally listless condition. The supposed culprits are varied: wealth, leisure, and the consumerist culture of instant gratification. The proposed solutions, too, have been varied.

Yes, we must take all such assessments with a grain of salt—after all, they generally issue from older commentators waggling their fingers in the faces of the younger generation.[7] But ironically, we may also be encouraged by the very frequency of such exercises in sociocultural hand-wringing. A historian can't help but notice how he or she echoes the tone and content of those most earnest of believers, the late seventeenth- and early eighteenth-century Puritans. These persistent expressions of concern, even in supposedly "post-Christian" America, indicate that the cultural heritage of Christian moral thought is—in the immortal words of the Monty Python leper—"not dead yet."

## C. S. Lewis and the Medieval Moral Tradition

One of the most acute commentators on the modern moral morass was C. S. Lewis. Modern/postmodern distinctions notwithstanding, C. S. Lewis walked our cultural ground. He lived, as we do, in a society that denied objective value; lacked a coherent social ethic; wallowed in instant gratification, sexual license, moral evasion, and blame-shifting; and failed to pass on a moral framework to its children through the training of what he calls the "moral sentiments." He would point out to us, as he did to his own day, that it is no good skewering the younger generation's failures when we, their elders, have failed to teach them well. "In a sort of ghastly simplicity we remove the organ and demand the function. We make men without chests [that is, without well-trained moral sentiments] and expect of them virtue and enterprise. We laugh at honour and are shocked to find traitors in our midst. We castrate and bid the geldings be fruitful."

These are Lewis's words in his seminal extended essay *The Abolition of Man*.[8] And the same analysis echoes through the pages of his imaginative writings—yes, Narnia, but also, and more explicitly, *The Screwtape Letters*, *The Great Divorce*, and the Space Trilogy: *Out of the Silent Planet, Perelandra*, and *That Hideous Strength*. In such works, Lewis portrays not just the moral problems facing modern society but also their solution: the graced renovation of the human heart. Indeed, I would argue that in *everything* he wrote, whether nonfiction or fiction, Lewis wrote first of all as a Christian moral philosopher. And I don't think it's too much of a stretch to add that he was a *medieval* Christian moral philosopher. At least, Lewis's Christian moral philosophy owes much to medieval faith, in both its intellectual framework and its didactic use of story and imagination.

In chapter 4, I defined a philosopher as someone who seeks to understand and live life in light of Truth, Beauty, and Goodness. From early in his life, Lewis's thought was immersed in that tradition, although as a young man (before his conversion to Christianity) he struggled against aspects of it.

Lewis's training under William T. Kirkpatrick from age sixteen to eighteen prepared him to find in "old books" not only aesthetic pleasures but also a meaning and a morality for living. His stint at the front during World War II momentarily sundered his moral understanding from his imagination and from the Christian sources of the Western ethical framework. When he returned from the front after being wounded, he took up his studies again in January 1919, constructing a stoic creed he called his "new look"—the belief that this material world is all that we can know and that our job is to "bear its deep pains and cherish its moderate joys with as much courage as we can muster." This new "no-nonsense philosophy" denied the existence of any grounds for making objective judgments about value.[9]

### Lewis the Defender of Objective Value

Soon, however, Lewis encountered a set of ethical theories derived from the Western tradition of moral understanding handed down from Judeo-Christian Scriptures and Roman law. Shortly after his return to Oxford, and still a decade before his Christian conversion, Lewis began to defend objective value in ethics.

In 1922 he read that favorite of medieval readers, Boethius's *Consolation of Philosophy*, for the first time—its cadences no doubt still rang in his ears when, as a test essay for a fellowship in philosophy, he submitted an argument for the existence of natural law (prefiguring his later *Abolition of Man*). And as we've seen, when he briefly taught philosophy at University College, Oxford, he took as his subject "moral goodness."[10]

In 1925, Lewis entered what would become his long-standing teaching position at Magdalen College, Oxford. As we have seen, the dominant philosopher there, John Alexander Smith, stood solidly with the Western Christian moral tradition (a position we described as distinctly medieval). This likely reinforced the young professor's commitment to the traditional doctrine of an objectively real moral law and his resolve to make "intellectual war on the utilitarians, the idealists, and the moral subjectivists."[11]

When in 1931 C. S. Lewis came to Christian faith, it gave a new ground for his moral understandings; he could now see them as being created, along with all material creation, by God. However, he was far from insisting that only Christians or theists could be moral. In his early spiritual autobiography, *The Pilgrim's Regress* (1933), Lewis shows a "Landlord" (God) who makes rules not just for a particular religious tribe but for all people. Christianity innovated morally only by teaching that the redemption purchased for us by Christ brings the Writer of the rules into our hearts, thus helping us to keep them.[12]

As Lewis knew well, these assumptions thoroughly suffused ancient and medieval culture: "Aristotle had assumed it, and Plato. Cicero had spoken of it when he called it the law that is not written down. When St. Paul wrote that even the Gentiles knew that certain kinds of behavior were wrong, he was appealing to natural law. This same idea informed the thought of St. Augustine in the fourth century and St. Thomas in the thirteenth."[13]

### Virtue Made Concrete: Lewis's Use of Story in Moral Teaching

While Lewis continued making the intellectual argument for objective value after his conversion, he was also captivated by the typically medieval use of imaginative story in teaching morality at the affective level (training the "moral sentiments" or the "chest," two of the phrases he uses in *The Abolition of Man* for the ethical seat of humans, what the Bible calls "the heart"). The medieval devotional authors he read through the 1930s and 1940s—from Julian of Norwich and Walter Hilton to the anonymous author of the *Theologia Germanica*, along with Dante and Chaucer (ca. 1343–1400)—all painted the Christian moral life in image-rich narrative colors.

Late in his career, Lewis told his students at Cambridge that the medieval cosmos was a world of "built-in significance," its physical realities all shot through with meaning and the divine.[14] Medievals, unlike moderns, refused to sunder the realities of mundane existence from the highest ideals of Truth, Beauty, and Goodness. And his deep engagement in medieval literature gave Lewis a desire to tell stories that showed the virtues (and vices) in concrete form.

Medieval schoolboys, Lewis says in his *English Literature of the Sixteenth Century*, learned

> farriery, forestry, archery, hawking, sowing, ditching, thatching, brewing, baking, weaving, and practical astronomy. This concrete knowledge, mixed with their law, rhetoric, theology, and mythology, bred an outlook very different from our own. High abstractions and rarified artifices jostled the earthiest particulars. . . . They talked more readily than we about large universals such as death, change, fortune, friendship, or salvation; but also about pigs, loaves, boots, and boats. The mind darted more easily to and fro between that mental heaven and earth: the cloud of middle generalizations,

hanging between the two, was then much smaller. Hence, as it seems to us, both the naivety and the energy of their writing. . . . They talk something like angels and something like sailors and stable-boys; never like civil servants or writers of leading articles.[15]

It was no accident that reading a schoolbook for children triggered Lewis's most famous moral screed against utilitarianism, *The Abolition of Man*, or that the most lasting testament to his own moral vision is a set of children's novels. When Lewis began teaching morality by embedding it in the concrete details of story, he wielded one of the most venerable tools in the medieval ethical toolbox. For it was in writing stories that medievals most exercised that habit of mind, leading the imagination of the reader to dart "to and fro between that mental heaven and earth."

In Thomas Aquinas, one can see the philosophical grounds for this use of storytelling. Following Aristotle, Aquinas taught that the moral life is to be achieved not by education in the mode of memorization but instead by imitation leading to habit. It is a key principle of Aristotelian virtue ethics that imitation requires living examples, not lists of ethical principles. To become virtuous, our hearts must be shaped by the lives and stories of others. In Lewis's copy of Walter Hilton's widely used devotional guide, *The Scale* (or "Ladder") *of Perfection*, he marked the following: "This is the conforming of a soul to God, which may not be had unless it be first reformed by *fullness of virtues turned into affection*; and that is when a man loveth virtues, for that they be good in themselves."[16] It was to develop in readers the emotional taste for the inherent goodness of the virtues that Lewis wrote his stories.

### Imagination: The Organ of Meaning

In doing this, Lewis was imitating his master, the novelist George MacDonald. In the preface to his tribute volume *George MacDonald: An Anthology*, Lewis says this about his early encounter with MacDonald's imaginative writings:

The quality which had enchanted me in his imaginative works turned out to be the quality of the real universe, the divine, magical, terrifying, and ecstatic reality in which we all live. *I should have been shocked in my teens if anyone had told me that what I learned to love in* Phantastes *was goodness.* But now that I know, I see there was no deception. The deception is all the other way round—in *that prosaic moralism which confines goodness to the region of Law and Duty*, which never lets us feel in our face the sweet air blowing from "the land of righteousness," never reveals that elusive Form which if once seen must inevitably be desired with all but sensuous desire—the thing (in Sappho's phrase) "more gold than gold."[17]

This love of, and desire for, goodness mirrors exactly the ancient and medieval Christian way of grounding morality (and all theology) in love and desire for God. For more on this, see chapter 8 (esp. p. 171) of this book, and for a captivating portrait of how this dynamic worked in early Christian thought, see Robert Wilken, *The Spirit of Early Christian Thought.*[18]

In *Miracles*, Lewis reminds us of what John 7:17 teaches, "that only He who does the will of the Father will ever know the true doctrine." We need the concreteness of moral action, as of devotional action, to ground our ideas of God, lest they float off into abstractions. It's not that the high abstractions are not also true—they are. But the moral life both grounds us in the "pigs, loaves, boots, and boats" (the stuff of our actual lives) and also makes real our understanding of the God who is above all understanding: "One moment even of feeble contrition or blurred thankfulness will, at least in some degree, head us off from the abyss of abstraction."[19] In this, again, Lewis follows the medieval tradition, which follows the early fathers.

Nowhere is Lewis more medieval than in helping his readers reach out to the transcendent God and the life of "godliness" through the instrument of concrete, detail-filled stories. As we've seen, Lewis insists that "reason is the natural organ of truth; but imagination is the organ of meaning. Imagination, producing new metaphors or revivifying old, is not the cause of truth, but its condition."[20] What does he mean (so to speak) by "meaning"? I think Lewis intends by the term "truth" *truly* understood, by being internalized through concrete example and application. Virtue is only virtue when we see it applied and when we apply it ourselves in the plot and circumstance of life.

When Lewis encountered the medieval poet Dante Alighieri, he met the master of making the transcendent concrete, of creating meaning through poetic imagery. In a 1948 essay, "Imagery in the Last Eleven Cantos of Dante's *Comedy*," which he read to the Oxford Dante Society, he talks about Dante's imagery having "an almost sensuous intensity about things not sensuous." Through frequent use of images from gardens, arts, and crafts, the "continual reference both to the quiet, moistened earth and to the resonant pavements, workshops, and floors," Dante represents heaven and heavenly values—qualities otherwise very hard to get hold of in any concrete way.[21]

### Planetary Virtues

Lewis comes clean about his own medievalesque moral approach to fiction writing in the preface to *That Hideous Strength*, the third volume of his Space Trilogy. There he writes, "This is a 'tall story' about devilry, though it has behind it a serious 'point' which I have tried to make in my *Abolition of Man*."[22] In this concretizing of the moral life through narrative, Lewis was without doubt following Dante.[23]

In *That Hideous Strength*, Lewis explicitly uses the "seven medieval planets" (Mercury, Venus, Mars, Jupiter, Saturn, Sol, and Luna) to accomplish this. According to medieval understanding, these were not cold, distant conglomerations of rocks and gases. They were living beings whose associated virtues patterned and influenced our own. Our modern English words reveal these virtues: "jovial" hospitality for Jupiter (whose Middle English name was "Jove"), "martial" courage for Mars, even "venereal" (or sexual) love for Venus. Michael Ward also argues that Lewis used these planetary characters as the implicit structure for the seven books of the Chronicles of Narnia.[24]

In the Chronicles the planetary virtues appear subtly, woven invisibly into the fabric of each story (and the very hiddenness of this structure itself, as Ward shows us, is a medieval technique). But Lewis's science fiction novels came first. Here, the planets show up "in the flesh," coming down to earth to communicate their virtues to the protagonists at crucial junctures in the plot. *That Hideous Strength* culminates, in fact, with Venus herself descending to the marriage bed of Mark and Jane Studdock, healing their crumbling relationship by restoring their sexual intimacy. How medieval! No "middle cloud of generalization" here; this is angels and boots rolled into one.

## Precision, Practicality, and Passion

Lewis saw how the medieval tradition "made the transcendent concrete," and he imitated this approach in his own imaginative writing. But there is more we can learn about morality from medieval Christian tradition. For that tradition contains riches of precision, practicality, and passion that can equip us for tremendous progress in our moral lives.

Let's be honest: those of us in the evangelical camp today largely lack the inclination or ability to submit our moral lives to any precise, practical spiritual tradition. We do not ask how humans—created, fallen, and redeemed—actually grow and develop as moral beings or what our faith has to say that is detailed and helpful about what can make us better moral beings. These are questions that *par excellence* animated the medievals, especially scholastics such as Aquinas, as we glimpsed in chapter 4.

In this matter of the moral life, if we do not evade the questions altogether, we give ourselves over to the secular social science, to the psychological disciplines. In the words of Thomas Oden, "What curious fate has befallen the classical tradition of pastoral care in the last five decades? It has been steadily accommodated to a series of psychotherapies."[25] This is not to denigrate modern psychological approaches to soul care, yet much of the wisdom in those techniques—and there is wisdom in them—was anticipated by more than one thousand years, and better grounded in a Christian framework, in people like Gregory the Great, as Oden argues in *Care of Souls in the Classic Tradition*. The precision and practicality of that older tradition can help us in so many ways—yet we are cut off from it.

My own need for honesty and precision in the moral life came to me as lightning out of the clear blue sky. I was born in 1963 and came of age in the 1970s. I didn't even like the word "responsibility," let alone anything that cramped my freedom to self-express, to enjoy the good things of the world. My conversion in 1985 started to change that (slowly, painfully, and in an ongoing way), but a significant moment for me was the Calvin College Summer Seminar in 2010, "Seven Deadly Sins (Capital Vices) in the Christian Tradition," a gathering of scholars in philosophy, theology, and literature to discover and discuss this particular part of the medieval moral tradition.

Most of us sitting around that seminar table each day, engaging with the ancient and medieval materials of the seven deadly sins tradition through our teachers Rebecca Konyndyk DeYoung of Calvin College and Bob Kruschwitz of Baylor University, reported the same sort of thing. Evagrius Ponticus (345–99), John Cassian (ca. 360–435), Gregory the Great, Aquinas, and the rest shed a bright, uncomfortable, and challenging light on our own personal behaviors and tendencies, as well as on the dynamics of God's grace as he weans us from the foul habits of the "capital vices." Just as Lewis's friend Charles Williams exclaimed when he first encountered Dante, so also did we in our encounter with these great early and medieval teachers: "Why, that's just what I feel!" And at the same time: "Yes, I'm guilty of this, and now I understand it better." You might think this would feel oppressive, the daily anatomization of our own sinful hearts under the surgical lights of the tradition. But it was not. It was strengthening, even exhilarating.

### Precision

Again, the precision of the medieval tradition is worth noticing here. Medieval moral teaching is no blunt instrument. In fact, to identify a "seven deadly sins" tradition is already to blunt medieval thinkers' precision about sin. The tag "seven capital vices" better reflects these writers' insistence that pride, envy, sloth, and the rest constitute *patterns of behavior* (vices) rather than *single acts* (sins); each vice is a fountainhead of other sins ("capital" means "head").

In his inaugural address as the Cambridge Chair of Medieval and Renaissance Literature, Lewis reflected wryly on how counterintuitive this medieval precision is for most modern folks. So blinded have we become by the Enlightenment caricature of the Middle Ages as a time of unremitting intellectual and moral darkness (flat-earth belief, the use of cruel torture implements, barbarous crusades, and the rest) that we cannot see the evidence in front of our faces. Lewis recounted, "Only last summer a young gentleman whom I had the honor of examining described Thomas Wyatt [a sixteenth-century English poet] as 'the first man who scrambled ashore out of the great, dark surging sea of the Middle Ages.'" (One can imagine the face Lewis made at this point in his delivery.) "This was interesting," he continued, "because it showed how a stereotyped image can obliterate a man's own experience. Nearly all the medieval texts which the syllabus had required him to study had in reality led him into formal gardens where every passion was subdued to a ceremonial and every problem of conduct was dovetailed into a complex and rigid moral theology."[26]

The precision of medieval moral theology is something that can frighten evangelical Protestants today, inasmuch as we try to protect the priority of grace bequeathed to us by the apostle Paul via Augustine—and think incorrectly that such a priority cannot be combined with a precise and detailed understanding of moral psychology. Again, as Willard says, we are in danger of being not only saved but also paralyzed by grace.

Putting this in personal terms, when I think of my own habitual resistance to, for example, spiritual direction or confession, it seems to come from a feeling that it would be time-wasting to focus on my littleness and imperfection, and depressing as well, when there are so many grander things to think about and to do. And yet the little, the material, the psychological, the earthy: that is where I live. If I try to ignore my moral psyche, then my unsanctified thoughts and emotions and the ways in which I indulge them will hamstring me, preventing me from functioning well. My desires will be moved more and more toward things that are not God, which will destroy my effectiveness. I need to not ignore or bypass those niggling negative patterns in my heart and mind, but rather face them, and face how they have led me into sins—even though it means delving into petty and sordid details of my imperfect character. When I do that, there is a promise—a promise rehearsed with particular clarity in the medieval tradition—that precise, informed, honest moral reflection clears a path to reconnecting with God.

### Vainglory—Precision about Pride

How "formal" and "complex" the garden of medieval moral teaching actually was can be seen in the nuances of the traditional teaching about the pattern of vice called "vainglory." Aquinas, following the ancient desert fathers, made several useful distinctions between vainglory and pride that have been obliterated, in today's standard list of seven deadly sins, by their conflation into the single term "pride."

Much of the difference can be found in the meaning of the little root "vain" ("vanity" is another form of this term), which means empty, idle, or false. When we indulge in the vice of pride we really want to *be* better than anyone else. In fact, there are things that we do and are that may be worthy of pride in the positive sense. But when we indulge vainglory we don't care whether we *are* good at something—we just want to be *perceived* as good. In other words, it is a particularly flashy and empty form of pride; it's about display, fame, and the adulation of the masses. At its center, vainglory is hollow because that display hides the fact that the recipient is unworthy. The glory received is truly *vain* glory—glory in vain, glory given where there is nothing worthy of it.

At our Calvin seminar, Bob Kruschwitz related a story John Cassian told of a young monk in the desert monastic cells of Egypt. One day the daydreaming youth becomes caught up in the fantasy of being made a great priest in a big city because of his tremendous progress in sanctity. As he stands in his cell, he begins preaching to an enraptured audience in his imagination. He becomes so impassioned that he begins actually to preach out loud. Before long an older monk wanders by and hears what is going on. He stands at the door until the sermon is over and then knocks. The younger monk, sensing he has been caught, blushes and asks, "How long have you been standing there?" Replies the elder sensitively, "I only arrived when you were dismissing the catechumens" (that is, after the sermon's end, before the Eucharist).

Usually vainglory involves an audience, and the glory being given is disproportionate to the good that is being lauded. But sometimes the thing lauded is indeed worthy—it is just that the glory given is misplaced. For example: I am born with an athlete's body; I've got "all the right genes." As I grow up, I excel in sports. I love the attention and adulation this gets me, and I am proud of the skills that draw this attention. Well, what is wrong with that? Just this: Yes, I have trained and improved my skills, and there are elements in my athletic performance that come from my hard work and discipline. But ultimately, who gave me the gifts that I have? And to whom, therefore, does at least part of the glory rightfully go? To God. Inasmuch as I boast and preen and strut, directing all attention to myself, the glory being given is "in vain" because it is not being directed to the proper object.

A moment's thought will raise for most readers countless examples of vainglory in the contemporary entertainment industry. But my own tribe—academics and knowledge workers—need to look "at home" before pointing the finger. The great North African theologian Augustine, whose presence spread across medieval faith like a mantle, reflected in his

*Confessions* on the vainglory that marred his life before God got hold of him. In his career as a rhetorician, for example, he remembered bitterly that he had been nothing but a purveyor of gilded lies, a "vendor of words" in a civic marketplace rotten with vainglory and deceit.

The syndrome of vainglory was already fully present in Augustine's boyhood when he stole pears from a farmer's tree—not because he wanted the fruit but because he wanted to impress his friends. When he reached adulthood he lamented that his career only gave him more and greater opportunities to indulge this vice. "The same desire for approval," De-Young recounts, "drove Augustine to excel in school and become an accomplished rhetorician. Even then, however, he was more concerned that his speeches in the law courts had the proper style and erudition to win him applause than that they conveyed truth, even when human lives hung in the balance."[27]

### *"Vanity, All Is Vanity"*

Lewis faced his own struggle with vainglory (in its peculiarly potent academic form), as he recounts in a letter to his boyhood friend Arthur Greeves, penned a year before his conversion in 1930:

> The old doctrine is quite true you know—that one must attribute everything to the grace of God, and nothing to oneself. Yet as long as one *is* a conceited ass, there is no good pretending not to be. . . . I catch myself posturing before the mirror, so to speak, all day long. I pretend I am carefully thinking out what to say to the next pupil (for *his* good, of course) and then suddenly realize I am really thinking how frightfully clever I'm going to be and how he will admire me. I pretend I am remembering an evening of good fellowship in a really friendly and charitable spirit—and all the time I'm really remembering how good a fellow I am and how well I talked.[28]

But we may object: "What's wrong with a little vainglory here and there?" This objection contains a truth, which DeYoung, following Aquinas, admits: humans have a natural desire to be known—and especially for their goodness to be known. And Aquinas believed goodness by its nature tends to communicate itself to others. We can see this in God too.

But the problem lies in that "vain" dimension of vainglory—the falseness, the unworthiness of what is receiving glory. As DeYoung puts it, when we are subject to vainglory, we fall into patterns of "falsity, hiddenness, staging, and embellishment."[29] Human life is properly lived best in community with others. So here in this life and in the next, our proper end is to be in fellowship with God and other people. *This will require that we are acknowledged for who we truly are*, not for who we are pretending to be. The false display of vainglory blocks the true self-disclosure necessary for love.

Like all of the capital vices, vainglory is the fountainhead of many other sins and syndromes, such as boasting, hypocrisy (pretending to possess good qualities we don't actually have), and love of novelty (of course nobody in this "iAge" has that problem!). And oh, this vice is a slippery snake; it sneaks up on us so quietly while we think we are just acting within the bounds of healthy self-acceptance. An unhealthy attention to "publicity" erodes one's ability to value the actual virtue that one was trying initially to display, so that gradually we sacrifice our integrity, compromising our view of what is truly valuable. We begin to "believe our own press releases."

All of these aspects of the syndrome of vainglory are dangerous, but are we aware of the deepest danger—the place where vainglory tips over into that most pernicious of vices—spiritual pride? Vainglory and pride are similar in that the better or more virtuous we become, the more susceptible we are to turning in on ourselves and glorying in what we've achieved. Again, here is Lewis in his 1930 letter to Greeves:

> During my afternoon "meditations,"—which I at least attempt quite regularly now—I have found out ludicrous and terrible things about my own character. Sitting by, watching the rising thoughts to break their necks as they pop up, one learns to know the sort of thoughts that do come. [This is pure desert fathers language: the identification of "thoughts" as the problem and the use of battle language.] And, will you believe it, one out of every three is a thought of self-admiration: when everything else fails, having had its neck broken, up comes the thought "What an admirable fellow I am to have broken their necks!" . . . It's like fighting the hydra (you remember, when you cut off one head another grew). There seems to be no end to it. Depth under depth of self-love and self admiration.[30]

If a person recognizes in his or her life a syndrome of vainglory, spiritual pride, or indeed any of the other "capital vices" and wants to deal with it, an excellent place to look is the tradition that stretches from the

desert fathers through Augustine to the scholastics of the twelfth and thirteenth centuries—in particular, to that great medieval scholastic, Thomas
Aquinas.[31]

Aquinas deals with vainglory and the other capital vices with a precision
and a practicality that can carry us beyond modern Christian platitudes to
real understanding and real change in our moral lives. Of course, ultimately
we get nowhere without grace. But grace does not rule out intelligent,
rational understanding of our moral predicament, or effortful application
of disciplines to our unrighteous condition.

So far I have been talking about the "micro" of ethics—personal morality, character, vice, and virtue. And this is consistent with the early Christian
literature on ethics, the vast majority of which addresses personal moral
formation.[32] But Aquinas and the scholastics assembled a world-embracing
system—"the medieval synthesis"—that also includes a social ethic.

We see that social ethic at work in Dante, who was a politician and
political theorist as well as a poet. In the *Commedia*, he puts that political
acuity to work in an outraged, full-frontal attack on the corruption of
the church.[33]

## A Medieval Take on Social Justice and Leadership: Dante and His *Commedia*

Dante wrote very much in the prophetic mode of Micah (who taught that
to live faithfully with our God we must "act justly" and "love mercy"; Mic.
6:8). Dante used his great poem to reveal the corruption, irresponsibility,
and mercilessness of the church and of the supposedly Christian state.
More precisely, he speaks directly about and to individual leaders. This
poem is a harsh and detailed seminar on Christian leadership from the
heart of one who failed in leadership himself (having been ousted from
his high office and exiled from his city).

To be sure, there is grace here. We find in the poem many people who
have sinned grievously against their fellow humans, yet who by God's
grace make it into the cleansing place that is purgatory and from there into
the loving presence of the Father in heaven. But those who do injustice,
who love unmercifulness, and who walk in arrogance, end up (barring an
eleventh-hour repentance) in hell. There, some of the worst punishments

are reserved for those whose moral transgressions have not just harmed themselves, their neighbors, and their society but have corrupted the church itself. "What [Dante] is trying to do in the *Commedia* . . . is bring life to a dying church: A church that is more concerned with property, material things, than it is with its spiritual mission."[34]

### Dante's Prophetic Criticism of Church Leadership

One of the most famous moments in the poem is Dante's encounter (canto 19 of the *Inferno*) with a corrupt pope. In the gully where the "simonists" (sellers and buyers of church offices) are punished, Dante's pilgrim alter ego finds a number of holes in the ground. Out of the holes stick the legs of sinners, feet aflame. Dante speaks down into one of these holes, basically asking to know who is down there, and he discovers that the sinner is none other than Pope Nicholas III (Nicholas Orsini). His sins are simony (selling church offices) and nepotism (putting family members in positions of power). Believing Dante to be Pope Boniface VIII, who was still alive at the time the poem was being written, Nicholas asks, "Are you already done exploiting the church?" Thus the poet indicts two popes at one go.

> After Nicholas has said his piece, Dante (the pilgrim, the autobiographical character in the poem) bursts out in righteous anger: "Tell me: how much treasure did our Lord ask of Saint Peter before He gave the keys into his charge? Truly he asked for nothing, saying only 'Follow me.' Neither did Peter or the others take gold or silver from Matthias when he was chosen for the place vacated by the evil soul. Stay there, for thou art rightly punished. But for the reverence I feel for the sublime keys that thou didst hold in happier life, I'd use graver words still."[35]

The late great Dantist Barbara Reynolds (friend of Dante translator and Lewis associate Dorothy L. Sayers) finds in this scene "the very core of the purpose of the *Commedia*": the proclamation of an ethic of justice that should characterize the governance both of the church and of the world.[36]

What did Dante believe had caused the terrible corruption that was spreading out from the church to stain the whole world black? Simply put, the corruption of that great spiritual body's leadership, through their meddling in the secular power of government. When did this secular power-mongering begin? With the fourth-century document the "Donation of Constantine," in which the first Christian Roman emperor, Constantine, supposedly gave the church political as well as spiritual dominion over the Western Roman Empire. Dante believed the document was genuine (as did everyone else until, in 1440, it was revealed as an eighth- or ninth-century forgery).[37] Whatever Constantine had meant to accomplish by it, Dante saw in that fateful decree only disaster for the church, which would go on to bring misery on itself and on the world by claiming temporal power:

> Ah, Constantine, that was indeed a curse,
>      not thy conversion, but thy dower which
>      first filled with wealth the Holy Father's purse![38]

It would be easy for Western, especially American, religious leaders today to miss the modern force of this medieval poet's angry indictment of his church's political corruption. After all, in a country in which the church has been mostly decoupled from the state, Constantine and his supposed "donation" might seem a distant and irrelevant memory. Surely, the disgraced empires of money-grabbing televangelist empires and authoritarian megachurches built on the sway of single charismatic leaders notwithstanding, nothing in today's church parallels the corruption of the medieval papacy.

### Dante and the Leader's Inner Life

But not so fast. Dante's critique of ecclesiastical corruption may cut deeper than we think. The poet does not leave the prophetic finger-pointing at bad popes and well-intentioned emperors. There is something deeper and more personal about his great poem's assessment of leadership. The *Commedia* is not just a social or ecclesiological critique. It is also a story about the heart of the individual leader. And here we may learn an important lesson for our own moment.

By the early 1300s, when he was writing his great poem, Dante had established himself as a renowned poet. He had given years of his life to philosophical study at the Franciscan and Dominican schools of Italy and occupied a place at the top of the leadership pile in his native Florence, getting himself elected one of the six priors who briefly presided as the "supreme court" of his city.

But the machinations of church politics caught him up, and he was falsely accused and exiled from his beloved Florence, never to return. In the midst of these bitter circumstances, Dante descended into a sort of hopeless, sin-soaked funk.

So when Dante set out in his own midlife to write what on one level is the story of his own spiritual pilgrimage, he began his poem with what scholars agree is an autobiographical confession. The poem's protagonist, conventionally identified as "Dante the Pilgrim" (to distinguish him from the author, "Dante the Poet"), is wandering in a dark woods. He has lost his bearings—spiritually, morally, and intellectually. "Once upon a time," he writes of himself, "he had known the right way; but he lost it, let it get overgrown and rank."[39]

This, then, was the well from which Dante drew as he looked at the situation of the church's leadership at the dawning of the fourteenth century. But the core of his insight came not from his involvement in the tangled web of high-medieval Italian church and state; rather, it came from a surgically painful and effective anatomizing of his own prideful heart (an appropriate source for a Christian writer working in the tradition of Paul of Tarsus and Augustine of Hippo).

### Dante's Self-Criticism

Everything in the poet's history seemed to encourage pride. He had made a success of himself as a love poet, a political philosopher, and a high functionary in his beloved city of Florence. After his bitter exile, he succumbed to an idolatrous patriotism that was willing to stop at nothing to restore the "glory days" of his fair city (and, not incidentally, of his party and his carefully groomed civic identity).

But clearly Dante became convicted of his own pride. As we get deeper into the poem, he begins dismantling the foolishness of his earlier life. Moving up from hell, ascending the terraces of purgatory, and finally entering paradise itself and nearing the beatific vision of God's own person, Dante the Pilgrim is faced increasingly with his own sinfulness. Woven through the verses of this epic poem is a kind of confession— a confession of a complex of habits and characteristics that had led him off of the "straight and narrow road" and on to the broad way to damnation.

Dante the Poet explains these habits as *"disordered loves,"* borrowing language both from Thomas Aquinas's virtue-ethics and Augustine's Pauline theology of sin and grace. Though Dante dedicated his life to pursuing ends that were truly right and good—*love, knowledge*, and *citizenship*—he pursued those ends by wrong means and to wrong degrees.

When, at the end of *Purgatorio*, he meets again his first love and muse, the young Beatrice, the self-exploration and self-critique that has been bubbling below the surface of the poem breaks out, and Dante comes to the central question of his life: If God's grace could free him from these partial loves—for romantic, sexual love; for learning; for political influence—how could he, with all of his talents, best do justice, and love mercy, and walk humbly with God? How could he serve God and love—and lead—others?

### Dante Emerges as a New Kind of Leader

The answer finally comes near the end of the *Commedia*. In *Paradiso* 17 and 18, Dante meets his great-great-grandfather, Cacciaguida, a martyr in the Second Crusade. Cacciaguida offers Dante a "new crusade," a war of peacemaking and perspective to be waged not with the sword but with the pen: Dante is to describe for the good of the world all the people he has met in the three afterworlds—their stories, sins, and virtues. Through their stories, Cacciaguida says, all parties will learn a new and compelling "universal view," a God's-eye view, beside which their damaging petty squabbles will pale. Dante accepts Cacciaguida's proffered quest, thus inheriting a mantle from the Old Testament prophets themselves.

This is a new, more moral calling: to rise above selfish agendas and the building of petty empires and to be a new kind of person and a new kind of leader. Surely this is a calling that, for all the differences between the medieval world and our own, we can still hear and heed with profit. It is a calling not just for official "leaders" but for every Christian. The reason Dorothy Sayers devoted the last years of her life to Dante's great poem was because she found the great Florentine telling her wartime world—a world far gone in moral paralysis, irresponsibility, and blame-shifting—what it most desperately needed to hear. In her friend Barbara Reynolds's words, this was that "good and evil exist, that . . . the will is free to choose between them, that, consequently . . . the individual, even though in part conditioned by heredity and environment . . . nevertheless remains morally responsible."[40]

Of this medieval wisdom, Sayers herself says: "We must also be prepared, while we are reading Dante, to abandon any idea that we are the slaves of chance, or environment, or our subconscious; any vague notion that good and evil are merely relative terms, or that conduct and opinion do not really matter; any comfortable persuasion that, however shiftlessly we muddle through life, it will somehow or other all come right." We must, in other words, truly believe in God's gift to us of free will, for "The Divine Comedy is precisely the drama of the soul's choice."[41]

But could it be that we, now, need to hear Dante's stringent moral-spiritual message more even than Sayers's readers did? After all, they had at least the bracing shock of a world war on their own doorsteps (unlike today's distant and more limited conflicts) to keep them alert to moral and spiritual realities.

This chapter began with a sober look at the "sanctification gap" in our churches, the dilemma of finding a moral teaching and practice that does not descend into graceless legalism but that guides us firmly as we seek to serve the Lord of love who came not to destroy but to fulfill God's law. Then we took a sort of "moral tour" of the Middle Ages. Through Lewis, we started with the medieval commitment to objective, transcendentally grounded moral reality. Then we peered into medieval imaginative literature's vividly concrete embodiment of that reality. We moved on to sample the seven capital vices—tradition's precision and power in anatomizing our inner moral lives. Finally, we explored Dante's poetic social ethics of leadership. In each of these medieval vignettes are glimpses of a complex, coherent, and theologically grounded morality—a quite different portrait from the Monty Python caricature of this era as a Dark Age of thumbscrews, Crusades, and Inquisitions. Here again, it seems the faith-informed cultural legacy of the Middle Ages may have some wisdom to offer us, after all.

# 6

# Getting Merciful

## *Why Medievals Invented the Hospital*

If we don't know anything else about the Middle Ages, we know that life then was "nasty, brutish, and short."[1] In the West, medical science had not advanced from the classical era—in fact, it had perhaps regressed. Feudal societies suffered under petty wars, abject poverty, and the plague. For the modern imagination, "getting medieval" means brutality, torture, and disregard for human life. Rarely is the counter-story (the other side of the suffering) told: Christians since the very earliest centuries of the church had taken seriously not just the salvation of the soul but the healing of the body. Nor was this concern of a mysterious or anti-scientific sort. Yes, occasionally healing might take miraculous form—through a prodigy of the sick person's faith or the power of some saint's relic. But most often healing meant simple nursing care, often at great risk to the caregiver's own life. And it also meant the creation and development of the world's greatest institution of mercy: the hospital.

When, in the first two centuries of the church, the pagan Romans watched the Christians rush into situations of pestilence and plague, caring not only for their own but also for their occasional persecutors, they had no categories for explaining this behavior. In some ways, not much has changed today. If a person does not believe in God, or does believe in God but lives like he or she doesn't (which amounts to the same thing), then there are two things that are ultimate in their life: health and wealth. Why would someone pour out his or her own resources and endanger his or her own health in order to help another in physical need? For us, busy climbing the ladder as we are, the parable of the good Samaritan stands as a challenge and perhaps even a scandal almost as deep as the scandal of the cross.

What drove the sacrificial Christian compassion of many (obviously not all) medieval Christians? This chapter is the story of how the virtue of compassion arose and was fostered and acted upon by thousands within early and medieval Christian society in the West. This was a society that most certainly *did* both believe in God and live as if there was a God. To most medieval people, it would quite simply be reckless foolishness not to worship God and try to live in a way pleasing to him. Any simpleton knew that eternity is unimaginably longer than one's evanescent mortal life, which appears for a moment and then fades like the grass or extinguishes like a guttering candle. To prioritize one's own health and wealth over the judgment of such biblical passages as the good Samaritan or the separating of the sheep and the goats was to "gain the world and lose one's soul"—the worst kind of bargain. Thus medieval people, acting on the example of some of their better leaders, poured out huge amounts of their wealth and endangered their own health in order to attend to the physical health of others. Theirs was not a merely rhetorical compassion but a habit of compassion in action, underwritten by a coherent theology of physical healing.

A reflective reader might compare this story with the current state of, for example, the modern American health care system. As the social nexus of health and wealth par excellence, the health care system has become for many a painful, confusing, expensive, and difficult system to navigate. Many would say it is the most bloated and unmanageable part of our bureaucratic society. What can we learn, if anything, from the story of the late ancient birth and medieval growth of this innovative institution in world history—the hospital? As I have researched this subject, I have wondered more than once: Do modern Christians really "get" the relationship of mercy and the gospel the way medievals did?

So let us open this study in Christian compassion with a question.

## Jesus, Illness, and Human Mortality

We might ask our medieval forebears: How central is mercy to the gospel? Or to put this more practically: Should Christians be known for lavish attention to the healing of human bodies, or is this a sideshow or even a sidetrack to the gospel?

A medieval person might answer with this familiar story.

Mary the sister of Lazarus got to where Jesus was. She fell down at his feet, overcome with grief and just a bit of accusatory anger: "Lord, if you had been here, my brother would not have died." The Lord saw and heard her weeping and the wailing and entreaties of the others with her.

What was Jesus's response? "He was deeply moved in spirit and troubled."

Lazarus's friends and family were facing the loss of their brother, friend, and son, and they were devastated by his mortality. Likely they were also, in the way people usually are in such situations, at the backs of their minds and in the dark corners of their hearts, terrified of their own eventual end.

Some sanctimonious Christian today might say: Well, what did they expect? The wages of sin is death! We are all under the same curse, ever since Adam! Not Jesus. He sprang into action. "Where have you laid him?" he asked. And they took him there. He saw Lazarus laid in the tomb, his life gone out of him. Once vital—smiling, working, resting, weeping, loving. But now cold and still and already decomposing.

And what did our Lord do? "Jesus wept."

"Then the Jews said, 'See how he loved him!'" (see John 11:32–36).

Modern Christians—especially evangelical Protestants—like to focus on Jesus's passion, his crucifixion, his resurrection. Maybe his preaching too. His "principles." His parables. This is all good. But what about his ministry? Jesus met people in the extremity of their need. He helped them. Healed them. What's that all about?

"Well done, good and faithful servant" (Matt. 25:21, 23). Those who earn this heartfelt commendation from the Lord are those who have compassion on others and then act on it. They give a thirsty person a cup of cold water. They clothe a naked person. They visit a sick or imprisoned person—not to "fix" them but to *be with* them. "Com-passion" (suffering *with*) equals sympathetic pity and concern for the sufferings or misfortunes of others.

## Bodily Healing: A Paradox for Christians?

How do the spiritual and physical dimensions of the gospel fit together? C. S. Lewis starts here: "God created the Natural—invented it out of His love and artistry—it demands our reverence." So far so good, but then he continues: "Because it is only a creature and not He, it is, from another point of view, of little account. And still more, because Nature, and especially human nature, is fallen it must be corrected and the evil within it must be mortified."[2] Oh, dear.

There is a balancing act going on here. Our "essence," like the essence of all created things (according to Genesis), is good. But some mortification, some discipline, is required because we *will* go running after "the things of the flesh," no matter how much we understand that God is our ultimate love and ultimate goal. Our bodies, affected by the fall, are not an unalloyed good.

Therefore, Christianity treads a middle way. "At first sight," says Lewis, "nothing seems more obvious than that religious persons should care for the sick; no Christian building, except perhaps a church, is more self-explanatory than a Christian hospital."[3] Yet what the Christian hospital reveals is a paradox.

Let's say, Lewis suggests, that there is a person who has never heard of Christianity, and he sets out to observe and decide what sort of religion this is. First, he sees a long history of quite earthy activities. Lewis knew that almost every aspect of the European civilization that grew out of the ashes of the Roman Empire was built by the Christian church: "agriculture, architecture, laws, . . . healing the sick and caring for the poor,"[4] the blessing of marriage, the arts, and philosophy—to which he could have added (as we've seen) science.

"If our enquirer stopped at this point," writes Lewis, "he would have no difficulty in classifying Christianity—giving it its place on a map of the 'great religions.' Obviously (he would say), this is one of the world-affirming religions like Confucianism or the agricultural religions of the great Mesopotamian city states."[5]

But this is only one side of Christian faith. Our observer might look, instead, at a different set of evidences: the central image of Christ tortured on the cross, the celebration of martyrdom, the many fasts on the Christian calendar, the constant meditation on our personal and cosmic mortality, the instruction to store up treasure not on earth but in heaven, and the strict and world-denying asceticism of many of the faith's most dedicated followers. "And here, once again, if he knew no more, the enquirer would find Christianity quite easy to classify; but this time he would classify it as one of the world-denying religions. It would be pigeon-holed along with Buddhism."[6]

To those of us who have been Christians for most of our lives, this "two-edged character" of our faith may seem obvious. Neither secular materialism nor gnostic denial of the body, says Lewis, "leaves you free *both* to enjoy your breakfast *and* to mortify your inordinate appetites." Christianity does. And, more important (for the theme of this chapter), "none of [the other religious options] leaves anyone free to do what is being done in the Lourdes Hospital every day: to fight against death as earnestly, skillfully, and calmly as if you were a secular humanitarian while knowing all the time that death is, both for better and worse, something that the secular humanitarian has never dreamed of."[7]

Lewis penned these words in that most earthy (and Christ-haunted) of settings, an Irish pub—to be specific, the White Horse Inn at Drogheda, Ireland. He had been asked to speak to the Medical Missionaries of Mary, founders of Our Lady of Lourdes Hospital in that town. Having laid the groundwork (as we've seen above), he sets up the central principle—a principle that led Christianity to affirm bodily healing as an essential good. Not surprisingly, that central principle has to do with Jesus, and Lewis takes us straight to him, to the Lazarus story with which I started this chapter. "We follow one," he reminds us,

> who stood and wept at the grave of Lazarus—not surely, because He was grieved that Mary and Martha wept, and sorrowed for their lack of faith (though some thus interpret) but because death, the punishment of sin, is even more horrible in His eyes than in ours. The nature which He had created as God, the nature which He had assumed as Man, lay there before Him in its ignominy; a foul smell, food for worms.[8]

Physical suffering and death, Lewis reminds us, are *unnatural*. Christ, who loves us more than we can even love ourselves, spent significant time on earth ministering healing to people's bodies and then by the power of his passion and resurrection rescued us from this unnatural and alien thing called death. Because of that triumph and because our bodies are part of God's good creation, "we cannot cease to fight against the death which mars it, as against all those other blemishes upon it, against pain and poverty, barbarism and ignorance." Ironically, "because we love something else more than this world we love even this world better than those who know no other."[9]

## The *Agape* Principle

So how does all of this translate into a Christian emphasis on bodily care? The early and medieval churches were notable for healing (sometimes miraculous but more usually scientific/naturalist in approach), particularly the poor and desperate. The pagans in the Roman world of Christianity's birth had no such distinctive. They had "no religious impulse for charity that took the form of personal concern for those in distress."[10] Indeed, the pagans taught neither compassion nor active mercy as virtues. To be merciful only helped the weak—those drags on society.

"In the cramped, unsanitary warrens of the typical Roman city, under the miserable cycle of plagues and famines, the sick found no public institutions dedicated to their care and little in the way of sympathy or help."[11] The Roman gods did not act out of compassion, and Rome did not teach its citizens a duty to help the poor or ill. Family usually helped, though if a family was poor and someone became chronically ill, they might well abandon that person to die. Unwanted children were often left to die of exposure at a local temple or public square. For those without family—discharged soldiers or freed slaves, for example—there was no social safety net.

The principle that set the Christians apart in this matter of physical illness and healing was *agape*: love that looks like the self-giving love of Christ for humanity. Such love reflects God's own nature (1 John 4:8), for God loves humans enough to send his own Son to us—even to die for us (John 3:16). How could we do less for one another?

So it was indeed the powerful scriptural vision of how their Lord acted on earth that birthed the medical philanthropy of Christ's followers. Christians acted on the ancient Hebrew law, articulated anew by the apostle James: "Religion that God our Father accepts as pure and faultless" is to care for "orphans and widows" (James 1:27). Moreover, this "mercy imperative" was not to be directed only to others in one's own community. The early Christians looked to the parable of the good Samaritan (Luke 10:25–37), in which Jesus breaks through ethnic and religious categories to affirm that it is the hated Samaritan who acted as a true neighbor when he happened upon the beaten and wounded man on the road.

## The Hospital: Late Ancient Precursors and Medieval Emergence

Before Christians developed—slowly, over many centuries—the institution that became the modern hospital, they did plenty of healing and helping, especially on behalf of the community's most needy members: widows, orphans, and the poor. Actually, they did it right there *in the church*—specifically within parish networks. From their earliest years, as a regular part of their worship, Christians had gathered alms to be distributed by deacons for the help of those in need. By the mid-200s, the benevolence mission of the church had birthed a complex of minor clerical orders. Cornelius (d. 253), bishop of Rome, reported in 251 a strategic system that divided the city into seven districts, with deacons and subdeacons appointed to care for the people in each one. Gary Ferngren relates that the Roman church in that day spent up to a million *sestercii* a year—a huge amount of money—in supporting and caring for fifteen hundred needy people.

While this benevolence work included much more than healing, healing became an increasingly large part of it. Christian medical philanthropy and the Christian institution of the hospital always focused on caring for the poor.

Something soon triggered more concerted efforts and greater organization. That something was the plague. The fifteen- to twenty-year epidemic that spread across the empire from North Africa starting in AD 250 devastated many areas of the West. At its peak, the plague killed five thousand people in one day in Rome.

The authorities launched no organized effort to "prevent the spread of the disease, treat the sick, or even bury the dead."[12] In fact, when the plague hit Carthage in North Africa, the Romans, in an attempt to appease their gods, turned to punish the Christians, sparking the cruel empire-wide persecution under Emperor Decius. Bishop Cyprian (ca. 210–58) of that city, however, urged the Christians not to return evil for evil but rather to bring aid to all who were suffering, whether believer or pagan—a first in imperial history.

### Organizing for Mercy

Another first was the level of organization required to pull off the relief effort. For example, in this and subsequent plagues, Christian "ambulance corps" went where the pagans would not, to the houses of the sick, thereby endangering their own lives.

How successful were such efforts? While the level of medical knowledge at the time was rudimentary, basic nursing care alone can reduce mortality in an epidemic by as much as 60 to 70 percent. This success did not go unnoticed. People saw the real *physical*, as well as spiritual, benefits of joining the Christian community.

In the early 300s, lay orders arose in such cities as Alexandria and Antioch, dedicated to caring for the many sick homeless people literally dying in the streets. These groups would "distribute food and money to them and take them to the public baths, where their basic hygienic needs could be met and they could find warmth in winter."[13] The hospital itself, it is generally agreed, emerged in the fourth century from the compassion of a well-known monk—Basil of Caesarea (329/30–379), now called "the Great." C. S. Lewis's "two-edged" description of the faith (body affirming and spirit affirming) characterizes monks as well as laypeople in a way that many people find surprising. Timothy S. Miller concurs: "If monastics really thought of the body as evil, then how is it that some of the greatest strides in the history of healthcare arose within monasticism? Monks cared for the ill in Benedictine monasteries, Franciscan leprosaria, the institutions of the monastic 'hospitallers,' the many hospitals of the Augustinians, and so on throughout the history of monasticism." Basil started it all, and his story "decisively dispels" our "myths of body-hating monks."[14]

Born in a wealthy and prestigious Christian family, Basil strayed from the faith as a young man, seeking fame and glory in the competitive field of rhetoric and political oratory. After his conversion, he decided to become a monk, leaving the tempting city to devote himself to prayer and fasting. After touring the then-flourishing desert monasteries in the east, he created a new monastic community in the mountains north of Caesarea.

After a few years, Basil envisioned a new, urban mode of monasticism, very unlike the desert model. This way would combine the customary ascetic disciplines with service to others—specifically, care for the sick and poor in the thick of the city. Little did he know he was pioneering a way of doing medical care that would blanket the Western as well as the Eastern landscape—and that still guides us more than a millennium later!

### Lepers and the Gift of Medical Knowledge

The community that ran Basil's "monastery and philanthropic complex" in Caesarea ministered to the sick and to travelers, effectively creating a hospice setting in which not only physical but also spiritual needs were addressed. In particular, they reached out to a despised class, whom Basil's friend Gregory Nazianzen said were "dead before death and have already perished in most parts of their bodies. They are driven from cities, homes, market places, and sources of water, even from their best friends." That is, the lepers.[15] The inclusion of lepers was a radical step even for Christians of Basil's day. Another radical aspect of Basil's proto-hospital was its emphasis on medical science as a good gift from God. Greek medicine was associated, in the minds of some Christians, with the cult of the healing god Asclepius. But Basil argued that God gave us the good gift of medical knowledge, and we are to use it. He staffed his institution not only with nurses but also with physicians who studied the fairly sophisticated Galenic tradition of classical medical science. This was the birth of the hospital.

After Basil, Christian institutions of medical philanthropy thrived and spread across Christendom as the newly legal Roman church increasingly took on public functions. In the last decades of the 300s, a wealthy and pious Roman woman, Fabiola, established the first hospitals in her city. Then in 526, Benedict founded his monastery at Monte Cassino and made hospitality to the stranger a linchpin of his influential Rule (which would become the "master rule" of Western monasticism after Charlemagne's reforms in the 800s). Quoting Matthew 25, chapter 36 of Benedict's Rule says: "Before all things and above all things . . . special care must be taken of the sick or infirm so that they may be served as if they were Christ in person; for He himself said 'I was sick and you visited me,' and 'what you have done for the least of mine, you have done for me.'"[16]

In the decades and centuries immediately after Basil, most institutions that cared for the sick looked more like poorhouses than modern hospitals. Medical care (despite Basil's example) was rudimentary, the focus was on the indigent who would otherwise be without help—often including long-term tenants—and the church in a particular region often set aside a percentage of its funds to provide this sort of care.

The ninth and tenth centuries saw a lull in the hospital's development as unrest and lack of funds sometimes led to the closing or destruction of European hospitals. Nonetheless, the church, led by its bishops and clergy, continued to do what they could for the poor. Meanwhile, Benedictine monks copied and handed down ancient medical manuscripts, developed herbal lore, and experimented with medicines.

Oddly, the next major impetus in the history of the hospital was the Crusades. When the First Crusade took Jerusalem in 1099, one of the first orders of business was to build what would become the "poster hospital" of the age, the Hospital of St. John of Jerusalem, funded by private donations—largely from Crusaders. In the twelfth century, the continued conflicts also birthed orders dedicated to caring for travelers and the ill, including the Hospitallers. By this time, we have accounts from those who visited the Jerusalem hospital describing a complex capable of serving nearly a thousand patients spread across as many as eleven wards. Suitable to the multicultural nature of the city, the hospital welcomed Muslim and Jewish patients, feeding them chicken instead of pork.

### Monks, Illness, Demons, and Sin

The distinctly monastic flavor of health care during the Middle Ages— even when it was provided by lay orders like the Hospitallers—deserves a bit more attention. From the beginning, monasteries in the West took Benedict's cue and made caring for not only ill monks but also needy travelers one of their primary tasks. The "stranger" was always an object of monastic charity. This "rather broad category," says medical historian Gunter Risse, included "jobless wanderers or drifters as well as errant knights, devout pilgrims, traveling scholars, and merchants." Monastic care for the stranger and the ill was formalized in the 800s during Charlemagne's reforms, as assemblies of abbots gathered to reform and standardize that aspect of monastic life. At that time, many of the scattered church-sponsored hostels (*xenodocheia*) across the Holy Roman Empire were given *regula*, quasi-monastic rules, and "monasteries . . . assumed the greater role in dispensing welfare."[17]

Ubiquitous, organized, stable, and pious, the monasteries of the West became sites of care and of medical learning. As Benedict says in his Rule: "For these sick brethren let there be assigned a special room and an attendant who is God-fearing, diligent, and solicitous." These infirmary attendants were chosen for their personality as well as their knowledge (gained by poring over manuscripts) and their skill in the arts of healing (gained through experience). As Risse explains, "The *infirmarius* usually talked with patients and asked questions, checked on the food, compounded medicinal herbs, and comforted those in need."[18]

Monks even practiced basic surgery (called "touching and cutting") to heal the "lacerations, dislocations, and fractures" that came with daily life. However, "the *infirmarius* may not have always been comfortable practicing surgery on his brothers, for it was always a source of considerable pain, bleeding, and infection. Complicated wounds or injuries may have forced some monks to request the services of more experienced local bonesetters or even barber surgeons."[19] Other popular healing practices of the Middle Ages were integrated into the monastic medical routine, including herbology, bathing (not otherwise common), preventive bloodletting, and diagnostic examination of pulse, urine, stool, and blood.

Woven through the physical care in a monastic infirmary was another, higher sort of care. Often lying within sight of an altar containing the consecrated bread and wine of the Eucharist, patients were encouraged to make regular confession and pressed (if able) to join in the prayer rituals of the monastic hours. They were also surrounded by other physical signs of their spiritual faith: relics; devotional pictures portraying spiritual and physical health; praying nurses; and the monastic gardens, pools, and streams. All of these contributed to an environment of holistic healing.[20]

Note, however, that the care available in monasteries was holistic, not "merely" spiritual. Just as some still credit the fabrication that medieval people believed in a flat earth, some assume that medievals did not know, and were not interested in, the physical causes of illness. As the story goes, they assumed that all illness came from devilish or demonic sources or (a variant) from some hidden sin in the sick person.

To be fair, this impression sometimes seems to be supported by misleading evidence in the sources themselves. Medieval Christians certainly did, in an ultimate sense, understand illness as having a spiritual dimension. Gregory the Great, for example, viewed illness and other causes of suffering as a particularly strong instance of God communicating with us through the natural realm.[21] Here, as in so many areas, C. S. Lewis agrees with the medieval theologians: "We can ignore . . . pleasure. But pain insists upon being attended to. God whispers to us in our pleasures, speaks in our conscience, but shouts in our pains: it is his megaphone to rouse a deaf world."[22]

Sin did play a role in illness for medieval thinkers. The fallenness of the world, originating in human sin, was in a general sense considered the source of illness (as of all dysfunction in the world). But medieval sources only very rarely mention a sick person's particular sins or even his or her general sinfulness as the cause of illness.[23]

Finally, certain afflictions might be attributed wholly or (more often) partially to demonic activity, particularly in the case of mental illness. But, perhaps surprisingly, even "mental and spiritual illnesses were attributed as much to overwork, overeating, and overindulgence in sexual activity as to climatic conditions, magic spells, and demonic possession."[24] Medievals were not blind to the natural causality of depression and other mental troubles. Both priests and physicians might help a troubled person, and we often find in medieval texts an acute awareness that a spiritual explanation of these psychological illnesses is not enough. The eleventh-century bishop Fulbert of Chartres (ca. 960–1028), for instance, wrote that "it is a physician's duty to offer those who are suffering from depression, insanity, or any other illness what he has learned in the exercise of his art."[25] In general, although "sin was certainly regarded by early medieval authors as the cause of sickness in the sense that without sin there would have been no material evil," the linking of a person's sickness to some specific sin in that person's life "is very seldom encountered."[26]

In short, though demons were often mentioned in medieval accounts of affliction, they were by no means considered to be the cause of all illness. "As a general rule," says Darrell Amundsen, "when early medieval sources mentioned direct demonic involvement, which they frequently did, the condition was clearly regarded as possession, whether accompanied by sickness or not." Furthermore, many venerated saints experienced frequent and terrible illness, and indeed "seemed to gain a high degree of sanctity through their sicknesses"—not the sort of people, nor the sort of effect, that medieval thinkers associated with demonic activity.[27]

### At Death's Door: The Whole Community Caring for the Whole Person

There was one situation in which the monks *did* focus on the spiritual dimension of illness, though in a more positive way. When a patient in a monastic hospital neared death, the monks sprang into action, visiting the dying inmate regularly and even staying with the person around the clock, "praying and reading from the Scriptures by candlelight."[28] In a culture so alive to the true spiritual meaning of death as a passageway to the eternal, such vigils were meant to usher the dying into God's presence, for the monks believed that this ultimate, momentous human event should not take place in solitude.

When the patient neared his or her final moments, "the whole monastic community was summoned and the monks congregated around the sick *on both sides of the bed*" (a wonderful detail), praying and singing, "using music to 'unbind' the pain and thus provide the departing with spiritual nourishment for the journey to the beyond." When the passing finally happened, bells were rung or boards clapped to announce it, and soon after, the body was buried in the monastic cemetery. But the care for the dead did not end there; the monks wrote the departed's name in a book as a reminder to include him or her in their daily intercessions.[29]

When, in the twelfth century, hospitals increasingly became separate and distinct from monastic guest houses, such special attention to the needs of the dying continued to be an important part of their function. Meanwhile, monastic hostels provided "prayer, rest, food, and the administration of sacraments" to tired and sick pilgrims, the poor, and other "strangers." What was the experience of those under monastic care? We can imagine with Guenter Risse:

> Resting on straw-covered floors, some of the guests must have felt protected behind the monastery's walls and reminded of their Christian identity and the redemptive quality of their suffering. Acceptance and understanding were important. At a minimum, these routines would have had a calming and reassuring effect as the visitors socialized with each other and with members of the caring monastic community.[30]

This spiritual environment also permeated hospitals not attached to monasteries, even before Charlemagne's reforms in the 800s. In those early centuries, most hospitals were just shelters for the indigent and travelers. They tended to cluster in cities or near significant roads, and they usually were small, with not many more than a dozen beds, a kitchen, and a chapel. Those who stayed there, for however long, were considered to be "members of a new spiritual community,"[31] temporarily living a monastic-esque life.

By the eleventh century, the separation of health care from monasteries was nearly complete. As thousands of destitute refugees crammed the burgeoning cities, clergy and monks began to invite laypeople into the holy task of succoring the sick and poor. Thousands of confraternities—lay "clubs" dedicated to charity, mutual support, and Christian devotion—sprang up, along with lay penitential groups that also performed charitable acts.[32] This new movement amounted to the creation of a public social safety net in European cities, as care for others' physical needs increasingly came to be seen as the Christian duty of all people. Popes even issued "plenary indulgences"—time off from purgatory—for visiting the sick.

### The Medieval Charitable Revolution: Healing as "the Jesus Thing to Do"

The de-monasticization of health care, however, did not mean its secularization—at least not as we moderns use the term "secular." By the twelfth century, a new theology of sickness was springing up among the scholastics and spreading to the parishes. This theology stressed how caring for the sick (and other needy) could contribute to one's salvation. For one thing, to minister to the suffering was to minister directly to Christ. For another, caregivers and benefactors of the poor sick could expect in return the valuable prayers of their charges: "Like monks, martyrs, saints, and finally apostles, the sick could function as mediators between God and His people."[33]

In the twelfth century's more urban, economically stable, and flourishing Europe, laypeople spurred by this new theology joined in a new "charitable revolution." Soon there was a massive uptick in the foundation of hospitals by wealthy lay donors. Initially the new lay institutions—leper houses, hospitals, and hostels—operated alongside monastic and parish-based houses. By the 1300s, however, lay organizations increasingly replaced church-led ones.[34]

At the heart of this new movement stands the Matthew 25 parable of the sheep and the goats. Preached all over the West by Franciscan and Dominican friars, the "Seven Corporal Acts of Mercy" spurred laypeople to charity. Six of the seven came from Matthew 25:31–46: feeding the hungry, giving drink to the thirsty, clothing the naked, visiting and ransoming the captive (prisoners), sheltering the homeless, and visiting the sick. The seventh, burying the dead, derived from the book of Tobit. Most catechisms and devotional guides joined the chorus.

"Charity," which today usually means giving money to a good cause, was a key theological term in this period. Quite simply, it meant self-giving love (*agape*) directed first and most importantly toward God and then (as a result) toward one's neighbor. For medieval Christians, its special objects were "those within society who were regarded as vulnerable, degraded, or in serious material need."[35] For the early and medieval church, alms (money given to the poor) were only one part of the real meaning of charity. Hospitals became "the concrete expression, in bricks and mortar, of Christ's teaching on charity."[36]

Laypeople flocked to this concrete expression of Christ's teaching: lords, knights, and townspeople founded hospitals, left bequests to them in their wills, and worked in them. England boasted only 68 hospitals in 1150, but numbered 252 in 1200, 389 by 1250, and close to 500 by 1300. By the time the Black Death devastated that nation in 1348, it had reached a peak of 541 hospitals.[37] Many were small, but all were animated by the list of seven "corporal mercies" mentioned above. Some were leper houses, some served a wider (and often poor) constituency, and some dedicated themselves exclusively to the succor of the poor.[38]

### Medieval Lay Ministry to the Sick: Joining in Their Sufferings to Meet Christ

A paragon of the new model of lay involvement in health care was Elizabeth of Hungary (1207–31). A wealthy laywoman in the tradition of the ancient Roman Christian hero Fabiola, the thirteenth-century saint Elizabeth began, after her husband's death, to feed, wash the feet of, sew clothes for, and bury the sick poor. No arm's-length philanthropist, she delighted in the unpleasant, humiliating labor of personally attending to even the messiest physical needs of her charges.

One might interpret such devotion to healing tasks as self-interest, since the theology of the day at times seemed to virtually assure salvation to those so engaged. No doubt this was a motivator, but theologians also stressed the attitude of the heart in ministering to others. Because Matthew 25 clearly shows that charitable acts to the needy are, in fact, done to Christ himself, physical charity weaves itself into the fabric of one's heart relationship with Christ. In fact, Elizabeth's actions represented (and promoted) a new, strongly affective theology of health care: in compassion, the empathetic experiencing of others' pain and suffering, she—and increasingly the Western church at large—found redemptive value because it brought them closer to Christ.[39]

From the eleventh century on, a new emphasis on the personal, emotional dimensions of faith arose. We see it in Anselm of Canterbury's intimate prayers and devotions and Peter Abelard's love-centered atonement theory. Most laypeople in this period heard many impassioned sermons from traveling Franciscan evangelists. From portable outdoor pulpits and in chapels where the walls were often covered with life-sized passion scenes (painted as graphically as possible so as to elicit emotions of compassion and empathy from the viewer), the preaching friars stressed as never before the emotions of Jesus during his ordeal—and the answering emotions of the worshiper. But this emotion was to be expressed in worship as well as action. "Don't spend all your time meditating on the Passion to the neglect of your fellow Christian," warns the fourteenth-century English Augustinian Walter Hilton. "Wash Christ's feet by attending to your subjects and your tenants."[40]

We hear this new language from those leaving money to hospitals in their wills. Often the benefactors would say that they gave "to sustain the poor compassionately" or were "moved by the zeal of compassion."[41] When Jacques de Vitry (ca. 1160/70–1240) wrote model sermons intended to be preached to hospital workers, he emphasized that the appropriate motive for caring for others in this way was not a thirst for public reputation or a desire to secure a place in heaven but rather a pious empathy with the sufferings of others.

Working in a hospital for the poor and lepers became the quintessential expression of holy compassion: "Many of the saints canonized during this period were laywomen who devoted themselves to working in hospitals for the poor and lepers."[42]

The "laicization" of health care in this period did not, however, mean its secularization. As in the earlier, monastic period, one's experience as a hospital patient—sick or injured, perhaps traveling, without the luxury of a private physician—would have been a thoroughly religious one. As described by Jennifer Woodruff Tait in her article "The Hospital Experience," most likely "you would find yourself in a setting with fifteen to thirty other patients," largely adults, though "some hospitals did take in abandoned babies and orphans." Your accommodations would probably have been some distance from the center of a town, in the "suburbs," where land was cheaper and "there was more space for buildings and gardens and more quiet for prayer and contemplation." If a stream was nearby, then so much the better, not only because running water was a useful commodity but also because the ritual service of prayer and confession that attended your entry to the institution might involve foot washing.[43]

After the initiation ceremonies, which likely included taking communion, you would be given a bed, either private or shared. A small chest of drawers might house your personal belongings, and a tray would stretch across your bed for supporting the meals served to you while you recuperated. Most important was the proximity of your bed to worship spaces, as "the round of worship in a medieval hospital was considered to be one of its most important functions." In these facilities, more often run by lay than cloistered orders, all seven of the "hours" (the traditional monastic prayer times) were likely observed, and "mass was usually said every morning as well, provided the hospital had a priest on staff (most did)."[44] There would have been no confusion about which God was being honored and served in the serving of your needs.

## Lewis's Own Ministry of Mercy and the Meaning of "Charity"

What can we derive today from this medieval witness? For one thing, I believe we can see in it a clear reminder of the supreme role of mercy in living out the gospel. C. S. Lewis, who knew the tradition well, insists that "if one virtue must be cultivated at the expense of all the rest, none has a higher claim than mercy."[45] He understood, of course, the teaching of the scholastics that mercy both is and is not Christianity's highest virtue. It is not the highest virtue, as Aquinas taught, because the theological virtue of *caritas* (charity, or love for God) must be counted greater since its object (God) is greater than that of mercy (humans). But as far as "external works" are concerned, we know that "the sum total of the Christian religion consists in mercy."[46] This puts individual acts of mercy in the right context. As Lewis puts it in a letter to a Mrs. Ashton (who took in a poor, illegitimate child), acts of mercy are "Agape in action. . . . Charity," he explained, "means love. It is called Agape in the New Testament," which is the kind of love that "God has for us." It is "all giving, not getting." It is not just throwing a few dollars at a problem—though giving money can be one kind of charity—but actualizing one's love, which is why "to give time and toil is far better and (for most of us) harder."[47]

The unfortunate history of the word "charity" actually illustrates the breaking of this unity that joined acts of mercy (social ethics) and Christian love (personal ethics, character). Charity started as a theological virtue with social implications. It has become now a purely social activity that anyone can achieve or practice no matter their relationship or lack thereof with the Creator and Redeemer God. In our post-Christian society we still speak freely of "charity," but we measure it in dollars and donations. Corporations talk about "charity" when they set aside 1 to 2 percent of profits to generate goodwill in the community—sometimes quite duplicitously, since they are purveying products or services that only extract value from the world rather than truly improving anyone's life. This is a bastardization of the traditional Christian understanding (certainly the medieval one) of what charity is.

There are hints scattered throughout Lewis's writings (and more crucially, in his life) of how important he took compassion and mercy to be in the life of the Christian. And when we find him talking about it, his reflections often have a distinctively medieval flavor. For example, in *The Problem of Pain*, while he admits that suffering is not a good in itself, it can work a tremendous good for the sufferer by leading him or her to submit to the will of God, just as it can work a good in those who witness it in the form of "the compassion aroused and the acts of mercy to which it leads."[48]

### Letters and Prayers

Lewis, like the medievals, grounded his understanding of compassion and mercy in Christ. In a letter to an American invalid, he affirms that "our Lord suffers in all the suffering of His people (*see* Acts 9:6)."[49] We see the same principle in the story of Lazarus, which Lewis used in addressing the sisters of Lourdes Hospital. The scene of Jesus weeping at his friend's death before raising him was in fact quite commonly found painted on the walls of medieval leper hospitals, which led to the common term for the leprosariums: "lazarettos."

Lewis did not stop with mere understanding—nor can we. To the same American woman he observes that the New Testament, in particular 2 Corinthians, contains much about prayer for others who are suffering. Two months later, responding to a letter from her that clearly told of some bad medical news, he signs off: "I shall pray for you whenever I wake in the night. . . . Yours, Jack Lewis."[50]

This demonstrates one of the ways Lewis acted out *agape* (charity) in his life,[51] tirelessly corresponding with a multitude of people and providing spiritual counsel (again, often accompanied by prayers for the correspondent). His friend Owen Barfield writes that people "wrote to him from all over the world with their personal religious or moral problems. And I doubt if any of them . . . went without a reply."[52] Lewis, as Barfield testified, did not like writing letters, considering them an interruption to his "real work" of reading and writing books. Yet he got into long, pastoral exchanges with people he had never met. After Lewis's death, the invalid woman in America to whom he was writing sent Barfield a box of more than a hundred letters Lewis had written to her in his last years. And she was only one of many who benefited from his spiritual counsel.

The medievals would have considered this sort of activity an actualization of *agape* in mercy, similar to caring for the physically sick. In fact, there was a parallel medieval tradition to the seven works of corporal mercy called the seven works of spiritual mercy. Those were to instruct the ignorant, counsel the doubtful, admonish sinners, bear wrongs patiently, forgive offenses willingly, comfort the afflicted, and pray for the living and the dead. Lewis spent much of his life doing these sorts of things.

### Alms

More concretely, Lewis was lavish in his almsgiving. In *Mere Christianity* he writes:

> Giving to the poor is an essential part of Christian morality. I do not believe one can settle how much we ought to give. I'm afraid the only safe rule is to give more than we can spare. In other words, if our expenditure on comforts, luxuries, and amusement, is up to the standard common of those with the same income as our own, we are probably giving away too little. . . . For many of us the great obstacle to charity lies not in our luxurious living or desire for more money, but in our fear—fear of insecurity. This must often be recognised as a temptation.[53]

Barfield, who was Lewis's trustee as well as his friend, observed how Lewis followed this principle in his own life.

> He gave two-thirds of his income away altogether and would have bound himself to give the whole of it away if I had let him. . . . There were substantial donations to charitable institutions, but what he really liked was to find someone through a personal connection or hearsay whose wants might be alleviated. He was always grateful to me for suggesting any lame dog whom my profession [as a lawyer] had brought to my notice.[54]

What's more, Lewis did not worry about wasting his money on undeserving types. Instead, he reflects, "It will not bother me in the hour of death to reflect that I have been 'had for a sucker' by any number of impostors; but it would be a torment to know that one had refused even *one* person in need." Then, like the medievals, he ties the principle back to Matthew 25: "After all, the parable of the sheep and goats makes our duty perfectly plain, doesn't it."[55]

### A Partial, Not Ultimate, Solution

Another lesson we may derive, as Lewis did, from medieval medical ministry is that we cannot expect to do away with suffering altogether through some utopian program or scientific advancement. We are often in the position of being able to provide only limited, palliative care. It is simply a fact of life that pain and suffering will always be with us. Part of our health care approach must be to address that persistent fact. Lewis accused the social-scientific schemers and dreamers of his time of "assuming that the great permanent miseries in human life must be curable if only we can find the right cure." From that belief, he argues, comes "the fanaticism of Marxists, Freudians, Eugenists, Spiritualists, Douglasites, Federal Unionists, Vegetarians, and all the rest."[56]

Instead of wasting resources and energy on such utopian schemes, Lewis counsels, "the best results are obtained by people who work quietly away at limited objectives . . . not by those who think they can achieve universal justice, or health, or peace." In the end, he concludes, "the art of life consists in tackling each immediate evil as well as we can."[57]

We see the pastoral and practical force of this in a recorded conversation Lewis had with a group of workers at an industrial company office in Middlesex: "Christianity really does two things about conditions here and now in this world," he said to the workers: "(1) It tries to make them as good as possible, i.e., to *reform* them; but also (2) it *fortifies you against them* in so far as they remain bad."[58]

It *does* matter, Lewis reminds us, whether we do our works of mercy from a Christian or a non-Christian perspective. While

> a Christian and a non-Christian may both wish to do good to their fellow men . . . the one believes that men are going to live for ever, that they were created by God and so built that they can find their true and lasting happiness only by being united to God, that they have gone badly off the rails, and that obedient faith in Christ is the only way back. The other believes that men are an accidental result of the blind workings of matter, that they started as mere animals and have more or less steadily improved, that they are going to live for about seventy years, that their happiness is fully attainable by good social services and political organizations, and that everything else (e.g., vivisection, birth-control, the judicial system, education) is to be judged to be "good" or "bad" simply in so far as it helps or hinders that kind of "happiness."[59]

This sort of reflection brings us into the important realm of medical ethics, in which Christians should have a distinctive witness. But it also impacts the sort of medical care we provide to individuals, particularly when the story of the medieval Christian origin and operation of the hospital pulls us back toward a balance. It took the British Christian Cecily

Saunders (1918–2005) and her hospice movement to back us away from the medical obsession with taking every heroic, technology-assisted measure to keep a person alive, even to the detriment of his or her quality of life. Death happens, as does suffering, and there are kinds of pain to which medical science will never have an answer. What is needed in those cases is a different kind of care—something less like the gleaming machinery, tubes, and beeping screens of the modern palliative care unit and more like the brothers of the monastery lining up on both sides of the dying man's bed, praying and singing as he suffers and sinks toward death.

Lewis aptly summarizes: "The Christian and the Materialist hold different beliefs about the universe. They can't both be right. The one who is wrong will act in a way which simply doesn't fit the real universe. Consequently, with the best will in the world, he will be helping his fellow creatures to their destruction."[60]

# 7

## Getting Earthy

### God's Second Book—The Natural World

Modern Western Christians tend to approach the material world in two seemingly opposite ways. And these two ways end up, ironically, in the same place. The first has often been noted, and a bit inaccurately tagged with a term deriving from an early Christian heresy.

### Gnosticism

The early Christian gnostics disavowed the spiritual significance and goodness of the material world. According to the gnostics, the world was created not by our God, who called his handiwork "good," but rather by an inferior sub-god called a "demiurge." Thus one must set aside the material world if one is to reach God. The world cannot be in any way a channel of grace; rather, it is an impediment to grace.

Signs of gnostic thinking include (1) thinking Christianity is about "spiritual" things (only), (2) thinking of one's destiny only in terms of souls going off to heaven, (3) thinking of creation as "left behind" in the end, rather than redeemed in the new creation, and (4) believing that God neither gives material things as a means of grace nor cares about the earth at all—so neither should we.[1]

This syndrome of devaluing the material world, thereby sapping it of all spiritual significance, supports a number of modern Christian bad habits. One is the sort of "it's all gonna burn" end-times scenario indulged in the *Left Behind* novels. Another is the excuse baby boomers (and others) make for the fact that their faith makes no difference in their daily lives: "I'm 'spiritual but not religious.'"[2] A third is the complete compartmentalizing of our (Sunday) faith from our (Monday through Saturday) work and leisure. For example, even when we behave at work in a generally moral way or have the occasional conversation with a coworker about our faith, we don't have a clue why whatever goods or services we are helping to provide would matter to God. Because of this, our faith often becomes neutered, unfruitful in the real world.

## Materialism

In our culture, and thus also our churches, the "gnostic" attitude is mirrored by an equally destructive and ironically opposite-but-the-same attitude toward creation that I'll call "materialism." It can manifest as consumerism, hedonism, or greed, but at its base is an attitude that treats material goods as ends in themselves.

We meet the hedonistic form of this syndrome in *Perelandra*, where the hero Ransom tries to protect the Edenic Green Lady against the sin of desiring over and over again to have the same pleasure—to have no restraint. Elsewhere, C. S. Lewis says:

> The books or the music in which we thought the beauty was located will betray us if we trust to them; it was not *in* them, it only came *through* them, and what came through them was longing. These things—the beauty, the memory of our own past—are good images of what we really desire; but if they are mistaken for the thing itself, they turn into dumb idols, breaking the hearts of their worshipers. For they are not the thing itself; they are only the scent of a flower we have not found, the echo of a tune we have not heard, news from a country we have never yet visited.[3]

In another place, Lewis puts it like this: "You can't get second things by putting them first; you can get second things only by putting first things first."[4] One is reminded of Matthew 6:33: "But seek first his kingdom and his righteousness, and all these things will be given to you as well."

What Lewis is saying here is based on Augustine's crucial distinction between enjoying (*frui*) something and using (*uti*) it: "to enjoy something is to hold fast to it in love *for its own sake*."[5] What's wrong with doing that, say (in the obvious case), with our family relationships? Isn't the word "use," with its connotations of abuse, inappropriate in that case? For Augustine, the problem is—bluntly speaking—that when we treat any created good as lovable *for its own sake*, we are in fact committing idolatry. That is, we elevate that good to a place only God can occupy in our lives. Plus, it separates that good from its source and meaning, which is God.

Oddly enough, the result of this inappropriate elevation of material goods (even our good human relationships) and the separation of those goods from their real source and meaning is pretty much the same as the result of the gnostic attitude: when we pursue elements of our material life as their own end, we lose their origin in God, who is the ultimate source of their value. Thus, materialism just as surely as gnosticism devalues the material world.[6]

Another "materialist" syndrome is to approach the natural world only in terms of its utility (either as something to be exploited or as a useless realm to be ignored and circumvented). Lewis's Ransom Trilogy, which in many ways is a modern reimagining of some very medieval values, shows this in each of its books. In *Out of the Silent Planet*, Weston and Devine plan to exploit Malacandra. In *That Hideous Strength*, Weston and the New Element at Bracton plan to eliminate (as much as possible) all bodily aspects of human life. Rather than treating the natural, organic world as having any inherent value, they consider it something to be exploited or as a nuisance. The book *Perelandra* perhaps even more strongly enfleshes Lewis's understanding that worldly pragmatism, utilitarianism, and triumphant industrialism are truly evil, in part because each fails to see the divinity in the material world—the ways the material world still pulses with life and still leads us back to God. The material world is something we are responsible to curate, to steward, and to connect with in a much deeper way than modern capitalist industrial society seems to allow.

Whether or not we call these two syndromes "gnosticism" and "materialism," if we are honest we can see them in our own lives and churches. And frankly, they point a big red arrow at our screwed-up theology.

So how do we fix screwed-up theology? We learn good theology, just as Lewis had told those wartime Oxford students that good philosophy must exist to combat bad philosophy. And Lewis knew where at least some of that good philosophy—and theology—was to be found. "Most of all, perhaps, we need intimate knowledge of the past . . . because we . . . need something to set against the present, to remind us that the basic assumptions have been quite different in different periods."[7]

I'm going to argue in this chapter that a particular medieval understanding of creation offers a theological solution to both problems, putting the material world back in a more helpful relationship with "spiritual things."

## Protestantism and the Arts

Let's put a finer point on the issue by looking briefly at modern Protestant churches and the arts. Where are the arts in modern orthodox Protestantism? Richard Wilkinson looks at the century from 1860 to 1960 and finds only C. S. Lewis and T. S. Eliot practicing the creative art of literature to a high degree from an orthodox Protestant stance, noting that both were "Anglicans with a strong emphasis on sacramental spirituality." During the same period, the Catholics produced an embarrassment of literary riches, from Tolkien and Flannery O'Connor to Gerard Manley Hopkins and Evelyn Waugh. All of these writers are considered "world-class," and all were orthodox Christians. The details of this argument are open to debate—everyone has their own list of "greats"—but something like this seems to have been true for much of the modern period, not only in literature but also in other fine arts. It is probably fair to say, as Wilkinson does, that "evangelical Protestants, especially, have not only not shone in the fine arts, they have often opposed such arts or valued them only as vehicles for evangelism, objecting to much of their subject matter."[8] Similarly, few evangelicals have excelled in the worlds of film and television drama. Wilkinson concludes that the problem for Protestants vis-à-vis Catholics in the arts stems from a difference in approach to creation. Whereas

Protestants often emphasize how fallen creation and human society are (a source of our "gnosticism"), the theology of the Roman Catholic Church has proven to be more creation-positive and thus more likely to affirm and create images of the world, whether in the literary or visual arts.

Perhaps counterintuitively, it was a form of Platonism—the Neoplatonism of the second century AD and beyond—that helped the church overcome Platonic dualism with a countervailing teaching that one can gain access to the spiritual world *only* through the material world. Couple this with the Aristotelianism that (as we'll see) entered the medieval scene during the twelfth and thirteenth centuries, which also believed that knowledge of the truths beyond nature might be gained through the study of nature, and you get not only a positive view of creation but also an almost riotous flourishing of the arts—both in and out of the church.

For the actual riots, though, we must turn to the early Protestants, who tended not only to dismiss all of this earthiness as extrabiblical and suspect but also to marshal Old Testament texts prohibiting the use of images as idolatry. This led to iconoclastic (image-smashing) riots in the mid-sixteenth century that destroyed much church art in cities across Europe.[9] As late as 1643, during the English Civil War, we see the same impulse at work in the account of Bishop Joseph Hall of Norwich, who describes iconoclastic mob action in England:

> What clattering of glasses! What beating down of walls! What tearing up of monuments! What pulling down of seats! What wresting out of irons and brass from the windows! . . . What demolishing of curious stonework! . . . And what a hideous triumph in the market-place before all the country, when all the mangled organ pipes, vestments, both copes and surplices, together with the leaden cross which had newly been sawn down from the Green-yard pulpit and the service-books and singing books that could be carried to the fire in the public market-place were heaped together.[10]

## Medieval Sacramentalism

What, then, did the medieval church have, theologically, that the Reformation church seems to have lost? What was the bridge from the material to the spiritual world that not only avoided both gnosticism and materialism but fostered the arts as well?

This missing link turns out to be one of the most central theological ideas of the Middle Ages: the idea of sacramentalism. Sacramentalism is the concept that the outward and visible can convey the inward and spiritual. Physical matters and actions can become transparent vehicles of divine activity and presence. In short, material things can be God's love made visible.

Put another way, sacramentalism is a linked set of beliefs that (1) transcendent spiritual reality manifests itself in and through created material reality, that (2) all creation is in some sense a reflection of the Creator, and thus that (3) God is present in and through the world. A correlative of these beliefs is that religion is not separated or compartmentalized from the rest of life. It's not something left for the ephemeral words of a Sunday morning sermon. God can and does manifest himself through the creation that he's made. It is not an overstatement to say that this principle enchanted everyday life for the medievals.

Why should Christians affirm sacramentalism? First and most important, *because God incarnated himself in Christ.* The transcendent God dug down and took on human flesh. The purely spiritual became human, two natures in one person. In late medieval Christianity, far from the incarnation being seen as a kind of one-time, bizarre aberration with no connection to the rest of salvation history, it's the paradigm, the model, for everything that follows. Lewis saw this and embedded it in *Perelandra*: "With the incarnation of Christ as man on the earth, the universe has turned a corner."[11]

The incarnation was the linchpin of medieval theology, and sacramentalism was the extension of that doctrine in its expression of God's mysterious presence in and through the created world. God is at the same time transcendent (above our cultural and material world) and immanent (dwelling and working in our cultural and material world).

Just below the surface of life, then, there hovers the constant presence of the holy. God is present in more places than just the traditional seven sacraments of the church (baptism, penance [confession], Eucharist [communion], confirmation, marriage, Holy Orders [ordination], last rites). Sacramentality is a much broader category.

Sacramentalism teaches that the material world contains in it much meaning that is not obvious "to the naked eye," so to speak. The world points always to the mystery of its origins and its sustenance in God. "The reason for the mysterious character of the world—on the understanding of the Great Tradition, at least—is that it participates in some greater reality, from which it derives its being and its value."[12] The world "participates" in the greater reality of God the Creator, even as it points to God. "In him we live and move and have our being" (Acts 17:28). In Christ, "all things hold together" (Col. 1:17). "The whole earth is full of his glory" (Isa. 6:3). The church subsides in Christ, who is "the fullness of him who fills everything in every way" (Eph. 1:23). Not only is this the real, actual nature of creation—which is sustained constantly by God and participates in God's Beauty, Truth, and Goodness, despite the damaging effects of the fall—but our own inner terrain, our yearnings, point us back to the Source to whom the sacramental nature of reality also points: "We do not want merely to see beauty, though, God knows, even that is bounty enough. We want something else which can hardly be put into words—to be united with the beauty we see, to pass into it, to receive it into ourselves, to bathe in it, to become part of it."[13]

### The Affirmative Way in Early Medieval Christianity

Until the twelfth century, although sacramentalism provided a space for the affirmation that the material world can help a person get to God, this affirmation could get dragged down by the Platonic dualist suspicion that the natural world is not only incapable of communicating truth but is also a distraction from contemplating the divine. Though sacramentalism laid the groundwork for a true body-spirit holism, that promise did not come to full fruition until the scholastic movement birthed in the twelfth-century renaissance of men like Anselm and Abelard.

Prior to this time, however, several things helped Christian theology along the Affirmative Way—that is, the kataphatic ("image-positive") path that looks to images and natural phenomena as conduits to theological truth, as opposed to the apophatic ("image-negative") path that requires us to strip away all images and metaphors en route to a direct mystical apprehension of God.

The end of the ancient and beginning of the medieval era—usually dated to between AD 450 and 500—was a time of de-secularization, or sacralization, of society.[14] Ancient Christianity grew up within the late Roman city, with all its civic and pagan political mechanisms and educational institutions. Medieval Christianity, on the other hand, grew up in the wake of the dissolution of Old Roman culture, out in the countryside under the ministrations of the clergy and in the cloisters of the monks and nuns.[15] From AD 400 to 800, Christianity soaked into every nook and cranny of Western culture,[16] creating a "pervasive and concrete" sense of God's presence in every area of daily life. Saints, visions, miracles, trial by ordeal, relics, and pilgrimage—every square inch of the landscape was at least potentially inhabited by the spiritual.

One catalyst moving Western society away from the more dualist attitudes toward the material world of the ancient period to the more sacramental understanding of the world in the medieval period was the monk-pope Gregory the Great. It is hard to overstate Gregory's influence on the faith of the Middle Ages, since throughout that period he was the most read of all the Western fathers.[17] If Augustine of Hippo was the father of medieval theology, then Gregory was the father of medieval spirituality.[18]

### Gregory the Great's World-Sacramentalism

This is important because Gregory's spirituality differs from Augustine's at just this point of attitudes toward the created world. Both shared, according to historian Carole Straw, "the late antique universe populated by Principalities, Thrones, and Powers," with "an energetic traffic of visitors" across the boundary between our visible world and the invisible world.[19] Yet Gregory's world differs subtly from the late antique world of Augustine, for in Augustine's time, "one is still cautious of crossing these boundaries, still conscious of how the dull life differs from the shimmering brilliance of the other side."[20] Augustine separates "the transcendent world of the spirit and the visible world of daily experience" in ways that Gregory does not, namely because the omnipotent God is often hidden to us: "Of necessity signs are ambiguous because God's mysterious majesty remains inscrutable."[21]

Those same signs, for Gregory, become more translucent (though not quite transparent); the whole world is sacramental and reveals spiritual truth, at least to those with discerning eyes to see and ears to hear.[22]

It is easy to see why Gregory so vigorously promoted the lives of the saints, relics, and miracle stories. For the monk-pope, "the . . . boundaries of late antiquity have all but vanished. The supernatural is mingled with the world of ordinary experience, and in surprising ways. Visible and invisible, natural and supernatural, human and divine, carnal and spiritual are often directly and causally connected." A storm is not just a storm but also a herald of God's wrath or a trial sent to man; indigestion might be caused by cabbage or by "the devil lurking in its leaves." The invisible reality sustains and determines the visible; thus, visible things can help us read divine meanings. Rather than being left to struggle through the ups and downs of our material fortunes, guessing wildly at truth (fortune is not, as in the classical understanding, blind), God uses a person's worldly trials and blessings to shake or soothe them. Straw shows us that Gregory "anticipates the *physicality* so characteristic of the later Middle Ages in figures as diverse as Anselm and St. Francis."[23]

Straw also recognizes that by promoting this more "physical" spiritual understanding of the created world, Gregory provided "an intellectual framework to integrate all aspects of life with Christianity." He "christened" the world so that "no part of life remains untouched by the sacred, no part of life need necessarily be excluded from the Christian."[24]

## Religion and Science: The Aristotelian Impact on Medieval Approaches to the Material World

Despite Gregory's much more physical approach, the underlying Platonic suspicion of bodily things continued to hamper a fully world-affirming spirituality and theology. That fuller Affirmative Way would await the time of Anselm and Francis, aided by the flourishing of some seeds planted by Augustine—seeds of trust in the human gift of reason (as we saw in chap. 4).

In the twelfth and thirteenth centuries, a recovery of Aristotelian science helped bring the powerful and useful discourse of science to bear in the deliberations of theology, both revolutionizing theology and laying the groundwork for the scientific revolution of the sixteenth through eighteenth centuries.

Essentially, the schools of the twelfth century were invigorated by a new interest in the scientific exploration of the universe. A "hunger of spirit" arose among the scholars of the twelfth century—a real desire to know what makes things tick. In a sense, the thinkers of that time were just beginning to discover nature itself, as something that was real, present, active, and above all intelligible. It was like they suddenly found another being on earth (and, in fact, they often personified nature in their allegories of this time) who had power and handed down decrees that must be obeyed or challenged. At the same time, they discovered that they themselves were caught up within the framework of nature, as bits of this cosmos they were readying themselves to master.

One High Medieval[25] image that captures this awareness is the "celestial sphere"—an imaginary, infinite sphere with the earth at its center and the stars, planets, and other heavenly bodies appearing to be located on its imaginary surface. In eleventh-century illustrations of the spheres, one can see a great deal of mythical illustration, with the heavenly bodies personified, as in astrology. This mixing of the material and the spiritual captivated C. S. Lewis, who used the personified planets again and again in his imaginative writings, using the spheres to represent a continuity with the older Neoplatonic sacramental view of the world.

Representing the new, more rigorous Aristotelian science of the scholastic era was the astrolabe, which used to measure the positions and altitude in the sky of celestial bodies such as the sun. Astrolabes were first developed in the Islamic world and came to the West in the same cultural transfer that brought Aristotle's scientific works. The fascination with which they were greeted in that time is hinted at in an odd fact: Peter Abelard gave the device's name to the son born of his illicit romance with his student Heloise. Compared to the mystical and personal quality of the celestial spheres, the astrolabe takes a much more mechanical, analytical approach to heavenly bodies.

Other major technological developments in the twelfth century include the windmill, the waterwheel, the use of keel and rudder, and the mechanical clock. With every new invention, people grew more aware that the world operated by orderly, natural laws. Suddenly the world was understandable and predictable. Order was no longer just an aesthetic or religious concept—you could see it all around you. And you could harness its power to your own ends.

The new scientists of this time still saw the natural world's operations as subservient to God, but they also understood that nature often contained its own causal explanations, as we have seen had long been the case in medieval understandings of illness (chap. 6). Scholastics were themselves pious Christians and certainly did not intend to deny God's creative, providential activity. They simply wanted to highlight the more and more evident fact that nature operates according to its own mechanisms, which are describable in naturalistic terms.

## Opposition and Complexity

The first responses of many in the church, however, were often not positive. Many got their first look at Aristotle through the eyes of Arabic scholars, who interpreted him in ways quite inconsistent with Christian theological understandings, implying that God had no knowledge of anything other than himself, that there was no afterlife, and that all human beings had only one intelligence. Thus the University of Paris, from 1210 to 1277, banned the study of Aristotle's works of science and their use in theology. Its leaders saw, quite reasonably, that there could be some problems with applying particular aspects of the scientific thought of the revered pagan philosopher to theology.[26]

Even so, the bans were ineffective. The study of Aristotle continued informally, and the philosopher's all-embracing system stimulated much fresh theological thinking. By the end of the thirteenth century, Aristotle was in wide use by the scholastics.

This robustness of Aristotelian presence in the universities illustrates the generally harmonious relationship between faith and science in those centuries. This puts the lie to the popular stereotype of benighted, obscurantist, reason-hating monks battling science-wielding scholastics for the right to interpret the faith. The fact is that conflict, while real, was peripheral to the real story of harmonization. It is fair to say that the monastic and scholastic theological styles did indeed differ, quite widely. But the bone of contention was not so much the intrusion of science into the theological task as the intrusion of logic into the realm of love. The pushback of the monastics was not *against* science and *for* faith; rather, it was against unwarranted, overreaching logic and for intimate knowledge of love.

## The Results of the Aristotelian Impact

Scholasticism sought to comprehend the whole sweep of human experience in a single system. As a theological movement, it clearly emerged as a response to a new, naturalistic worldview that was becoming dominant in the culture. According to Eugene Fairweather, it was

> the most daring constructive attempt in the Church's history to think of grace and nature, faith and reason, Christianity and culture, God and his creation, in terms that would neither separate nor confuse them, neither strip God of his sovereignty nor do violence to the integrity of his creatures. In other words, scholastic theology and philosophy are, at the very least, a noble effort to face the abiding problems raised by the correlation of Christian faith in God, Creator and Redeemer, with man's knowledge of himself and his world.[27]

For the medievals (and from this we should learn), theology was not just a pastime of theologians and religious scholars with time on their hands, squirreled away in their university libraries, Gollum-like with their pale skin and big eyes, safely removed from any interference with the public sphere. The medieval passion for theology was part of an all-embracing vision of the Christian faith as *the* truth that contributes most to human flourishing in the material, natural, economic, and political realms, through the application of "sanctified reason" to the perennial problems of humanity. The rational God who creates all that exists, who intones that all of it "is good," says that humans are "very good" and implants in us his very image. Most people in the medieval period identified human reason as the presence of God's image in us.

God desires that we live in full enjoyment of his creation as well as his fellowship. God will not allow this full enjoyment and flourishing to be completely destroyed by the disobedience of free humans in the fall, and so he works with and through human reason to improve every area of human life through law, medicine, education, and every other field of culture. As the "queen" of these sciences, medieval theology served as regal protector and fosterer of every science and art—the *quadrivium* of the maths and sciences as well as the *trivium* of the humanities.[28] But within and behind all the discussions of the Eucharist and the atonement is an abiding sense of wonder and love for creation. This wonder captivated Lewis at a deep level, as he related it in his *Discarded Image*. The medieval universe was "tingling with anthropomorphic life, dancing, ceremonial, a festival not a machine."[29]

In fact, it was the surge in scientific inquiry and economic activity in twelfth-century Europe that brought Christian theology into its full flowering in that age, leading to the towering and world-embracing accomplishment of Thomas Aquinas. This is "the medieval synthesis"—the arm-in-arm progressing of science, the arts, and theology in the peak period of the High Middle Ages.

In this period the great medieval poet Dante Alighieri (ca. 1265–1321), during an intensive period of education in the schools of the Franciscan and Dominican scholastics,[30] came to see the universe as "theomorphic," or God-shaped. "Through the joy of sheer knowing, philosophy introduced him to an objective cosmos, grander than any dream—an immense, unfathomable order of parts in a whole."[31] In the whole vast and mathematically, rationally, even musically structured universe, "God is revealed, if we can but see it, wherever we might turn."[32]

Dante expresses the theo-scientific vision of the medieval synthesis throughout his *Commedia*, which culminates at the end of the *Paradiso* with the pilgrim Dante seeing a vision of the universe as animated by a perfectly rational, perfectly loving being. The verses wrap within themselves both the mystical/imaginative and the intellectual/rational:

> My mind was struck by lightning
> Through which my longing was at last fulfilled.
>
> Here powers failed my high imagination:
> But by now my desire and will were turned,
> Like a balanced wheel rotated evenly,
>
> By the Love that moves the sun and the other stars.[33]

We are reminded of Lewis's assessment of the *Commedia*—that it contains, like Catholic theology, a perfectly rational, calibrated, nested set of truths, "wheel within wheel." This is a vision of the universe in which reason and love are unified so that, as Lewis once said, in the Middle Ages people could "love the universe as a man can love his own city."[34]

Such a theology proceeds by turning, in empirical mode, toward the world and then attempting to account for *every* element of what it finds there. This method resonates strongly with the recent work of contextual theologians (e.g., liberation, black, feminist, Asian, and eco-theologians). To be effective, and indeed true, theology must take into account our real experience as humans in the world—in not just our natural but also our social and cultural settings.

Commenting on Thomas Aquinas, Josef Pieper summarizes as follows: "faith presupposes and therefore needs natural knowledge of the world," and "moreover, the study of created things must be praised for its own sake, since these things are works of God."[35]

## Religion and the Arts

Medieval liturgical arts, like scholastic theology, manifest the medieval predilection for "sorting out and tidying up" that Lewis notes in his *Discarded Image*. Their carefully worked-out systems of conventional details amount to a meticulous science of representing the divine through the natural. To take just one example, "little figures of nude and sexless children, ranged side by side in the folds of Abraham's mantle, signified the eternal rest of the life to come."[36] Medieval artists and art were soaked in the sacramentality of all created things—the understanding that God is continually communicating to us in everything he makes.

For example, the medieval bestiaries (which Lewis also wrote about) give us some very odd and scientifically incorrect characterizations of actual animals (and some more fantastic imagined creatures, such as the unicorn and the phoenix) whose supposed habits may be read as direct symbols of holy things. Through a collection of model sermons for the main festivals of the liturgical year, the *Speculum Ecclesiae* ("mirror of the church") of Honorius of Autun (1080–1154), these stories of the bestiaries made their way into artworks in a group of European cathedrals of the twelfth century and beyond. At the cathedral tower at Strasburg, for example, we find an early fourteenth-century frieze of animals, all of whom have symbolic spiritual significance derived from the explanations of the bestiaries: "The eagle and its young, the unicorn taking refuge with a young girl, the lion reviving his cubs . . . the pelican feeding her young with her life blood, the phoenix in the midst of flames." These serve as "so many symbols of the Nativity, Passion, Resurrection, and Ascension," for as Honorius said, "every creature is a shadow of truth and life."[37]

Emulating the bestiaries, Honorius says of the eagle:

Of all creatures [the eagle is] that which flies highest, and alone dares to gaze straight into the sun. When teaching his young ones to fly he first flies above them, then takes them up on his widely spread wings. Even so did Christ ascend into Heaven higher up than all the saints to his place on the right hand of the Father. He spreads over us the wings of His Cross, and carries us on His shoulders like lost sheep.[38]

The unicorn, says Honorius,

is a beast so savage that it can only be caught by the help of a young maiden. When he sees her the creature comes and lies down in her lap, and yields to capture. The unicorn is Christ, and the horn in the midst of its forehead is a symbol of the invincible might of the Son of God. He took refuge with a Virgin and was taken by the huntsmen, that is to say, he took on human form in the womb of Mary and surrendered willingly to those who sought him.[39]

Quoting the bestiaries, Honorius writes "It is said that the lioness gives birth to lifeless cubs, but that after three days the roaring of the lion brings them to life. Even so the Saviour lay in the tomb as dead, but on the third day He rose awakened by the voice of His Father." According to the bestiaries, the pelican, "after having killed her young, revives them at the end of three days by opening her breast and sprinkling them with blood, even as on the third day God raised His Son," and the phoenix "burns itself on a pyre and on the third day rises anew from the ashes."[40]

Each of these creatures, found in the art and architecture of Gothic churches, spoke its deeper meanings to all who saw it, continuing the entire symbolic code used in the arts in that period.

In mediaeval art there are then intentions a knowledge of which is necessary to any real understanding of the subject. When for example in scenes of the Last Judgment we see the Wise and Foolish Virgins to the right and left hand of Christ, we should thereby understand that they symbolize the elect and the lost. Upon this all the commentators on the New Testament are agreed, and they explain it by stating that the five Foolish Virgins typify the desires of the five senses, and the five Wise Virgins the five forms of the contemplative life. To take another example, it is not as rivers that the four rivers of Paradise—the Gihon, Phison, Tigris, and Euphrates—are represented pouring water from their urns towards the four points of the compass, but as symbols of the evangelists who flooded the world with their teaching like four beneficent streams.[41]

## The Public Code of Medieval Art

For medieval artists and likely the majority of their audience, the "code" wasn't secret. It was a shared, public set of artistic conventions that acted as a key to the deeper, usually scriptural, meanings of a given natural phenomenon or work of art. Just as the ideas of the scholastics spread widely among laypeople through (for example) the preaching of Franciscan and Dominican evangelists, the web of natural and artistic symbols that encoded those ideas were also "not the property of the great thirteenth century doctors [theologians] alone, but were shared by the mass of the people to whom they had permeated through the teaching of the Church. The symbolism of the church services familiarized the faithful with the symbolism of art."[42]

As Lewis knew, medieval artists' use of natural symbols was considered a form of exegesis—a direct parallel of the medieval exegesis of Scripture. Dante, in a letter to his friend Cangrande della Scala (1291–1329), claims that his imaginative creation, the *Commedia*, is a multilayered allegory that should be interpreted according to the four senses—literal, allegorical, moral, and anagogical—categories that are usually reserved for the medieval study of Scripture. So, both in literature and in the visual arts, "the artist, as the [scholastics] might have put it, must imitate God who under the letter of Scripture hid profound meaning, and who willed that nature too should hold lessons for man."[43]

In fact, medievals spoke of nature as a "second book" that complements the book of Scripture. Since creation is nothing less than the thoughts of God realized through his *Logos*, the Word, "the world is a book written by the hand of God in which every creature is a word charged with meaning."[44] The wise know how to read its meanings, whether in nature or in art, thereby accessing God's thoughts. Thus, in a monastery refectory, Adam of St. Victor (d. 1146) held a nut in his hand and reflected: "What is a nut if not the image of Jesus Christ? The green and fleshy sheath is His flesh, His humanity. The wood of the shell is the wood of the Cross on which that flesh suffered. But the kernel of the nut from which men gain nourishment is His hidden divinity."[45] Similarly, Peter of Mora, the cardinal and bishop of Capua, saw in his garden of roses "the choir of martyrs, or yet again the choir of virgins. When red it is the blood of those who died for the faith, when white it is spotless purity. It opens among thorns as the martyr grows up in the midst of heretics and persecutors, or as the pure virgin blooms radiant in the midst of iniquity."[46]

As a whole, the sacramental symbol system of medieval art is not subject to individual interpretive fancy. Rather, we find ourselves "in the presence of an ordered system, an ancient tradition," which is detailed, closely knit, and founded on Scripture.

> In the Scriptures, indeed, as interpreted by the Fathers, the material world is a constant image of the spiritual world. In each word of God both the visible and the invisible are contained. The flowers whose scent overpowered the lover in the Song of Songs, the jewels which adorned the breastplate of the high priest, the beasts of the desert which passed before Job are at once realities and symbols. The juniper tree, the terebinth, and the snowy peaks of Lebanon are alike thoughts of God. To interpret the Bible is to apprehend the harmony which God has established between the soul and the universe, and the key to the Scriptures is the key to the two worlds.[47]

### Nature Loved for Its Own Sake

One might be tempted to say that the medieval writers and artists seem to have loved nature only for what it told them about God. But many animals and plants appear in their art with no particular symbolic purpose. For example, we may look at the facade of the cathedral at Laon, where

> a glance upward shows us vines, raspberries heavy with fruit and long trails of the wild rose clinging to the archivolts, birds singing among the oak leaves or perching on the pillars. Beasts from far-off lands side by side with homely creatures of the countryside—lions, elephants and camels, squirrels, hens and rabbits—enliven the basement of the porch, while monsters securely fastened by their heavy stone wings bark fiercely at us from above.[48]

There is a kind of riotous celebration of nature going on here, quite different from, though continuous with, the meticulous symbolism shown in the previous examples. Sometimes a plant is just a plant, celebrated for being marvelously what it is. The Gothic cathedrals, especially, "are all life and movement. The Church to them was the ark to which every creature was made welcome."[49]

In thirteenth-century art one can recognize the same thing that is apparent in Gregory the Great's sixth-century spirituality: the medieval understanding of the sacramental quality of the whole world, which holds that spiritual meaning is delivered through physical means in all of creation. The medieval use of universal representative conventions and "symbolic code" in their artwork is indeed, as Émile Mâle says, a kind of hermeneutic of creation that imitates the medieval hermeneutic of Scripture, an allegorical way of reading spiritual meaning from material realities. It is also a vivid illustration of Lewis's principle that the medieval mind was equally comfortable with and moved rapidly back and forth between pigs and eternal verities.

One might think that with all this symbolism going on in the arts, and with the sacramental approach to creation that reads divine meanings in ordinary things, medievals would never apply scientific reasoning independent of theological explanations. And in fact this has been a popular myth. But it is simply not true, as we have seen in how medievals interpreted the causes of illness. Thomas Aquinas's teacher Albertus Magnus, for example, wrote two scientific treatises that helped to found empiricism and the scientific method—"one on botany and one on zoology"—and sought empirical knowledge everywhere he went through observation and experiment. "He used his journeys through the Western world to further this interest, and was forever asking questions of fishermen, hunters, bee-keepers, and bird-catchers." Neither he nor his student Thomas found it necessary to inject theological explanations into these natural phenomena; God had given to each thing he created its own particular being, which must be understood on its own terms. "Albert and Thomas knew that the works of God cannot be grasped unless they are viewed as what they are in themselves. . . . Albert simply takes it for granted that theological arguments should be kept out of scientific investigations."[50]

Way back in 415, Augustine made the same point in his *Literal Commentary on Genesis*. To paraphrase: Don't import biblical reasoning to the sciences; it gets the science wrong and embarrasses the faith. In Augustine's words,

> even a non-Christian knows something about the earth, the heavens, and the other elements of this world, about the motion and orbit of the stars and even their size and relative positions, about the predictable eclipses of the sun and moon, the cycles of the years and the seasons, about the kinds of animals, shrubs, stones, and so forth, and this knowledge he holds as certain from reason and experience. Now it is a disgraceful and dangerous

thing for an infidel to hear a Christian, presumably giving the meaning of Holy Scripture, talking nonsense on these topics; and we should take all means to prevent such an embarrassing situation, in which people reveal vast ignorance in a Christian and laugh that ignorance to scorn.[51]

## Sacramentality Solves Gnosticism and Materialism

What lessons, then, can we carry away from this survey of medieval people's attitudes to creation? First, their sacramentalism helped them value creation neither less nor more than it should be valued—a salutary lesson for our simultaneously gnostic and materialist age. Second, their theological reading of creation allowed them to be attuned to God in all of life, including work, play, relationships, arts, and culture—an important practice in our age of compartmentalization between the spiritual and the material. Third, this sacramental attention to a creation that everywhere reflects its Creator underwrote a medieval cultural mandate, birthing a lavish growth of universities, sciences, and arts—a desperately needed correction to "gnostic" otherworldliness.

As Hans Boersma concludes in his study of medieval sacramentality, "only a heavenly minded Christian faith will do us any earthly good."[52] The seeming paradox is easily explained: only when we reassociate the natural and social worlds in which we live with the God who both created and sustained those worlds can we properly celebrate the blessings and address the maladies of those worlds.

Those in the evangelical Protestant stream might wish that their fundamentalist forebears had taken this lesson from medieval Christianity rather than retreating from culture when faced with a powerful new scientific language about the world, as they did with the Darwinian theory of evolution by natural selection. In fact, they very nearly did. The retreat was not sudden. At first we find evangelical Christians who were trying to harmonize Darwinism and Christianity, including some of fundamentalism's most prominent early leaders.[53] Unfortunately, their efforts were soon forgotten in the fearful, anti-intellectual rush to "defend the faith." The result was not only a tremendous cultural black eye on Christianity in America, which still remains today, but also the accelerated growth of theological liberalism as the only apparent remaining theological approach for intelligent, science-aware Christians.

Scholasticism was born out of a similar meeting between faith and science. But it was formed as a response of engagement rather than separation. The reaction of the scholastics was to accept much of the power of the new naturalistic paradigms at face value and to use the new tools of scientific thought to examine and explain the great truths of the Christian faith. In this process, a distinctively Christian worldview with a powerful naturalist philosophy came into being—the "medieval synthesis."

To put this another way: as the theologians of the twelfth-century monastic and cathedral schools and the thirteenth-century universities came face-to-face with new, powerful, naturalistic ways to describe their world, they began looking for more "down-to-earth" ways to study and understand their faith. They wanted to get answers from their study of the faith that were more satisfying to human reason than the old quasi-mystical answers provided by their teachers, which often amounted to "because God says so" or "because God did it that way." But even when using Aristotle, they still protected the faith's central mysteries (see the example of transubstantiation in chap. 4). A tree was both a natural earthly object with observable qualities and a window to heavenly meaning: tree of life, tree of knowledge of good and evil, "tree planted by streams of water" (Ps. 1), and so on.

To many evangelicals today, the myth that reason and faith as well as science and religion are essentially at odds is not only born of blind fear but is also a damaging diversion. That American evangelicals have in the past consistently been unable to forge such a synthesis as the scholastics did is obvious. There is today not one single evangelical-sponsored research university.[54] When we look back and see that the university itself came out of the scholastics' Christian synthesis, this lack of evangelical commitment to higher learning becomes an embarrassing fact.

I think that we have much to learn from the medieval scholastics in terms of addressing culture with Christ. And I think the scholastics would have agreed wholeheartedly with Mark Noll's conclusion: "The search for a Christian mind is not, in the end, a search for mind but a search for God."[55]

## Recovering a Common Sacramental Language

One more lesson emerges. I have argued that owing to our cultural syndrome of separating everyday natural and social experience from its divine meaning, we have lost an ultimate framework for our work, our play, our arts, our sciences, and so on. Both our gnostic and our hedonist/materialist approaches to the world sap the meaning from our created environments as well as from the social, economic, and cultural environments we build around ourselves every day.

Modern Westerners are characterized by an unrootedness, a dislocation, and a malaise that amount to an inability to find the "maps" to guide us in constructing stable selves.[56] We don't know who we are, either morally or metaphysically. The medieval system of artistic conventions reviewed in this chapter was a giant engine of meaning. It was a way of sharing truth socially. Because of the traditional, conventional nature of medieval art's visual language, *everyone* recognized the meanings of animals or objects; therefore, every time they saw a lion in a painting or a tree in real life they were reminded of the larger scriptural narrative to which these symbols point.

In other words, today we not only fail to find scripturally and tradition- ally grounded meaning in creation and our social-cultural environments but we also can't communicate even such rags of meaning as we *do* find in ways instantly recognizable to those around us. In a medieval era still soaked in oral tradition, where the details of a story delighted listeners in part because the story was told the same way each time, cultural com- munication fostered a communal sharing of meaning. The most vivid modern example was created not by C. S. Lewis but by his Catholic friend J. R. R. Tolkien, who wove throughout his tales of Middle-earth a fabric of songs and stories that clearly functioned to remind the people (in the story) who heard them of their shared experiences, values, and meanings. This famously creates a sense of cultural solidity and com- pleteness in the reader: we feel we have stepped into a coherent world with a coherent worldview. Said Lewis of his friend: "Medieval people, like Professor Tolkien's Hobbits, enjoyed books which told them what they already knew."[57]

In this sense, we find in the premodern era of the Middle Ages func- tioning maps for selfhood that come from an artistic use of creation and sociocultural reality to build a shared, recognized, conventional narrative anchored in a shared Christian understanding. *That's* what Lewis discov- ered in medieval literature and spent the rest of his life sharing with read- ers, whose individualism and rationalism (both then and today) make it so hard to access such socially shared meanings, especially meanings that reach beyond what we can see immediately with our eyes.

In other words, it's a good thing, in and of itself, to observe that medievals found in tradition something valuable. But it's also important to observe that the ways they discovered and shared that value were reinforced every time they observed something in nature, looked at a painting, or thought about a scientific phenomenon. The universe is alive with meaning. The material universe becomes a book of nature that reinforces the book of Scripture in ways that the Enlightenment and scientific revolution have largely destroyed for us today.

So tradition isn't something that we merely tell stories about—it isn't something that merely teaches us an ethic—but indeed it gives us structures of shared meaning that remind us at every turn of who we are as humans, of our *telos* and the *telos* of everything around us. As we take a walk in the woods, everything around us takes part in God's purposes and communication—it participates in that. We participate, as beings at the top of the hierarchy, but so do the trees, the rocks, the ants, the sunshine, and the rain. We are not walking in an interesting set of scientific facts. We are walking instead in a book—the book of nature. And that book reinforces the meanings we experience in the liturgy. In turn, the liturgical space not only hosts the liturgical communication of God's reality and perpetual presence but it also reminds us visually that the natural world, in its own powerful way, communicates the same reality and presence.

## Lewis on Enjoying Creation for What It Is as Well as Where It Points

How are we to derive new practice from the age of unicorns and self-mutilating pelicans? Isn't it a bit much to ask moderns to accept all this Neoplatonic mysticism and fanciful symbolism? Once again, C. S. Lewis is an excellent guide.

Just as medieval people did, Lewis appreciated both the material world's quiddity ("thatness") and its sacramentality (its quality of pointing beyond itself to another world). From his Oxford friend A. K. Hamilton Jenkin, Lewis received, as he puts it, an "education as a seeing, listening, smelling, receptive creature." Walking about with Jenkin, he learned "in a squalid town to seek out those very places where its squalor rose to grimness and almost grandeur, on a dismal day to find the most dismal and dripping wood, on a windy day to seek the windiest ridge," and so to "rub one's nose in the very quiddity of each thing, to rejoice in its being (so magnificently) what it was."[58]

Not only is this quiddity of things something to be enjoyed but it also points us to objective truth. The beauty of a waterfall is something inherent to the waterfall, not a trick of the subjective mind of a human. Lewis was actually concerned for the souls of those who did not see this.[59] He knew that when a person sees a waterfall, he or she sees both water and something infinitely greater. Toward the end of his life he wrote to a friend about his aging and increasingly malfunctioning body: "I have a kindly feeling for the old rattle-trap. Through it God showed me that whole side of His beauty which is embodied in colour, sound, smell and size."[60]

Lewis really did believe he could see God's beauty through his own sense perceptions of the material. Moreover, he believed that in the process of seeing in this way he was actually peering through the less real, the less solid, to the more real, since God is the realest and most solid thing there is (which is why the shades of *The Great Divorce* hurt their feet on the sharp grass of heaven). He was, in other words, an Augustinian, Pseudo-Dionysian, Neoplatonist (that is, a medieval) dinosaur thumping about in a modern materialist age.

Not only God's beauty but also God's personal and moral attributes become accessible to us in his creation. Lewis explains, in a letter, James's image of God as "the Father of lights" (1:17 NKJV): "He is pure Light. All the heat that in us is lust or anger in Him is cool light—eternal morning, eternal freshness, eternal springtime: never disturbed, never strained. Go out in early summer before the world is awake and see, not the thing itself, but the material symbol of it."[61]

Lewis's medieval, sacramental perception of matter emerges in various forms throughout his imaginative writings, from the creation narrative of *Perelandra* and the redemption narrative of *That Hideous Strength* to the talking animals of Narnia. In the latter case, as Michael Muth argues, Lewis built the world of Narnia on medieval bestiaries, which themselves functioned (as Lewis says in *Allegory of Love*) sacramentally.[62]

## Transposition: We Have Only Our Natural Experience to Lead Us to the Supernatural God

In so many ways, Lewis positioned the stuff and creatures of this world to act as symbols or sacraments of a higher reality (or, in the case of the endragoning of Eustace, a lower but still supernatural reality). As Lewis preached so powerfully in his sermon "Transposition," which was given on Pentecost 1944, the material world is the only way we can see the immaterial. That's just the sort of "rattle-trap" creatures we are.

The question that Lewis frames in "Transposition" goes like this:

> If we have really been visited by a revelation from beyond Nature, is it not very strange that an Apocalypse [the book of Revelation] can furnish heaven with nothing more than selections from terrestrial experience (crowns, thrones, and music), that devotion can find no language but that of human lovers, and that the rite whereby Christians enact a mystical union should turn out to be only the old, familiar act of eating and drinking?[63]

He answers this question at the end of the Chronicles of Narnia. Lord Digory, speaking of the Narnia that the children experienced, says:

> "That was not the real Narnia. That had a beginning and an end. It was only a shadow or a copy of the real Narnia, which has always been here and always will be here; just as our own world, England and all, is only a shadow or copy of something in Aslan's real world. You need not mourn over Narnia, Lucy. All of the old Narnia that mattered, all the dear creatures, have been drawn into the real Narnia. . . . And of course it is different; as different as a real thing is from a shadow or as waking life is from a dream." His voice stirred everyone like a trumpet as he spoke these words but when he added under his breath "It's all in Plato, all in Plato. Bless me! What do they teach them at these schools!" the older ones laughed.[64]

It is finally Lewis's apologetic from desire that points us to perhaps the most helpful modern appropriation of the medieval sacramentalist approach to the natural world. Lewis says in a letter to his brother, Warren, that "the 'vague something' which has been suggested to one's mind as desirable, all one's life, in experience of nature and music and poetry . . . and which rouses desires that no finite object pretends to satisfy, can be argued *not* to be any product of our own minds."[65] The sensing self, which interacts with the world through not only perception but also desire, leads us toward something real and objective beyond our subjectivity: it leads us toward God. Certainly, it can *hinder* us from God—as Plato, the Neoplatonists, Pseudo-Dionysius (late fifth or early sixth century), and Augustine all taught. But it can also *lead* us to God, albeit sometimes by negative example and suffering (by the sinfulness in ourselves that we stumble across as soon as we engage fully in that natural mode and world), as the Neoplatonists also understood and as Gregory the Great promulgated to the whole medieval period.

## In Defense of the Affirmative Way

Some medieval writers did lose the sense that the material world can lead us to the spiritual, insisting instead on an ascetic denial of all worldly things in favor of pure spiritual contemplation. The anonymous author of the *Theologia Germanica*, a book Lewis read and annotated heavily, and indeed appreciated for many of its emphases, is one of these. In one passage, the author describes Christ as being able at all times to keep one eye on "nature" and the other on God. But then the author turns and says that humans cannot do the same: we must "shut the eye of nature" (of our natural, material preoccupations and desires) if we are to open the spiritual eye that sees God. This explains why we must completely deny ourselves (our desires) if we are to come to God and achieve union. When Lewis came across this passage, he jotted a single, terse critical annotation: "In other words we must be essentially *unlike* the Lord?" He clearly recognized that the Christian warrant for traveling the Affirmative Way, encountering the material world as a place rich with sacramental meaning, was the incarnation of our Lord. Being perceptive about the natural world—keeping that "natural eye" open—was for Lewis an essential part of the way to God, and the incarnation of God in an actual, flesh-and-blood human being, Jesus Christ, proved it.

Again, it makes sense that Lewis would push back in this way. After all, he very famously taught that our natural desires—our yearning, which is triggered by our experiences of what is good and beautiful in the world— can lead us toward God. Indeed, he insisted that he came to God in this way, so that he called himself an "empirical theist."[66] And that, perhaps, is the most solid lesson we can learn from the medieval approach to creation. We must resist the modern proponents of the sterner side of the Neoplatonic stream; this includes the gnostics who suspect that since everything about the natural life can lead us away from God (as we've seen, Lewis agreed with this Augustinian point) we must do all we can to wean ourselves from any desire that would focus on the natural (or social) reality.

To that suspicion, the appropriate answer is the one Lewis gives in "Transposition": this world is finally the only one we know. If it cannot help us get to God along the Affirmative Way, then we are finally without help. Thus, it is possible to appropriately celebrate the many ways that created things meet and satisfy our desires and at the same time attend to that final reality to which this world points—the "beyond" that causes in us a yearning that the natural world can never fulfill.

This affirmative understanding of creation as conduit to God takes its most exalted form in Lewis's portrayal, in *That Hideous Strength*, of how a sanctified sexuality can play a role in bringing us to wholeness. In that book's culmination, in a thoroughly Williamsesque and indeed Beatrician way, Lewis shows us Mark Studdock returning to spiritual health and integrity as he joins with Jane in the marital bed, under the joyous superintending of Venus come down from the heavens.

This is *eros* in its most potent form, and it certainly seems to be a vote for continuity between nature and grace. Again, in "Transposition" Lewis explains that *only* our natural experiences can lead us to God, for we have no other mode or vocabulary with which to understand him. Humans vis-à-vis divinity are like "flatlanders"—people living in a wholly two-dimensional world—straining to relate to the three-dimensional world. It is finally only our prosaic experiences in this "flat," merely "natural" world, and the words and concepts we form to describe that world, that lead us upward, breaking us through our limitations and showing us—in a dim and imperfect way—that other, divine world for which we have yearned all along.

# 8

## Getting Passionate

### *Medieval Faith as a Religion of the Heart*

What does emotion have to do with knowing and serving the Christian God? For some today, this question raises distasteful images: television evangelists whipping up naive audiences and pulling on their heartstrings for fat donations; wild-eyed, gun-toting fanatics pronouncing holy wars against their enemies; crowds in a revivalistic frenzy—laughing, weeping, shaking, and falling on the floor. Or maybe the image is as simple as sappy singing and clapping that seems distant from the reverence due a holy God.

But strong emotion has been part of the Christian story since its very beginnings. Peter describes the relationship of worshipers to their God in this way: "Though you have not seen him, you love him; and even though you do not see him now, you believe in him and are filled with an inexpressible and glorious joy" (1 Pet. 1:8).

### You May Be a Mystic

In the Christian tradition, the emotions stirred up when people encounter the God of Abraham, Isaac, and Jacob have been described with the term "mysticism," which can be defined as follows:

Mystical experience involves an intense awareness of God's presence, accompanied by a knowledge and love of God that are recognized as extraordinary. Such awareness is difficult to put into words, and often results in a dramatic transformation in the one who receives it. Like every experience of grace, mystical experience is attributed to the utterly gratuitous love of God. It is not the result of any purely human activity, although it can be desired, petitioned, and even prepared for to some degree.[1]

By this definition, as medievalist Joan Nuth points out, some of your friends may be mystics. Or you may be a mystic.

As a young Christian in a Pentecostal church in Nova Scotia, I heard many prophecies spoken by people in the congregation. Often these were exhortations to enjoy the Lord, like a small child who basks, secure and happy, in the arms of her mother or father. In fact, much of the Pentecostal prophecy I experienced exhorted God's people to be comforted and assured of his love and to rest happily in his presence. What I didn't know at the time was that our church was recovering something that had been an everyday occurrence for medieval Christians: a living experience of devotion to God that elicited an affective (emotional) as well as a cognitive (rational) response.

If we agree with the medieval that our emotions and desires should come into play in our faith life—that something like "joy" should characterize a Christian in relationship with her or his God—then we are following a long tradition of "Christian eudaemonists" (the Greek *eudaemonia* refers to well-being, blessedness, or fulfilled desires). The classical philosophers asked, "What makes humans truly happy?" The Christian eudaemonists have answered out of the ubiquitous scriptural language of reward: we are happy when God transforms and fulfills our desires by leading us into the bliss of his loving presence.

Augustine cries out in his *Confessions*, "Our hearts are restless till they rest in thee."[2] He even goes so far as to say, "Come into my heart and *inebriate* it, enabling me to forget the evils that beset me and embrace you, my only good."[3] According to Augustine, the key to happiness is to want the one right thing, which is God himself. And from the Middle Ages to modern groups such as the Puritans, the Pietists, and John Wesley's and Jonathan Edwards's (1703–58) early evangelicals, Christian thinkers and saints have picked up this emphasis on the transformation and fulfillment of spiritual desire.

Not all Christians share this emphasis on the transformation of desire, but it is to be found deep in the fabric of Christian history, through all ages of the church. And nowhere (not even among Pietists, Pentecostals, or charismatics) did it flourish more than among the medieval faithful of the twelfth to fifteenth centuries. Not surprisingly, as I will show, the voracious reader C. S. Lewis found it there too and made it a part of his own faith, most famously in his frequently deployed "argument from desire."

## C. S. Lewis's Medieval Doctrine of Desire

C. S. Lewis was a scholar of the medieval period, but his medievalism was much more than intellectual. As we've seen in chapter 2, he was medieval not only in his mind but also in his heart—in his love for the way medieval people viewed the world and their place in it.

At the center of this sympathy for the medieval way of seeing the world was a very particular understanding of how a person's emotions move him or her along a specific path to God. Significantly, in his apologetic writings, Lewis frames both his own movement toward faith and the usual human process of conversion as an Augustinian eudaemonistic quest of desire.

Lewis found the modern ethic of absolute abnegation of desire to be unchristian: "If there lurks in most modern minds the notion that to desire our own good and earnestly to hope for the enjoyment of it is a bad thing, I submit that this notion has crept in from Kant and the Stoics and is no part of the Christian faith." Instead, he argues, "our Lord finds our desires not too strong, but too weak." Following Augustine, he affirms that "we are half-hearted creatures, fooling about with drink and sex and ambition when infinite joy is offered us, like an ignorant child who wants to go on making mud pies in a slum because he cannot imagine what is meant by an offer of a holiday at the sea."[4]

This doctrine of desire emerged first of all from Lewis's own experience of his path to salvation. But like all his experiences, he applied to this one a strong set of philosophical and literary filters. As we've seen in chapter 4, Lewis places on the first page of his allegorized spiritual autobiography, *The Pilgrim's Regress*, twin quotations from Plato and Boethius, which together make the same point about how people on the path to truth proceed through a kind of desire.

> This every soul seeketh and for the sake of this doth all her actions, having an inkling that it is; but *what* it is she cannot sufficiently discern, and she knoweth not her way, and concerning this she hath no constant assurance as she hath of other things. (Plato)

> Whose souls, albeit in a cloudy memory, yet seek back their good, but, like drunk men, know not the road home. (Boethius)

He adds to these two a third quotation, from Anglican theologian Richard Hooker (1554–1600): "Somewhat it seeketh, and what that is directly it knoweth not, yet very intentive desire thereof doth so incite it, that all other known delights and pleasures are laid aside, they give place to the search of this but only suspected desire."[5] This language of desire, of eros, would become crucial for Lewis's developing Christian apologetic. Indeed, when he honed the story of his own conversion for a wider audience, in the more accessible *Surprised by Joy*, this Platonic-Boethian language of desire and its fulfillment remained prominent.

### Lady Philosophy's Sweet Song

Lewis's reading of Boethius, quite a while before his Christian conversion, revealed to him a particularly Christian understanding of the role desire plays on the path to God. Lewis's knowledge of this tradition led him to craft a form of a traditional apologetic argument for Christianity—the argument from desire.

Since *The Consolation of Philosophy* was one of the most translated, most influential books of the whole Middle Ages (Lewis's own copy was one of many medieval translations), let's look for a moment at how this influential argument from desire appears in Boethius's book. Boethius— the character in the allegory—begins the book in a very agitated state. His fortunes have turned for the worse, he has been accused of political skulduggery, his goods have been confiscated, and he is under arrest. With the righteous fervor of a Job and the melancholy of a psalm of lament, he says, "I seem to see the wicked haunts of criminals overflowing with happiness and joy."[6] How is it that the wicked can be enjoying themselves, and he, who has lived an upright life as a faithful servant of the Germanic king Theodoric, has had happiness snatched away from him?

Now Lady Philosophy spends much of the first half of the book convincing Boethius that the things he thinks will bring him secure happiness—money, fame, power, pleasure—are actually will-o'-the-wisps, that is, pale shadows of true happiness. But she does not disagree with Boethius's premise that happiness is our proper end.

This can be seen in book 3 of the *Consolation*, which begins with Lady Philosophy singing an argument about the mutability and ultimate uselessness of all worldly things. Boethius responds with a kind of rapt ecstasy. "She had stopped singing," he says, "but the enchantment of her song left me spellbound: I was absorbed and wanted to go on listening."[7]

"You're eager to hear more," responds Lady Philosophy. "You'd be more than eager if you knew the destination I am trying to bring you to." Boethius asks what this is, and she answers, "*True* happiness."[8] She is going to move him from false happiness to true happiness, which is the proper end (the *telos*) of human beings, for which we yearn as the caged bird yearns for the woods.

What Boethius teaches us here—and, it seems clear he taught Lewis—is a Christianized Platonic understanding of the purpose and end of human beings. The Platonists taught that the real and perfect essence of each of us "first exists as an Idea in God's mind." This idea is "a Platonic form" that is also our *end*, our *telos*, our *perfection*—and thus the "measuring stick by which all creatures are individually judged and measured."[9]

### Coming to God and Becoming More Ourselves

Even more important for Lewis's reading (and, I might say, *ingestion*) of Boethius is that when created things are given existence—when God's ideas are actualized in creation—they are instilled with Platonic *eros*, which causes them to desire to be whole or to become like the idea God has of them: "Everything," Lewis summarizes in his copy of *Consolation*, "desires to realize its own proper nature."[10]

Adam Barkman comments on Lewis's argument that "all creatures become more themselves—attain more happiness and are more fully actualized—the more they look to, and act like, God; that is, the more they exercise 'creaturely participation in Divine attributes.'"[11] And Lady Philosophy argues, this time drawing from the Neoplatonists more than Plato, that we can achieve that realization of our nature only through union with the sum of all good and the source of all happiness—God himself. Thus God is the true end of the desires that we pursue in partial and flawed ways through money, high office, fame, pleasure, and beauty.[12]

The positive form of the principle of desire may be found everywhere in Lewis's life; it even peeks out before his conversion in his rich imaginative life and his appreciation for common, everyday things.

If we accept that ordinary things can lead us to God—a belief Lewis seemed to arrive at by temperament, literary taste, and philosophical commitment—then we must affirm that our desires (which I take to be an affective concept with both cognitive and physical elements) serve a positive function in God's economy of salvation. In his sermon "The Weight of Glory," Lewis tells us that our problem is not that we desire too much but that we desire too little. In fact, he insists that "unselfishness" (or more explicitly, the denial or abandonment of self) is a dangerous virtue for Christians to make the highest one: "If you asked twenty good men to-day what they thought the highest of the virtues," says Lewis, "nineteen of them would reply, Unselfishness. But if you asked almost any of the great Christians of old he would have replied, Love. You see what has happened? A negative term has been substituted for a positive, and this is of more than philological importance."

Of course, Lewis goes on to say, the New Testament does contain injunctions to "deny ourselves and take up our crosses." But, he insists,

> nearly every description of what we shall ultimately find if we do so contains an appeal to desire. If there lurks in most modern minds the notion that to desire our own good and earnestly to hope for the enjoyment of it is a bad thing, I submit that this notion has crept in from Kant and the Stoics and is no part of the Christian faith. Indeed, if we consider the unblushing promises of reward and the staggering nature of the rewards promised in the Gospels, it would seem that Our Lord finds our desires, not too strong, but too weak.[13]

## Medieval Affective Devotion: Roots and Fruits

C. S. Lewis was not idiosyncratic among twentieth-century Christian imaginative writers on this matter of desire's role in bringing us to the gospel. Lewis's close friend Charles Williams was captivated by Dante's belief that he had been led to salvation by a young woman with whom he had become infatuated when he was a boy. From Dante's vision of Beatrice, Williams elaborated a "romantic theology." Another key Christian influence on Lewis, G. K. Chesterton, discovered a similar romantic dynamic in the life of "God's troubadour," Francis of Assisi. Each of these writers, and Lewis himself, was drawing from a distinctively medieval tradition of affective theology, exemplified in such Lewis favorites as Francis, Dante, and Julian of Norwich. In turn, each of these figures drew from a tradition of heart religion with roots in the church fathers and the Bible.

Clarissa Atkinson traces the evolution of affectively charged devotion from "the first outpourings of private, emotional response in the prayers of Saint Anselm [1033–1109]" to "Saint Ailred's [1110–67] meditations, in which rapturous emotion was directed toward Jesus and his Mother," and then to Bernard of Clairvaux (1090–1153), who made "adoration of the sacred humanity . . . the basis of a grand scheme of mystical theology." She reads Francis (1181/82–1226) and the Franciscans as adapters of Bernard, transforming that adoration into "a popular passion focused on the details of Christ's birth and death and used it to preach penitence to large numbers of lay as well as religious people." Stepping back, she identifies the central elements of this tradition (in affective terms) as *compassion*, which "enabled Christians to participate in Christ's life and death"; *contrition*, which "produced repentance and conversion"; and the various *emotional and sensory feelings* that came with "an experience of the divine."[14]

### Origen and Those Who Followed

Although affective piety was "a mood and form of expression which advanced over all of Europe between the eleventh and the sixteenth centuries,"[15] from the earliest years of the church "nothing is more characteristic of the Christian intellectual tradition than its fondness for the language of the heart." Even in the densest and most abstract theologizing of the early and medieval fathers, "the goal was not only understanding but love."[16]

The very first systematic commentator on Scripture, Origen of Alexandria (185–254), interpreted the Song of Songs as an allegory of the believer's relationship with God, erotic emotions and all. In Origen's reading, the song's male lover is God or Christ, and its female lover is Israel, the church, or the believer. Augustine, Gregory the Great, and a long line of medieval interpreters picked up Origen's approach to the Song of Songs, using similar sexual language for our desire for God. As Gregory muses, "What force of love exists in the bedchamber of the Bridegroom."[17]

These writers knew that the comparison of our love with Christ to married love has the highest biblical authority. Think, for example, of Paul's allegorical treatment of the church, comparing it to marriage in Ephesians 5:31–32; or of the book of Hosea, in which Hosea becomes a living object lesson of God as the cuckolded husband who nonetheless takes his adulterous wife back again and again; or indeed of the many passages in the major prophets that speak of Israel as God's beloved.

### Augustine

Once we have a sense of the background of this type of language, we can begin to grasp Augustine's (354–430) famous image of the human heart, which is restless until it rests in God. Later in the *Confessions* we read more of the same: "By God's gift we are set on fire and carried upwards; we grow red hot and ascend. We climb 'the ascents in our heart'" (Ps. 83:6). Augustine says that "the 'flame on the altar of the heart' is the 'burning fire of love.'"[18]

It is not a stretch to say that Augustine's theology is most essentially a theology of love. He saw God as a persistent lover who pursues us until we finally cannot elude his loving arms. This emerges from his own life experience as a sex addict and fame-seeker; he found out that when he was at his worst, God embraced him with grace and would not let him go. It is no wonder that when Augustine came to write his *Confession*, he did so as a kind of "love song to God." It is in prayer form, and it narrates brilliantly the shift in young Augustine's affections from the sins of the flesh to God himself. For Augustine, original sin is a problem of "disordered love." He even, famously, describes the Trinity in terms of love: the Father is the Lover, the Son is the Beloved, and the Holy Spirit is the Love that passes between them.

In short, it was Augustine who pioneered the "argument from desire" that we see Lewis (and other modern apologists) making—the idea that we have a "hole in our hearts" that, if we are honest about it, we will realize only God can fill, and that we will, as desiring creatures, run around trying to fill it with other things until we come home to God.

## GREGORY THE GREAT

We have seen already a bit of how the hugely influential Christian philosopher/educator Boethius Anicius developed that theme of earthly and heavenly desire in his allegory of Lady Philosophy, I would now like to turn again to arguably the most influential father for the medieval period after Augustine: Gregory the Great (540–604).

Gregory's chief contribution to the tradition of heart religion is his formulation of the virtue of *compunctio* ("compunction").[19] Often thought of as a kind of godly sorrow (2 Cor. 7:10–11), the Latin word literally means "piercing." It is rooted in Acts 2:37, which tells how Peter's hearers at Pentecost were "pierced to the heart" (NASB). Cassian, Benedict, and others followed up this concept by closely associating compunction with conversion, but it was Gregory who made it a central value in Western spirituality.

Gregory deepened and elaborated Augustine's simple experience of restlessness leading to rest. Our desire for union with God operates in a kind of cycle, never to be fulfilled on this earth. Every time we come closer to God, our desire for him is amplified; in the very fulfillment of the desire, there is planted a deeper yearning to experience more of the Beloved.

Gregory quotes the bride of the Song of Songs, who says, "I am wounded by charity [that is, by the love of God]." And when we are so wounded, we "burn with the desire of contemplation," which God's wounding stirs to life. That desire "burns, it pants, and it already longs to see him whom it [formerly] fled."[20]

This complex experience involves, according to Bernard McGinn, "sorrow for sin, religious awe before the divine judge, detachment from the world, intense longing for heaven, contemplative self-awareness, and even the sweet sorrow that accompanies the necessary descent from the heights of the immediate experience of God."[21]

## ANSELM

There is no better example of the uniting of love and logic, theology and devotion, in the medieval period than Anselm of Canterbury (1033–1109). Anselm wrote a series of highly evocative, meditative, imaginative prayers focused on the lives and personalities of Christ, Mary, and the saints, designed for people to use in their private devotions. His stated purpose in publishing these was "to inspire the reader's mind to the love and fear of

God" (love and fear being the two sides of Gregorian compunction) and to inflame the desire to pray.[22]

In this devotional guide of Anselm's we see a shift in biblical focus from the early medieval (500–1000) spiritual focus on the Old Testament (especially the Psalms) to the high and late medieval (1000–1500) fascination with the Gospels.[23]

These prayers open the door to a slow, thoughtful, and heartfelt *lectio divina* mode of reading and meditating not only on the Bible but also on written prayers and other devotional works.[24] Introducing the prayers, Anselm says: "They are not to be read in the midst of an uproar, but in quiet, not quickly or rapidly, but gradually, attentively and painstakingly meditated." The reader need not start at the beginning but rather can read bits and pieces, making use of whatever he feels "will be effective in inflaming his desire to pray."[25] Everything in the text and the reading style is aimed at arousing a certain personal experience of connection with God, and it would do so out of the writer's own experiences and emotions. Toward that end, Anselm's "language was powerful, and his mood, intense," writes Clarissa Atkinson.[26]

A good sample is Anselm's sixteenth prayer, addressed to Mary Magdalene, "the model of the weeping lover": "Saint Mary Magdalene, who came with a spring of tears to the spring of Christ's mercy, from which, thirsting greatly, you were refreshed abundantly, through which the sinner is justified, through which she grieving most bitterly is most sweetly consoled."[27]

Anselm's words then take his readers to the empty tomb in their imagination and encourage them to weep along with Mary, then share her elation when she understands that Jesus has risen again. This sort of imaginative identification, this "com-passion" (suffering with), was also critical in the twelfth-century charitable revolution that swept through Europe, resulting in the founding of hundreds of hospitals. Again, affective devotion went beyond the purely private.

### BERNARD

Probably best known today for hymns such as "O Sacred Head Now Wounded" and "Jesus, the Very Thought of Thee," Bernard of Clairvaux (1090–1153) was by any measure a formative figure in medieval devotion.

A reforming monk of the Cistercian order, Bernard returned to the simplicity of the Rule of Saint Benedict, preached to recruit participants in the

Second Crusade in 1146, and later in life held so much power that he was the virtual pope of the Western church. Throughout his career, Bernard's teaching focused on love in a positive, personal vein but not a sentimental one; he talked about the relationship between the self and God. Borrowing a good deal from Augustine, Bernard presents four degrees of this love in his treatise *On Loving God*: first, the self loves only itself; second, the self loves the neighbor and God but only for its own sake; third, the self loves God for the self's sake; and finally, the self comes to love itself for God's sake (fleetingly on earth but constantly in heaven).

Bernard preached for eighteen years on the Song of Songs, spending eight sermons on chapter 1, verse 2 alone: "Let him kiss me with the kisses of his mouth— / for your love is more delightful than wine."[28] In each sermon, he takes the sensuous, erotic metaphors of the poem to describe the joys of spiritual intimacy with God: "What a close and intimate relation this grace produces between the Divine Word and the soul, and what confidence follows from that intimacy, you may well imagine. I believe that a soul in such condition may say without fear, 'My Beloved is mine.'"[29]

In the fourth of these sermons, Bernard elaborates on the verse "Let him kiss me with the kisses of his mouth" with a reflection on our progress toward intimacy with God, in which we move from the kiss of the feet (the ascetic or "purgative" way) to the kiss of the hand (the "illuminative" way of knowledge) to the kiss of the mouth (the "unitive," the final mystical goal of personal union with God). Here again, ascetic discipline is the first step, the baby step, in the affective path toward union: "The first is the sign of genuine conversion of life, the second is accorded to those making progress, the third is the experience of only a few of the more perfect."[30]

Bernard emphasizes the importance of the human Jesus for Christian spirituality, pushing high and late medievals further into their fascination with the Gospel accounts. In his twentieth sermon on Song of Songs, Bernard argues that the incarnation was actually for this purpose: to attract our affections.[31]

### FRANCIS OF ASSISI AND DANTE

Francis of Assisi, on top of all his other distinctions, gave the affective tradition a great boost in the thirteenth century. The sheer ubiquity of the evangelizing, teaching movement he started ensured that anything he emphasized would deeply penetrate the Christian culture of that century and many centuries to come. By the latter part of the thirteenth century, almost every town of any size had a community of Friars Minor (Franciscans). Within fifty years of the saint's death there were more than fifty such communities in England alone and more than five hundred in Italy.[32]

No influence shaped popular devotion in the high and late Middle Ages more than the Franciscans. They reached into the psyche of the people, appealing to them directly through art, literature, and impassioned preaching on the homely details of the nativity and the stark and gritty narrative of the passion. The Franciscans taught that tears were a gift from God, cleansing and cathartic—a worthy daily discipline for those who "keep watch over the perfection of their life."[33]

Francis experienced, and acted extravagantly upon, an overwhelming passion for the person of Jesus. In his biography of the "little poor man," G. K. Chesterton insists that Francis's religion "was not a thing like a theory but a thing like a love-affair."[34] Following the tradition of the chivalrous knights and troubadours of his day, Francis was spurred by this love to extravagant deeds for his Beloved. His life, says Chesterton, was one long "riot of rash vows."[35]

From the beginning of Francis's calling, as he roamed the streets begging alms for stones with which to repair the broken-down St. Damian's church, he was "so completely absorbed by this new life, so certain of his vocation and so much aware of the divine compulsion, that he went about as if in an ecstasy of joy. The chroniclers speak of him at this time as 'one drunk with the Spirit,' or as if driven forward by 'a very intoxication of the divine love.'"[36]

Out of this intense, mystical experience of communion with the person of Christ, Francis desired to follow in the very footsteps of his Lord, whatever the physical cost or the austerity of the resulting lifestyle might be.[37] His followers were marked by what may seem to us an odd combination of intense joy and an equally intense penitential mind-set. They "gave up all pleasures for one pleasure of spiritual ecstasy,"[38] and their commitment to ascetic discipline indicated not (as many moderns assume) some underlying masochism or fear of the body but rather "the secret of some actual power or experience," which Chesterton likens to a heady wine.[39]

This was the dynamic of Francis's prayer:

Therefore,
let us desire nothing else,
let us want nothing else,
let nothing else please us and cause us delight except our
Creator, Redeemer, and Saviour,
the only true God,
Who is the fullness of good,
All good, every good, the true and supreme good,
Who alone is good,
Merciful, gentle, delightful, and sweet,
Who alone is holy,
Just, true, holy, and upright,
Who alone is kind, innocent, clean,
From whom, through whom, and in whom
Is all pardon, all grace, all glory
Of all penitents and just ones,
Of all the blessed rejoicing together in heaven.[40]

Dante, trained as he was by the Franciscans, reflected their affective devotion in his own "romantic theology" (as Charles Williams identified it). At one point in Dante's poem the pilgrim character (who is Dante himself) asks his beloved Beatrice why God would choose to redeem us by coming to us in the incarnation. Beatrice, who has already died and gone to heaven and is talking to Dante with the certainty of one who has seen the face of God, responds "that what she is about to explain to him 'is buried from the eyes of everyone whose intellect has not matured within the flame of love.'"[41]

If what Dante says here is true, then it means that the religion of the heart, the religion of love, is not just some nice add-on to the religion that concerns itself with doctrinal truth. It is in fact, as Lewis also saw,[42] the only way we can even come to truth in the first place.

### The English Affective Tradition: Devotional Writers

Affective devotion came of age in late medieval England. For some reason, it seems the English were particularly good at retaining the earthy and emotional elements of the Christian tradition, from relics and saints to mystery plays and mystical experiences. Let's look for a moment at the English affective tradition, first in overview and then through four of its leading figures: Richard Rolle, Walter Hilton, Julian of Norwich, and Margery Kempe.

Importantly, the English were no less scriptural in their faith than other parts of Christendom. They read the Bible aloud (or had texts read to them), meditated on what they read or heard (ruminated, chewed, and digested it) until they memorized it, prayed through what they read, and finally rested in God's presence, praising him for the privilege of union with him (*lectio*, *meditatio*, *oratio*, and *contemplatio*). Having read, however, they also poured out their hearts in the tradition of affective piety, loving Christ's humanity as Mary Magdalene did.[43]

### RICHARD ROLLE AND WALTER HILTON

Richard Rolle's (1290/1300–1349) spiritual writings are striking for the earthy, empirical way he describes the physical experience of passionate concourse with the Lord. In *The Fire of Love*, Rolle describes actual bodily warmth he felt while in prayer. John Wesley, eat your heart out (so to speak)! "I cannot tell you how surprised I was the first time I felt my heart begin to warm. It was real warmth too, not imaginary, and it felt as if it were actually on fire. . . . I had to keep feeling my breast to make sure there was no physical reason for it!"[44]

As if this weren't enough, Rolle also experienced audible song wafting down from heaven: "the joyful ring of psalmody. . . . In myself I sensed a corresponding harmony at once wholly delectable and heavenly. . . . The effect of this inner sweetness was that I began to sing what previously I had spoken; only I sang inwardly and that for my Creator."[45] Rolle was exuberant in his joy; he spoke and wrote about his experiences not for educated clerics or monks but for "the simple and unlearned, who are seeking rather to love God than to mass knowledge."[46]

Walter Hilton and Julian of Norwich were late medieval English mystics whose writings C. S. Lewis loved, recommended to many, and rated highly as great and useful Christian books. Hilton was an Augustinian canon in Nottinghamshire. Lewis marked his *Scale* ("Ladder") *of Perfection* copiously, particularly noting (in a jotting on the endleaf) Hilton's simile that "mere knowledge" is like water, but Jesus turns that cold, logical water into wine, as he did at the wedding at Cana: "cold naked reason into ghostly light and burning love, by the gift of the Holy Ghost."[47] In another passage Lewis marked, Hilton insists that "because he loved us so much, therefore

He giveth us His love, that is the Holy Ghost. He is the giver and the gift, and maketh us then by that gift to know and love Him."[48]

### Julian of Norwich

Possibly Lewis's favorite devotional writer and certainly one whom he quotes often (in a half dozen of his books and many more of his letters) is the English anchoress Julian of Norwich. Julian had many visions, which she called "showings," as well as the sorts of direct, physical evidences of God's love that we see in Rolle. In Julian's words, "There will be many secret touches that we shall feel and see, sweet and spiritual."[49] Unperturbed by this almost sexual intensity in Julian's experience of God, Lewis brings her visions up again and again in his books and letters. In particular, her arresting vision of holding all creation in her hand like a hazelnut and hearing Christ say "All shall be well" struck Lewis as genuine and powerful. "He thought it just the right balance to say that the material world is not evil, as the Manichaeans taught, but merely little."

In *The Four Loves*, Lewis uses Julian's image to show how even "the most magnificent things" in creation are far beneath God's majesty. The phrase "All shall be well" that Julian heard from God also arrested Lewis's imagination, and it emerged again and again in such books as *The Great Divorce*, *The Problem of Pain*, and his essay "Psalms." As David Downing suggests, Julian seems to be "the sort of person Lewis had in mind when he described mysticism (in the same paragraph where he discusses the hazelnut vision) as 'wonderful foretastes of the fruition of God vouchsafed to some in their earthly life.'"[50]

### An Uncomfortable Witness to Divine Love

Unlike Lewis, today's readers seem hesitant to embrace the English anchoress and her visions. The reasons for this get to the heart of the modern discomfort with affective devotion. Modern Quaker spiritual writer Richard Foster describes having taught Julian's *Revelations of Divine Love* to a classroom of undergraduates. Unlike the other books he assigned, this one sparked a controversy—even an uproar—with students not only disagreeing with each other but even shouting at one another.

Foster was puzzled. Surely this language of devotion was familiar to these students—even from the movies and television shows of their experience. But *Christian* devotion seemed an alien concept (ironic, given the romanticism, not to say sentimentalism, of much modern worship music). In Julian's words, "The Trinity is our everlasting lover, our joy and our bliss, through our Lord Jesus Christ." And again, "In his love he wraps and holds us. He enfolds us for love, and he will never let us go."[51] Somehow this seemed "too much" for Foster's students.[52] "We found it hard to believe that this relationship of deep, holy intimacy could be right, could be true, could be ours." Puzzling over this, he concluded that our society's eroticized, sexualized concept of love and passion is to blame.[53]

Plumbing beneath the surface of Julian's visions, we find a spirituality and an accompanying theology that delight in assurances of God's everlasting love. Assurance of salvation has been a perennial issue for Christians throughout history—no less for medieval anchoresses than for modern Pentecostals. Though Julian enumerated a number of subjective, approximate barometers of one's spiritual state—"tears of contrition, devotion and compassion"—a gap remained.

Into this gap stepped God, communicating his love to her directly in visions and sensations. Other mystics wished to instruct; Julian wanted to comfort. Throughout her book we have direct words from the Lord: "I am keeping you very securely." "You will not be overcome."[54] Similar to the congregational prophecies of my charismatic church, God urged her to respond with particular emotions to these assurances: "Because I love you, enjoy me! This will please me most of all."[55]

### Mother God

One of the things that has made Julian controversial in my own classroom is that she refers to God—even to Christ—as feminine: a mother to us children. As the translator of the Penguin edition notes, we may find biblical warrants for this "feminizing" of God and Christ in Isaiah 66:13 and Matthew 23:37, but it still makes many Christians uncomfortable. It seems, however, to be a natural development of affective devotion: not just the married sexual relationship but the child-mother relationship is an obviously close, intimate relationship that can provide a fruitful parallel for our devotions—perhaps even more appropriate than the sexual one, since Christ is indeed he (or she) through whom we were created. We owe our being to him as we do (in a different way) to our mothers, and when we return to his arms, it can certainly feel similar to how we felt as children, nestling in our mothers' arms.

And in answer, we have a Jesus who weeps over us, who is nothing like the impassible God of the Greek philosophers (and Christian theology). Julian portrays not just her own emotions but also God's emotions[56]—his "thirst" and "yearning" for us, how he is "cheered" by our prayers[57] and looks for them expectantly. This is a very human Jesus indeed—vividly embodied, strongly emotional.[58] Julian recommends that in answer to that vivid humanity, in our devotions to Christ we should use all five of our senses.[59] God is in our sensuality![60] While this is a challenge to Protestants (perhaps especially to those in the free-church and Reformed traditions), couldn't we stand to focus more of our contemplation and worship on bodily, visual themes and to respond to God in a bodily, visual way? The genuflections, holy water, and incense of the medieval worship experience served this purpose of wooing our "deep places"—our very embodied emotional lives—by means of our often distractible senses.

On the other hand, Julian recognizes (as Lewis does) the ways that our emotions can lie to us—can lead us astray in their extremes. She urges a kind of detachment that balances the emphasis on emotion's role in our devotions. For example, she describes swinging twenty-five times from depression to joy and back again and then relativizes these emotions by saying, "I should not be made glad by anything specially, nor on the other hand should I be much distressed by anything else, for 'Everything will be all right' [as she had heard God say to her]. The fullness of joy is to see God in all things."[61] This echoes what we have already heard from Boethius: our earthly fortunes—their ups and downs—may mislead is in the unavoidable limitedness of our perspectives. Providence is behind it all. We need to raise our heads to the higher, God-perspective. This provides a kind of joy, even bliss (Jesus is for her "King of bliss"[62]), but it is a supernatural kind, which is different from our paltry, protean, and passion-driven emotions.

Another struggle some have with Julian is that her God never seems to be wrathful. In her visions we are forgiven, really, at the very moment of the fall.[63] In the Augustinian tradition of seeing evil as only a privation, not a positive force, Julian portrays sin as having no reality; indeed, sin is something for which God will not ultimately blame us.[64] We have an original, sinless will that the fall has not destroyed. Julian seems Pelagian in her insistence that this will is "why we can always do what pleases him,"[65] though she stops short of saying that this will is the source of our

salvation. Her famous line, which Lewis took as something of a motto—
"All will be well, and all manner of things will be well"—may seem to
wink at the fall by simply bringing all people back into the good graces
of God without question.[66]

### MARGERY KEMPE

Margery Kempe (ca. 1373–after 1438) was a middle-class laywoman
(and mother and business owner) who lived in the late fourteenth and
early fifteenth centuries and provided us with the first biography of a
woman written in English.[67] This, by the way, was probably dictated to a
clergyman, since she was almost certainly either illiterate or barely literate.

Margery is a great example of a layperson with an impassioned, even
mystical piety who influenced the clergy and monastics of her day, although plenty of people simply wrote her off as a crazy lady because of
her effusive emotional expression during church services. But in that very
trait, she was a reflection (if extreme) of the late medieval tradition of
affective devotion:

> Her spiritual life was centered, from the beginning and throughout her life,
> on the human Christ, the object of her prayers and her love. She identified
> very closely with the Virgin as woman and mother, and her participation
> in the Passion was enlarged and inspired by sharing Mary's grief. Her en-
> thusiasm, her "boisterous" emotion, and her conspicuous humility were
> borrowed from the Franciscans and legitimated by their authority. And
> her method of meditation—that is, her personal involvement in the bibli-
> cal story, placing herself among the holy figures—was exactly the method
> prescribed by writers of affective devotion.[68]

Margery's book is earthy at points—even bawdy. She tells a particular
story about an episode of sexual temptation in her life that is R-rated, and
her language of intimacy with Christ is also direct and frank. When she
sees a "comely man" in the streets, it sets her to meditating on Jesus. And
when she talks about her times of inner dialogue with her Lord, she uses
a term usually reserved in her time for the kissing and cooing of young
lovers: "dalliance." We have not moved far from Bernard's spiritual use
of the Song of Song's eroticism here!

And though we may not be entirely comfortable with this type of erotic
imagery, its trajectory continues. A century and a half after Margery,

through the words of Catholic Reformation hero Teresa of Avila (1515–82), we encounter the almost lurid description of being pierced again and again by the flaming spear of God's love. It is easy enough to see the whole late medieval fascination with this affective tradition as a kind of, if not sexual repression than at least transfer of, overheated erotic energies from human sexual outlets and relationships to God himself.

The first thing to say here is that this way of speaking about our relationship to God in the language of human sexual attraction and intimacy was no new thing on the horizon of Christianity, even in Bernard's day. It dates back at least to Origen and has plenty of warrants in both the Old and New Testaments.

The second thing is drawn from something Lewis told his friend Arthur Greeves in a letter the year before his conversion (January 30, 1930). After confessing that he has been struggling mightily with pride and vainglory, he admitted that he had experienced "the most delicious moments of *It*." Clearly "it" (some sort of mystical frisson of joy) had been a topic of conversation between Lewis and Greeves in the past. Lewis goes on to describe one such moment, triggered by a particularly charged experience of nature, which had brought "such a sudden intense feeling of delight that it sort of stopped me in my walk and spun me round. Indeed the sweetness was so great, and seemed so to affect the whole body as well as the mind, that it gave me pause—it was so very like sex."[69]

Now this description of a mystical experience would fit comfortably into the writings of a Richard Rolle or Walter Hilton. But Lewis immediately says that he recognizes the obvious Freudian interpretation: that his experience is "just" sublimated sex. But he counters, "Why is it not open to me to say that sex is undeveloped *It*?—as Plato would have said."[70] In his *Symposium*, Plato explains the friendship of two lovers as transcending the physical pleasures of their sexual relationship. They, according to Plato, could "hardly account for the huge delight they take in one another's company." That delight must be explained in terms of a longing in both of their hearts for something else, "a something to which they can neither of them put a name, and which they can only give an inkling of in cryptic sayings and prophetic riddles."[71] In other words, why not understand sex as a sublimated mystical yearning for and connection with God, in the mode of the English affective tradition, with its Neoplatonic, Augustinian roots? This is the sacramental perspective on sexual pleasure that Lewis develops more fully in the context of a larger argument about the sacramentality of marriage (a Catholic belief he came to later in his life) in *That Hideous Strength*.

## Medieval Devotion to the Passion of Christ

Perhaps the most intense and long-lasting dimension of medieval affective devotion was that era's devotion to the passion of Jesus, the God-man. Martin Luther, the founder of Protestantism and a thoroughly medieval man, acted on the repeated urgings of his Augustinian confessor, Johann von Staupitz (1460–1524), to "look to the wounds of Jesus."[72] And soon after posting his "Ninety-Five Theses," he announced that the only man who deserved to be called a theologian was he "who comprehends the visible and manifest things of God seen through suffering and the Cross."[73] Throughout Luther's life, his sermons and hymns contained striking images of that event. Where did this come from?

The roots of Luther's passion devotion are to be found in the tradition of medieval affective piety that we have been examining. Anselm of Canterbury (d. 1109) asked Christ to forgive him "for not having kissed the place of the wounds where the nails pierced, for not having sprinkled with tears of joy the scars." Abelard (d. 1142/43) focused on the supreme example of Christ's love and forgiveness in his passion, in order to foster in the unbeliever emotions of horror and godly sorrow when confronted by this death. Bernard of Clairvaux (d. 1153) gave lavish attention to the emotions of the believer captivated by the love of God.

And then, of course, there is Francis of Assisi, whose all-consuming imitation of Christ seemed rewarded on September 17, 1224, in the hermitage on Mt. Alverno, when he is said to have received the gift of Christ's wounds in his own flesh—the stigmata.

Francis's disciples in the next two hundred years brought the humanity and sufferings of Christ into the mainstream of devotion. From portable outdoor pulpits and within chapels whose walls were often covered with life-sized passion scenes, the preaching friars stressed as never before the emotions of Jesus during his ordeal—and the answering emotions of the worshiper.

They also championed an ascetic approach that sought to follow Paul, who says, "I fill up in my flesh what is still lacking in regard to Christ's afflictions, for the sake of his body, which is the church" (Col. 1:24). In the late-medieval heyday of passion piety that followed, many monks, nuns, and layfolk tried in various ways to imitate Jesus's passion or to experience something of the same extreme suffering as their Lord.

### The Complexity of Passion Devotion

Fourteenth-century passion literature was supposed to evoke four primary reactions: gratitude, penance, compassion, and imitation. But these responses did not appear simply or discretely. Rather, terror, awe, sorrow, and joy might mix in one experience. At the center of all this emotion was the single goal that every believer sought: "a sense of profound contact with the deity that was joined with [Christ's] humanity."[74]

From the time of Bernard of Clairvaux through Ignatius of Loyola (1491–1556), Christians wrote and read increasingly elaborate accounts of the passion events. The man whose exegetical work opened the floodgates to these newly detailed narratives was Rupert of Deutz (ca. 1075–1129). A Belgian who died an abbot in Germany, Rupert mined not only the Gospel accounts and a number of apocryphal accounts, all of which had been used before his time to tell the story of the passion, but also a host of obscure passages in the Old Testament.

By an allegorical method of exegesis, Rupert found in the pages of Job, Psalms, Isaiah, and other books new and little-known details of the "Secret Passion" of Christ—the exact number of times he fell down en route to the cross, the drunken condition of Jesus's tormentors in Caiaphas's court (Rupert was no friend to the Jews), and so forth. The detail of the executioner's ropes pulling Jesus's body taut, for example, come from Psalm 22:17. Historian Gerard S. Sloyan says, "A legion of visionaries took their lead from [Rupert's] writings," elaborating an expanding cast of characters and litany of details of Christ's suffering.[75]

Authors from the late thirteenth through the fourteenth century went one step further with entire comprehensive biographies of Christ that contained details from outside of the Gospels—most famously, the *Vita Christi* of Ludolph of Saxony (ca. 1295–1378). It was this book that eventually reached a swashbuckling young Inigo (later Ignatius) Loyola, founder of the Jesuit order, in his convalescence from a war wound and turned his heart toward Christ. Ignatius wrote in his widely used *Spiritual Exercises* a set of directions on how to place oneself imaginatively in the scene of Christ's crucifixion.

Loyola worked in the same tradition as the anonymous thirteenth-century author who wrote under the name of the early eighth-century historian Bede, who urged readers to place themselves on the scene of Christ's trial—to plead with his tormentors, offer their own bodies to be beaten in his stead, and wait with him as he sat in chains, offering their shoulders for him to rest upon.

This same tradition founded such long-standing devotional practices as the Passion Play and the Stations of the Cross. And it was in this period that disturbingly graphic crucifixion paintings (by Hieronymus Bosch [1450–1516], Albrecht Dürer [1471–1528], and Matthias Grünewald [1470–1528], for example) became much more common.

At the same time, the laity picked up another spiritual practice that was once the preserve of the monastics: the regular discipline of private prayer. The wealthy commissioned beautiful books of the hours and other aids to help them meditate on the crucifixion. And when a full-blown literature of the passion developed in the fourteenth century, laypeople such as Margery Kempe flocked to that as well.

### Passion and Christ's Passion in the Fabric of Medieval Devotion

The typical critique of such intense devotion to the passion is that it unduly separates the human and divine natures of Jesus, concentrating exclusively on the former. But for medieval believers, with their sacramental understanding of God's presence in the material world, depictions of Christ's wounded body only drove home the truth that in this man the divine became human.

Finally, underlying this very tangible, imaginative piety was the belief that the best way to gain understanding is through experience. Both intuitive emotion and practical imitation infused wisdom into one's very heart and body in a way that speculative theology could not, leading to charitable as well as devotional action. Spiritual leaders like the fourteenth-century English mystic Walter Hilton continued to teach—as Francis of Assisi had—that the Christian life must be lived out, practically, by imitating Christ's example of charity.

## Spiritual Time Travel

The desire for a tangible experience of God's love has not dissipated with the discovery of the atom or the invention of the automobile. Modern Protestantism has given relatively little attention to our imaginative and emotional lives, yet the past century saw a dramatic upsurge in charismatic spirituality.

With its devotion to the person of Jesus, its impassioned worship, and its physical experiences of God's intimate presence (such as tongues and "slaying in the Spirit"), this movement first sprung up at the turn of the twentieth century in a poor, multiethnic Los Angeles neighborhood, from the Wesleyan holiness movement's continuation of the long-standing Christian "heart religion" tradition. Then at midcentury it reemerged in mainstream Christianity, springing first from the Anglican and Roman Catholic confessions, with their sacramental and historical emphases.

But one doesn't have to be a charismatic to awaken imagination and senses in devotion to Christ. Those who feel a lack in this area could do worse than to begin a time-traveling "spiritual research trip" to the roots of cross-centered piety. Not everything you find there will be helpful. Few of us will wish to emulate certain Irish monks by standing for long periods in a bucket of ice water, arms outstretched in a cruciform position. But it couldn't hurt to look, with Martin Luther, "to the wounds of Jesus" to "comprehend the visible and manifest things of God seen through suffering and the Cross."[76]

Western Christians today need to hear the medievals on this: we tend to hurry over the incarnation, seeing it as a necessary step to get Jesus to the cross where he can die as a substitutionary atonement for our sins. In general, we miss out on the rich historical and theological resources on creation and incarnation, and we focus instead on sin and salvation. But Margery Kempe, for example, was captivated by the fact that God has *really become human* and *really has been tempted and has suffered in all the ways we have.* Jesus's stark human suffering affected her most not by illuminating the legal, substitutionary mechanism of salvation (as is true today in many evangelical circles) but by revealing the unimaginable love of a God who would go to such extremes to reach us, even taking on the deepest physical and emotional sufferings to which we fallen folk are heir.

A second reason for connecting with Margery and the other medieval mystics is that their affective piety may be a medicine for a peculiar ailment of many (post)modern Christians—the spiritual torpor and indiscipline induced by lives of material gratification and "amusing ourselves to death."[77] To such inaction and spiritual flabbiness, the ascetic discipline of the medieval offers an intriguing tonic. But our modern spiritual illness involves not just spiritual inaction but also spiritual and emotional distance. By this I mean a sort of "flatlining" of the spirit: We may so easily fall into an attitude that says, "There may be a God. There may be a Jesus who died for our sins. And while I believe these things, they do not touch my heart." How different this reaction is from Margery who, when the archbishop of York asked her the rough question, "Why do you weep so, woman?" replied firmly, "Sir, you shall wish some day that you had wept as sorely as I."[78]

Margery's life and book remind us that such intensely emotional piety focused on the humanity (and thus also the deity) of Christ was not merely an inward-focused "kick." Both intuitive emotion (her weeping) and practical imitation (her late-life acts of mercy) can infuse wisdom into our very hearts and bodies in ways that speculative theology can never do.

### Reclaiming the Physical

Finally, among the varied aspects of our human nature, our emotions seem especially closely tied to our physical bodies. We use the same words, "feeling" or "being touched," for the physical senses and for emotional experiences. But reading *The Book of Margery Kempe* prompts me to ask: Where has the sense of the spiritual importance of touch or physicality gone in today's culture? Are these human senses allowed to communicate anything true or spiritual to us? We have plenty of the visual in our television- and movie-soaked culture, and even in our churches. But how often do we experience anything spiritually significant through touch? The most intense, ecstatic touch-experiences, those of our sexuality, have been devalued and dehumanized through obsessive attention and commodification in the impersonal marketplace. I think that like the Mel Gibson movie *The Passion of the Christ*, Margery's life of devotion and the whole English mystical tradition can help to draw today's Christians back to the sort of visible, physical devotion epitomized in the medieval pilgrimage.

In the mid-1990s I was giving a lecture on Pentecostalism at an evangelical seminary in New England. I was describing the huge influxes of eager believers, every day, by the busload, to the Azusa Street Revival that launched Pentecostalism in 1906 and again to the modern Toronto Airport Vineyard revival and the Brownsville/Pensacola revivals. One student put up his hand and asked, with skepticism in his voice: "Why do Pentecostals and charismatics feel that it's so important to actually *go* to the place where a revival is supposedly happening, to 'bring back' that revival to their home churches?"

At the time, I didn't have an answer. Now, having encountered Margery and studied her time, it seems to me that these trips to modern charismatic revivals resonate with medieval pilgrimages. Theologically speaking, people have always gone to places where God is reputed to be moving in a special way because at some level they recognize the essentially personal, visual, and physical nature of this historic faith of Christianity. That is, they see that the God who incarnated himself in history as a first-century Jew continues to make himself incarnate, though imperfectly, in the *body of Christ*—in his people, his "living stones" (the very tactile image of 1 Pet. 2:5), wherever he chooses to build them together.

Many of us may not venerate saints or go on pilgrimages to seek out their relics (which were the focal point of many medieval pilgrimages), but we *do* crave the kind of contact with Christ that comes to us in special gatherings of his people—his body—where he seems to be doing special things uniquely for our time and place. That we can come away from those gatherings changed reflects the fact that the church is the continued incarnation of Christ.

Of course, we will only consider the "coolness" of much modern devotion a problem if we agree that our emotions and desires *should* come into play in our faith life. If we do, then we find ourselves in the camp of Augustine and the "Christian eudaemonists," who find in emotions of joy and fulfillment an important clue to our *telos* or ultimate purpose in God.

Other sorts of emotion do tend to show up in our churches: emotions that are whipped up, self-centered, spiritually and morally useless. But in Margery we meet a different sort of religious emotion, rooted in a "full boisterous" acceptance of Jesus's real human nature. Her spirituality sprang from a theology that bled to death before her eyes. It drove her not only to strong feelings but also to strong spiritual action. If only we could come to the same balanced, physical/emotional/cognitive devotion to the three-person God and the two-natured Christ. For the help toward that goal that Margery gave many in her own time, I would say she is still well worth reading today.

Margery, Richard Rolle, and the rest of the medieval affective devotional tradition teach us to approach Christianity as whole persons, physical and emotional as well as intellectual. It is a lesson worth (re)learning.

# 9

## Getting Human

### How the Incarnation Lifts Up Our Humanness

I was working at Christianity Today in the early 2000s, editing *Christian History* magazine.[1] After my first year, I hesitantly offered the suggestion that we do an issue on "Mary in the Christian Imagination." Though the idea met with more support than I expected (at that distinctively evangelical Protestant magazine), our art director did hazard the prediction that we would lose readers if we did the topic. Imagine my surprise when, in the end, not only did we not lose any readers but we also actually won the Evangelical Press Association's award that year for "best single-topic issue." This recognition told me we'd hit a nerve with our evangelical Protestant readers. Apparently, there's "something about Mary," even for the descendants of Protestant fundamentalists.

By the time I'd finished working on the issue, I had an inkling of what that "something" might be. As I wrote in the issue's editor's note:[2]

> It's a sleepy Wednesday night and I'm the only one left in the office, on the top floor of CTI's modest Carol Stream, Illinois facilities, across from the Aldi's grocery store and the McDonald's restaurant. I've been looking

through the images on the layouts for this issue—picture after picture of scenes starring Mary, the mother of Jesus—until they have all begun to blur together in one big scene. . . . And I'm wondering: Do I know the mother of Jesus—the *theotokos*, or "the one who gave birth to the one who is God"³—any better now than when we started this issue?

I'm just not sure. Part of me still feels like a kid in a museum: The Renaissance masterpieces, the Byzantine icons, the 15th-century German wood carvings . . . these are all too lofty and alien—something from a different age and a different religious sensibility. Can all of this really mean anything to me: a college-educated twenty-first century suburbanite, an "evangelical," used to thinking of Mary for only a few days around Christmas?

## The Flabbergasting Fact

Although I hadn't become convinced by the lavish Marian devotion and theology of the Roman Catholic Church, I had been captivated by one aspect of the Mary story: the "flabbergasting fact . . . that God himself came down and chose to be conceived, and carried to term, and born the son of a real, living woman."

The Reformation scholar Timothy George, a Protestant who had just written a book called *The Blessed Evangelical Mary*, reminded me in a conversation that "God didn't have to do it that way. He could have descended from heaven as a little fresh baby God just made and plopped down on earth."

"But he did choose to do it 'that way,'" I reflected in my editor's note, "the normal, *human* way. Aside from the divine conception, he came the same way we all do: through pregnancy, labor, birth, infancy." That single fact, I mused, "elevates all of humanity."

I concluded, "I hope 'meeting' Mary will face you, as it has me, with the extraordinary truth of the incarnation. Look: Here is the flesh-and-blood woman who bore our savior, suckled him, clothed him, taught him, and followed him. Then, at the cross, she sorrowed over him. And then at last, in the Upper Room, she participated in the birth of his church. No wonder his church has dwelt on her so lovingly."⁴

In the second half of the medieval era, an age infatuated with the details of the Gospel accounts, no scene was painted more than the annunciation—the angel's announcement to Mary that the Son of God would be incarnated in her womb. What we miss today about the devotion to Mary that rose to new heights in that period is that it was first and foremost a devotion to the incarnation as the key fact of salvation history. We tend today to skip over Christ's incarnation, seeing it as merely a necessary step to his cross and the substitutionary atonement. Though late medieval Christians also paid devotional attention to the crucifixion, their focus (as with their devotion to the incarnation) was squarely on the miracle that God, in his love, became flesh for us, suffering all that we suffer, in solidarity with us.

## Lewis's Incarnational Spirituality

The very fact that C. S. Lewis needed to see Christianity as satisfying not just to his intellect but also to his imagination shows us that he saw our full humanity as important in our faith. He had been taught well in that by the Romantics—among them William Wordsworth (1770–1850), whom Lewis listed as one of the writers who most influenced him, and George MacDonald (1824–1905), who reveled in nature and its sacramental function of pointing to God. Lewis's affinity to these authors predisposed his post-conversion self to dwell lavishly, as the medieval authors he studied had done, on the wonder of the incarnation.

### Christ in the Midst of Our Joy and Our Suffering

We will see how that fascination with the incarnation—the enfleshment of the Creator God as a human being—emerged in both his nonfiction and fiction writings, but it also gained a new and powerful meaning for him when he lost the love of his later life, his wife, Joy. The fact that Christ shared not only his humanity but also his suffering helped Lewis get through that experience of grief.

In *Letters to Malcolm*, he writes: "We all try to accept with some sort of submission our afflictions when they actually arrive. But the prayer in Gethsemane shows that the preceding anxiety is equally God's will and equally part of our human destiny. The perfect Man experienced it. And the servant is not greater than the master. We are Christians, not Stoics."[5]

This was more than a general observation. After the medieval manner, Lewis attended to every detail of the passion of the human Christ, drawing succor in his hour of need. He continues:

Does not every movement in the Passion write large some common element
in the sufferings of our race? First, the prayer of anguish; not granted. Then
He turns to His friends. They are asleep—as ours, or we, are so often, or
busy, or away, or preoccupied. Then He faces the Church; the very Church
that He brought into existence. It condemns Him. This also is characteristic. . . . There is, then, nothing left but God. And to God, God's last
words are "Why hast thou forsaken me?" You see how characteristic, how
representative it all is. The human situation writ large. These are among
the things it means to be a man. Every rope breaks when you seize it. Every
door is slammed shut as you reach it.[6]

Lewis saw that Christ's passion experience was "the human situation
writ large." He found this a comfort and sought to comfort others in turn:
"Some people feel guilty about their anxieties and regard them as a defeat
of faith. I don't agree at all. They are afflictions, not sins. Like all afflictions, they are, if we can so take them, our share in the Passion of Christ."[7]

When he wrote to people who had brought their life troubles to him
in letters, he offered them the same comfort, born of Christ's willingness
to share our humanity: "You needn't worry about not feeling brave. Our
Lord didn't—see the scene in Gethsemane. How thankful I am that when
God became man He did not choose to become a man of iron nerves; that
would not have helped weaklings like you and me nearly so much."[8] And
to another woman: "Fear is horrid, but there's no reason to be ashamed
of it. Our Lord was afraid (dreadfully so) in Gethsemane. I always cling
to that as a very comforting fact."[9]

One of Lewis's most complete and imaginative renderings of the theme
of the incarnation appears in a chapter titled "The Grand Miracle" in his
book *Miracles*: "The central miracle asserted by Christians is the Incarnation. They say that God became Man. Every other miracle prepares for
this, or exhibits this, or results from this . . . every particular Christian
miracle manifests at a particular place and moment the character and
significance of the Incarnation."[10]

### Ennobling Human Choice and Culture

Part of understanding and affirming the wonder of who we are as human
beings, affirmed by the fact of the incarnation, is being clear about ourselves as creatures capable of *choice*, who are responsible for the choices

we make. Free will is a crucial part of Lewis's anthropology and his case for hewing to the morality of the Western (Christian) tradition. Our wills are as essential, ordinary, and marvelous as our bodies. The choices we make on earth have transcendent, cosmic, and divine (or infernal) consequences. Lewis loved Dante's *Commedia* and appreciated Sayers's take on that great poem. Sayers (as I've noted) called it "the drama of the soul's choice."[11] Drama, acted out by humans in all their earthy but exalted embodiedness. Full of color, life, and substance.

It may be fair to say that Lewis was a "Christian humanist" in this respect. That is, our arts, sciences, cultural activities, and personal choices all contribute to heaven or hell on earth, as well as to the story of our salvation; many are *preparatio evangelii*—they lead us to God's doorstep. In his essay "Christianity and Culture," which I refer to in chapter 3, Lewis reflects: "Culture is a storehouse of the best (sub-Christian) values. These values are in themselves of the soul, not the spirit. But God created the soul. Its values may be expected, therefore, to contain some reflection or antepast [foretaste] of the spiritual values."[12]

This means that the "older" values of courage, fortitude, prudence, and self-control are crucial to who we are as humans. Thus, as Christians, we can hear from pagan sources on ethics without worrying that we are giving up the Christian farm. But it also means that the whole cornucopia of human culture-making is a divine directive.

Through the incarnation, God affirmed the value and importance of bodily human life and all that goes with that, including the moral decisions we make over against the temptations that we face. We see Jesus faced with temptations in the wilderness and successfully navigating those. We see him eating and drinking with the disciples, eating and drinking with sinners, to the point that some called him a wino and a glutton. In his earthly—and often quite "earthy"—ministry we find Jesus as model.

Lewis repeatedly held up Christ's earthly, incarnate life as an important guide to our choices and our moral lives. Do we need help in interacting with those caught in a variety of sins? See Jesus's interactions with the woman at the well and the woman caught in adultery, or his brazen habit of eating with the "tax collectors and sinners."[13] Help with trials and temptations? Then, as Lewis says in *The Four Loves*, we can reflect on "the Jesus . . . of the workshop, the roads, the crowds, and the clamorous demands; the Jesus who faced surly opposition, the Jesus who lacked all peace and privacy, who constantly experienced interruptions." *This* is our picture of the divine life, lived under earthly conditions. As he considered the role of free will and choice for the Christian, Lewis followed such influential medieval traditions as the Franciscans who emphasized the imitation of Jesus's earthly life.[14]

In the wonderful *The Great Divorce*, we find perhaps Lewis's most eloquent exploration of free will and moral choice. The entire story is a defense of the importance of choice, strongly echoing Dante's similar tale. "[Lewis] terms it a 'disastrous error' to believe that 'reality never presents us with an absolutely unavoidable "either—or,"' or to imagine 'that mere development or adjustment or refinement will somehow turn evil into good without our being called on for a final and total rejection of anything we should like to retain.'"[15]

In other words, *The Great Divorce* is also, like the *Commedia*, a drama that aims to show that we must, unavoidably, make choices and that those choices will, unavoidably, affect our eternal destinies. We are at the top of the chain of (natural) beings—given reason and free will by God, and then ennobled further by his incarnation to live a human life, which itself demonstrated the importance of choosing well.

### Drawing Us to Our "Best Selves"

As well as illuminating our moral nature and demanding that we choose well, for Lewis the incarnation performs an astounding work of drawing us up into the divine presence. Lewis launches into his key apologetic work *Mere Christianity* with this observation: "At the beginning I said there were Personalities in God. Well, I'll go further now. There are no real personalities anywhere else. Until you have given up your self to Him you will not have a real self."[16] This is a version of the classical Christian teaching of *theosis*, formulated by Athanasius, who said that "God became man so that we can become gods."[17] That startling language does not mean that we become what God is in his essence but rather that we are reattached to the divine life, which overcomes the death at work in us because of the fall. God came to earth, to flesh, in order to lift us back up with him.

Lewis has a couple of unique ways of describing the incarnation. As Will Vaus points out, Lewis suggests in *Letters to Malcolm* that

the Incarnation can be described as Heaven drawing Earth up into it. He asserts that when God the Son took on the human body and soul of Jesus, he took on with it the whole environment of nature—locality, limitation, sleep, sweat, aching feet, frustration, pain, doubt, and death. The pure light walked in the darkness and the darkness, thus received into the heart of Deity, was swallowed up. In his uncreated light the darkness was drowned.[18]

In other words, by not just creating us but also *becoming* one of us, Christ ennobled and raised up all of humanity. The truest things about ourselves reflect the image of our Creator—not just as he is in the Trinity but also as he is in the incarnation. "Our own composite existence," says Lewis, is "a faint image of the divine Incarnation itself—the same theme in a very minor key."[19] The fact that each of us is a spirit dwelling in a body parallels Christ's divine spirit dwelling within his human spirit.[20]

To get a sense of Lewis's deep devotional engagement with the theme of the incarnation, remember that *Miracles* was published in 1947, and Lewis had first read his Greek edition of Athanasius's *De Incarnatione* on Christmas Eve 1942 (years prior to writing the introduction to his friend Sister Penelope's translation). The holy day of this and a subsequent reading (Good Friday 1958) indicate that he read the book not only with a scholarly interest but also devotionally.

Moreover, Lewis started reading his friend Dorothy Sayers's earthy sequence of radio plays on the life of Christ, *The Man Born to Be King*, sometime around 1943. Writing to Sayers soon after (May 1943), he confesses his properly medieval affective response to her appropriately earthy portrayal of the incarnation: "I shed real tears (hot ones) in places: since Mauriac's *Vie de Jesus* nothing has moved me so much. . . . I expect to read it times without number again."[21]

This he indeed did. At Sayers's funeral in 1958, Lewis said that he read it "in every Holy Week since it first appeared, and never re-read it without being deeply moved." This means that by the time of his eulogy for Sayers, he had read *The Man Born to Be King* at least sixteen times, and likely read it five more times before his own death on November 22, 1963.[22] In a letter written in response to an American Nazarene man's question about modern authors, Lewis says that although he usually didn't read modern authors, "I think D. Sayers['s] *Man Born to be King* has edified us in this country more than anything for a long time."[23]

### Deep-Sea Divers, Living Statues, and the Great Dance

Lewis engages the doctrine of the incarnation on a deeply imaginative level. He uses a set of striking images for the incarnation and what it did for us and for all of creation. One is that of the deep-sea diver. Like the diver working on a salvage project, Christ goes down into his own creation "in order to bring the whole ruined world up with him to new life."[24]

The beautiful, organic, mutual vision of this coming down and drawing up seemed to Lewis like a great dance: "The partner who bows to Man in one movement of the dance receives Man's reverences in another. To be high or central means to abdicate continually: to be low means to be raised: all good masters are servants: God washes the feet of Men."[25] The entire final section of the fall-redemption story *Perelandra* shows us this dance, a dance of incarnation that was the turning point of the universe.

> All which is not itself the Great Dance was made in order that He might come down into it. In the Fallen World He prepared for Himself a body and was united with the Dust *and made it glorious for ever*. This is the end and final cause of all creating, and the sin whereby it came is called Fortunate and the world where this was enacted is the centre of worlds. Blessed be He![26]

Again, these images evoke the old idea—rooted in Athanasius's thought and dominant in the East but shared as well by Augustine and the Western tradition—of salvation as *theosis*, usually translated in English as "deification" or "divinization." What happens to us in that process is akin to what happens to the creatures who were turned to stone in the White Witch's courtyard: though we now may be only static pictures of God, made in his "sculptor's shop," "some of us . . . some day [are] going to come to life"[27] under the vivifying power of the breath of the dying-and-rising Aslan.

> We are not begotten by God, we are only made by him: in our natural state we are not sons of God, only (so to speak) statues. We have not got *Zoe* or spiritual life: only *Bios* or biological life which is presently going to run down or die. The whole offer which Christianity makes is this: that we can, if we let God have his way, come to share in the life of Christ. If we do, we shall then be sharing a life which was begotten, not made, which always has existed and always will exist.[28]

Paul Fiddes notes that "this is touching doctrine with the glow of imagination. Lewis's fundamental insight is that, by entering the dance or drama of the Trinity, we truly become sons and daughters of God; we truly become persons. This is mainline Christian doctrine, expressed in an imaginative form."[29]

### Our Embodied Life Here and Beyond

Another facet of the incarnation that captivates Lewis is the way that it ennobles our humanity, even our very materiality. To try to abstract mind from body, spirit from matter, is to commit the gnostic error and destroy (or at least falsify) what we truly are as human beings. *That Hideous Strength* shows us in imaginative form how modern technocrats (the National Institute of Coordinated Experiments, or N.I.C.E.) might try to eliminate that crucial materiality in a gnostic quest for pure spirit. In an attempt to eliminate their bodily natures (as well as all biological life on earth) and retain only the mind, N.I.C.E.'s agents lose their morality and their very selves. A sample of the dialogue gives a sense of the chilling vision at work here. Mark Studdock is querying Feverstone, whom he is trying to impress in his effort to be counted one of the "inner circle." Studdock asks, "And what is the first practical step?" Feverstone responds:

> "Yes, that's the real question. As I said, the interplanetary problem must be left on one side for the moment. The second problem is our rivals on this planet. I don't mean only insects and bacteria. There's far too much life of every kind about, animal and vegetable. We haven't really cleared the place yet. First we couldn't; and then we had aesthetic and humanitarian scruples; and we still haven't short-circuited the question of the balance of nature. All that is to be gone into. The third problem is Man himself."
>
> "Go on. This interests me very much."
>
> "Man has got to take charge of Man. That means, remember, that some men have got to take charge of the rest—which is another reason for cashing in on it as soon as one can. You and I want to be the people who do the taking charge, not the ones who are taken charge of. Quite."
>
> "What sort of thing have you in mind?"
>
> "Quite simple and obvious things, at first—sterilization of the unfit, liquidation of backward races (we don't want any dead weights), selective breeding. Then real education, including pre-natal education. . . . [He continues:] Of course, it'll have to be mainly psychological at first. But we'll

get on to biochemical conditioning in the end and direct manipulation of the brain. . . ."

"But this is stupendous, Feverstone."

"It's the real thing at last. A new type of man: and it's people like you who've got to begin to make him."[30]

Over against their machinations, the redemptive community found at the household at St. Anne's is so *everyday, earthy, prosaic, and ordinary* in its routines, its mundane talents, and especially its morality—leftover great Western morality. Throughout the book, this prosaic, common, ordinary, and traditional morality is threatened, along with the goodness of the body and material life. Again, though Mark and Jane's sexual intimacy has been progressively destroyed as Mark is drawn into the gnostic machinations of N.I.C.E., in the end, the gods come down to save their embodied, moral lives.

As it says in Genesis 1:27, "male and female he created them." Christ came not just as a man but as a fetus in a woman's womb. Throughout *That Hideous Strength*, women serve to draw the characters back to the divine in human embodiedness; Mother Dimble, an "earth mother" who represents fertility, serves Jane in this way. Mother Dimble and Jane herself are channels of charity, agents of salvation. Jane becomes a *theotokos*—a "God-bearer"—to Mark, saving him in something very much like the way Beatrice saved Dante. This was a theme in Dante's life and work that fascinated Charles Williams, whom Lewis draws from throughout *That Hideous Strength*.

### Friendship, Salvation, Pigs, and Boots

To ignore the "earthiness" of human beings—our embodiedness—as if what is important to us is only our rationality, is to remove traditional understandings of what human beings are, and thereby to destroy traditional morality. It is, in fact, to "abolish humanity"—to unmake us as creatures of God (think of the demonized "Un-man" in *Perelandra*), and thus prevent us from reaching God as well (we end up with the *abolition* of man).

Medievals did not do this. They kept the sublimely metaphysical and the crassly physical together in the simultaneously exalted and earthy interplay between, "death, change, fortune, friendship, or salvation" and "pigs, loaves, boots, and boats."[31]

This simultaneous exalted spirituality and physical earthiness came together for medieval Christians in their emotional devotion. They knew that among the varied aspects of our human nature, our emotions seem especially closely tied with our physical bodies—and they tuned their worship and spirituality accordingly.

We know God only through analogy, that is, through our sense experience. Why is it so important that we affirm our embodiedness in our relationship with God? Because we receive everything we know about God through our bodies, our senses, our experiences. We have no other way to understand him. Analogy is more than analogy; it is sacrament. To use Lewis's word in his title of a key essay (to which I will return), it is "Transposition."

Sense-knowledge about God through his creation is not second-class knowledge. Lewis expresses this idea memorably in his poem "On Being Human," which compares the angels' incorporeal way of knowing with our way—to the advantage of the latter. While angelic minds can directly behold the Platonic forms of things—"pure Earthness and right Stonehood" and the essence of a tree—they cannot know the blessedness of that tree's shade on a sunny day, for they have no skin or sense of touch. Air they know intellectually, but the smells of "the field new-mown" and "the wood-fire smoke that whispers Rest" escape them, for "an angel has no nose." The poem concludes:

> Here, within this tiny, charmed interior,
> This parlour of the brain, their Maker shares
> With living men some secrets in a privacy
> Forever ours, not theirs.[32]

### The Resurrection Body

Lewis returns to the spiritual significance of bodies in his reflections on the new bodies we will have at the resurrection. Not only will the life of the senses be preserved in those bodies (in some way beyond our understanding), but the experience of the material world that we had in this life will somehow also be "drawn up" into that world: "I can now communicate to you the vanished field of my boyhood—they are building sites today—only imperfectly by words. Perhaps the day is coming when I can take you for a walk through them."[33] What's going on here? According to

Paul Fiddes, it seems that, for Lewis, "there is continuity between nature and spirit in the redemption of sensations or sense-memories."[34]

Lewis admits, "How far the life of the risen man will be sensory, we do not know." But, he says, "it will differ from the sensory life we know here, not as emptiness differs from water or water from wine, but as a flower differs from a bulb or a cathedral from an architect's drawing."[35]

Famously, Lewis argues that our pets will somehow appear in that new earth as well because, in their physical presence, they are close to our hearts in this world. Their importance to us in this world will be reflected in the next. Mere months before his death, in a letter to Mary Willis Shelburne, he muses:

> My stuff about animals came long ago in *The Problem of Pain*. I ventured the supposal—it could be nothing more—that as we are raised *in* Christ, so at least some animals are raised *in* us. Who knows, indeed, but that a great deal even of the inanimate creation is raised *in* the redeemed souls who have, during this life, taken its beauty into themselves? That may be the way in which the "new heaven and the new earth" are formed. Of course we can only guess and wonder. But these particular guesses arise in me, I trust, from taking seriously the resurrection of the body: a doctrine which now-a-days is very soft pedaled by nearly all the faithful—to our great impoverishment.[36]

One might add that the resurrection of the body is soft-pedaled today precisely because we no longer believe our bodies have any spiritual importance. And this is tied up with the fact that we no longer value the humanity of Christ in his incarnation. While Lewis admits that we do think of Christ's humanity once a year at Christmas (which, not coincidentally, is the only time most Protestants ever think of Mary), for the rest of the year, "it's almost as if we think Christ once became a man and then presently reverted to being simply God." But that is of course not so. "Once the second Person of the Trinity takes on humanity, he will not lay it down again."[37]

### The New, Even More Material Creation

In *Miracles*, Lewis muses on the post-ascension moment in which Christ went "to prepare a place for us," which Lewis understands to entail Christ creating a "new Nature which will provide the environment or conditions for His glorified humanity and, in Him, for ours." Remember that the church—and certainly the medieval church—understood that Christ's humanity did not disappear after he rose from the dead; his ascension was not some divine escape act out of nature and into "some unconditioned and utterly transcendent life." Rather, says Lewis, "It is the picture of a new human nature and a new Nature in general, being brought into existence. . . . The old field of space, time, matter, and the senses is to be weeded, dug, and sown for a new crop. We may be tired of that old field: God is not."[38]

Not only did Lewis affirm the materiality of the new creation that the incarnate and risen Christ prepared for us to share with him, he thought of it as *more solidly material* than this one. To Arthur Greeves he writes:

> I agree that we don't know what a spiritual body is. But I don't like *contrasting* it with (your words) "an actual, physical body." This suggests that the spiritual body wd. be the opposite of "actual"—i.e., some kind of vision or imagination. And I do think most people imagine it as something that *looks* like the present body and isn't really there. Our Lord's eating the boiled fish seems to put the boots on that idea, don't you think? I suspect the distinction is the other way round—that it is something compared with which our present bodies are half real and phantasmal.[39]

Lewis stresses that though "we know and can know very little about the New Nature," the New Testament accounts of the resurrected Christ don't leave us the option of seeing that nature as immaterial: "The local appearances, the eating, the touching, the claim to be corporeal, must be either reality or sheer illusion. The New Nature is . . . interlocked at some points with the Old." The incarnation, played out in the nativity, crucifixion, resurrection, and finally ascension, paved the way for a new and still (in some sense) physical reality. And for this reason, we may not dismiss materiality with a gnostic wave of the hand, as if it didn't matter to God and shouldn't to us.[40]

Lewis's most direct statement of how important our bodies and senses are to us spiritually comes in his sermon "Transposition," which (as we saw in chap. 7) pressed home the undeniable reality that we finally have no other conduit to the divine besides our bodies and our senses. Simply put, we are sensuous creatures, and that's okay; we know it's okay because in the incarnation God shared that embodied sensuous reality with us.

To turn the connection on its head, Lewis also confesses that he found this sacramental principle of transposition—that we can approach God only through our earthly, sensory experience of a material reality that mysteriously participates in the spiritual reality of God—helpful in understanding the incarnation. We are told in one of the creeds (actually the one that bears Athanasius's name) that the incarnation worked "not by conversion of the Godhead into flesh, but by taking of the Manhood into God." How does the incarnation accomplish this? Lewis is careful here, professing that he "submit[s] all to the verdict of real theologians," but he seems to say that the incarnation provides that pathway through which our sense experiences become not mere representations of deity but actually the way (and the only possible way) that we are "veritably drawn into . . . Deity."[41] This is certainly Athanasian: "He became man that we might become gods."

### Aslan

We see this incarnational principle worked out in the lead character of the Chronicles of Narnia—the lion Aslan. However, one needs to be careful here: Aslan is not an incarnation of God in the exact way Christ is. In the words of Lewis scholar Paul Ford, Aslan "comes on the Narnian scene already and always a lion; he did not become lion to save Narnia," therefore he is not precisely a Christ figure.[42] Nonetheless, Aslan is truly "an incarnation": he is earthy, embodied, powerful in his materiality, and also the son of the Great Emperor. It was only a year after his extended reflections on the incarnation in *Miracles* that Lewis turned back to continue work on *The Lion, the Witch, and the Wardrobe*. In the chapter "The Grand Miracle" (the incarnation) in *Miracles*, Lewis "speculates on a springtime coming to the whole cosmos as the result of Christ's incarnation on earth." According to Ford, "Aslan, the incarnation of Christ in Narnian terms, represents in Narnia what Christ represents on earth: the God of the Chosen People, the 'glad Creator' of nature and her activities."[43] Lewis reveals his intention in a letter to a girl who asked about "Aslan's other name":

As to Aslan's other name, well, I want you to guess. Has there never been anyone in *this* world who (1) arrived at the same time as Father Christmas (2) Said he was the Son of the Great Emperor (3) Gave himself up for someone else's fault to be jeered at and killed by wicked people (4) Came to life again (5) Is sometimes spoken of as a Lamb (at the end of the *Dawn*

*Treader*)? Don't you really know His name in this world? Think it over and let me know your answer![44]

### Brother Ass and the Living Nativity

Returning to one of Lewis's favorite medieval figures, the earthy Francis of Assisi, we find a childlike wonder at the incarnation of Christ.[45] William Short, in *Poverty and Joy: The Franciscan Tradition*, provides an excellent example:

> Two weeks before Christmas in 1223, Francis was staying in the little hillside hermitage near the town of Greccio, south of Assisi. According to his contemporary, Brother Thomas of Celano, Francis called a friend of his, named Giovanni, to help him in preparing a special celebration of the forthcoming feast. He asked that animals and hay be brought to a cave at the hermitage, so that a scene could be prepared to show the people of the town and his own brothers the physical conditions of the birth of Jesus.
>
> He wanted people to be able to experience what it was like for the Son of God to be born in a stable, surrounded by the ox and ass, straw and cold. Francis's brothers and the people of the town of Greccio gathered in the cave on Christmas Eve lighting up the night with torches, singing hymns, with a priest celebrating Mass on an altar arranged over the manger. Francis himself, "dressed as a Levite," sang the Gospel "in a beautiful voice," and preached, full of emotion. Thomas tells us that it seemed as if the infant Jesus, long forgotten in the hearts of the people, came to life that night. And all of creation, the trees and stones of the surrounding mountainside, echoed the praises sung by the people.
>
> This simple kind of nativity scene was destined to be spread by Franciscans throughout the world as they moved out from Assisi in the following centuries. It is now a familiar feature of Christmas celebrations everywhere. Though it has suffered its share of commercialization, and its significance has sometimes become purely sentimental, at its origins the nativity scene was a striking affirmation of God's entry into the mundane, everyday life of poor people, the world of creatures, the world of straw and rocks.[46]

## Mystery Plays

In the centuries following Francis, the English mystery play (or "miracle play") picked up and elaborated this earthy, visual approach to the nativity—and indeed the whole incarnate life and passion of Christ and the story of salvation, all the way back to Genesis. Lewis appreciated the way these plays dealt with sacred subjects yet combined them with earthy farce.[47] The plays were developed and performed as an extended series— in the case of the famous York cycle, on wagons scattered around town. Each play was mounted by one of the local craft guilds, and this itself grounded the drama in the realities of the workaday world. For example, in the York crucifixion play, the nailers' guild (who had the hereditary responsibility for the play) had the men prepare the cross and pound the nails through Christ's hands and feet as they complained in a rough and jocular manner of the difficulty and boredom of the work, oblivious to the divine significance of what they were doing.

In his *Life of Christ*, Bonaventure (1221–74) counsels: "You must direct your attention to these scenes of the Passion, as if you were actually present at the Cross, and watch the Crucifixion of our Lord with affection, diligence, love, and perseverance."[48] The plays helped their audiences do this by marrying the sublime and the ridiculous, heightening the bizarre reality of a God who becomes human and dies at the hands of those he created.

Lewis's friend Dorothy Sayers picked up that same riotous combination in her own *Man Born to Be King* and her several successful stage plays, drawing quite consciously from the mystery play tradition. Likewise, the wonderful legends of King Arthur and the Holy Grail, Chaucer's ribald *Canterbury Tales*, and many other works of medieval literature appeal directly to our imaginations in ways that mere doctrine or even Protestant worship just don't do. This earthy quality in Medieval literature surely arises at least in part from the period's understanding that the incarnation demands we encounter our world, as well as God, in visual, physical, and embodied ways. Without the imagination and its storehouse of images, we don't seem to really be doing business with an incarnate God. In many ways, that's what Lewis's whole body of fiction is about.

# 10

## Getting It Together

### Responding to Our Medieval Heritage and Reflecting on the Ascetic and Monastic Paths

In the incarnation, we have discovered a sort of culmination of this survey of medieval wisdom for today. This seems to be the central point around which other medieval themes converge and cohere. Fortuitously, this same theme of the incarnation seems to promise a solution to one of our biggest problems as modern Christians: our anemic view of what it means to be human. Yes, the incarnation of Christ launches the redemptive plan that leads to the cross, the tomb, the resurrection, and the ascension. But it is more. It is the Creator God entering his creation. And not only entering creation but entering *the part of creation that is us*. In the incarnation, God experiences us from the inside.

This stunning event exalts two things: first, the humanity of Christ and second, the humanity of humanity, of ourselves. When we really "get" the incarnation, it releases us to live *all* of life in light of Jesus Christ and to affirm our own humanness—our own materiality, our own affectivity, our own rationality, our own cultural creativity. The incarnation wipes away the gnostic super-spirituality that is a serious problem of modern evangelicalism.

The medievals "got" the incarnation with a particular acuteness that we can learn from, and it affected everything else they did. It allowed them to value their bodiliness (although not always their sexuality), affectivity, and rationality. It allowed them to value their culture, to keep Word and world, science and religion, together.

The incarnation is the linchpin of medieval theology and the linchpin of medieval spirituality.

We don't get this incarnational correction, of course, just from medievals; we get it from Scripture and from Christian tradition—the two-thousand-year, worshipful, moral tradition of exegesis of Scripture. But Christians who wish to grasp the incarnation again are fighting upstream, and a selective appropriation of medieval understandings may provide a powerful towline to assist us.

## Reclaiming Christ's Body in Our Worship and Work

How radical a separating wall stands between modern Protestants (in particular) and our common heritage in the incarnational faith of the Middle Ages? I've suggested one quite formidable aspect of that wall for evangelicals—our immediatism. But the barrier stretches back much farther in history. In a *crucial* (quite literally) sixteenth-century moment, a central symbol of the incarnation was removed forcibly from the church. This was the point at which some zealous Reformers went beyond tearing down paintings and smashing statues to take the very body of Christ off of the crucifix—thus (they thought) defending the church against idolatrous images and defending the resurrection. Left behind was (arguably) only an abstract symbol of a judicial transaction.

The difference between worshiping in a space where there is no body of Christ on the cross and worshiping in a space where there is a body of Christ on the cross is that in the latter space worshipers cannot ignore the humanity of Christ—nor, thus, of themselves. In that space, our humanity—bodiliness, affectivity, rationality, community, society, culture—always stands (no, hangs) before us in the person of, the body of, the humanity of Jesus Christ the Lord.

In a sense, this entire book tells the story of what happens when we lose our hold on the incarnation. Here is a personal example from my own life.

Over the past two years I have been involved in founding and running two different centers for reengagement between our faith and our work.[1] I have realized: *The reason we have to have such centers at Christian institutions of higher learning is that by losing a vivid sense of the incarnation, we have lost the sacredness of our own work.* This realization has taken on particular poignancy for me as three of my children have reached their twenties, with all the vocational searching of that age.

How can we understand how our daily work is informed by our identity in Christ? I believe we can make significant progress if we meditate on the incarnation as the medievals did. We should get up every morning and look at a painting, a sculpture, or an image representing Jesus Christ in his fleshly existence.

We should meditate not only on how Christ's precipitous descent into the flesh and blood of humanity made possible his sacrifice for our sins but also on how it raises up the value and wonder and splendor of our own humanity. We humans are not explained in a Darwinian sense by biology nor in a Kantian sense by morality. Nor even, as if we were one with the angels, by spirituality. No, we must hear again the truth Athanasius so staunchly defended, the medievals so lavishly celebrated, and modern imaginative writers such as C. S. Lewis captured in the only way it really can be captured, apart from worship—that is, in stories that speak to our imaginations. We were created in God's image, and when that image was stained and saddened by sin, *God became man so that we could become (again) gods*—and reflect (again) that image.

Protestant readers in particular may want to ask: Why do we skip over the incarnation and downplay the embodied, human Christ in our theology and devotion? And what would happen in our lives if we returned to those crucial elements of medieval Christian thought and practice? Must we leave behind entirely the wisdom of the medieval period? While that period birthed both lavish Marian devotion and the eucharistic theology of transubstantiation, it did so in an attempt to get as close as possible to the physical, embodied Christ. (What, after all, is the modern, questionable theology of an imminent "rapture" but the attempt to recapture that closeness, if only in our imaginings of the future?) If we did recapture the wisdom of the Middle Ages, then how could this medieval learning be reflected in Christian practice?

- Renewed emphasis on physical aspects of worship, such as art and architecture?
- Openness to affective/imaginative modes of devotion?
- Once and for all getting over the fear of so-called works-righteousness to live our ethics in compassionate, public (and of course theologically informed) ways?
- Reclaiming ascetic spiritual disciplines as practices that, though subject to abuse in the past, hold crucial benefits especially for those of us accustomed to First World comforts and temptations?

All of these questions and possible answers are worth considering as an "ancient-future" path from weakness to strength.

## What a Difference the Incarnation Makes

The incarnation underwrites every facet of the medievals' faith that I have explored in this book: their high valuation of tradition, their passion for theology, their detailed and intentional morality, their compassionate ministry to bodies as well as souls, their understanding of the sacramental quality of the created world, their investment of emotion into their devotion to the Lord, and their willingness to discipline their bodies in service of that same devotion.

What would happen if we recaptured these medieval values?

### Incarnation and Tradition

By putting the "body" back into our understanding of Christ and his church, we would again see how fitting it is for us to study and value our own traditions. We would recapture the wisdom and truth in those traditions while never separating this truth from the primary revelation of Scripture—as most medievals understood for most of the Middle Ages! Tradition is nothing less than wisdom and truth passed down from generation to generation throughout history. How apt is this? Christianity is at its core *not* a list of timeless principles or abstract teachings. It is uniquely a historical religion, based on a historical person and the words of two "testaments" that are full of historical accounts.

Nineteenth-century liberal theologians liked to talk about the "essence of Christianity"—usually little more than a set of ethical teachings summarized under the rubric "the Fatherhood of God and the brotherhood of man"[2]—that needed to be extricated from the centuries of errant doctrines and practices of a church that never seemed to get it right. (The problem with this approach, as a wit once observed, is that those nineteenth-century liberals, when they read Christian history, looked down the well of nineteen centuries and saw their own faces at the bottom.[3]) But there is no "essence" that is not clothed in history, lived out bodily by God incarnate, and then lived out by "his body," the human beings whom he has constituted ever since as his church. Christianity is all about the incarnation of God's Second Person as a first-century Jew from Nazareth, and then the incarnation of his truth in his living, embodied disciples in all ages and places.

Naturally, then, the New Testament is no philosophical book of moral teachings but rather the narrative of a life, a sacrifice, and a resurrection played out on the stage of history. And the book of Acts and the letters, following the model of the Old Testament's historical books, just picks up the story from Easter. Tradition is the extension of the story beyond Acts—the continued faithful, often flawed attempt of the church to wrestle with its identity in Christ. When we (in effect) shout Henry Ford's foolish gibe—"History is bunk!"—and throw aside the lessons of that history, we cut ourselves off at the knees spiritually, intellectually, and practically.

### Incarnation and Theology and Ethics

Renewed attention to the incarnation can also renew our passion for theology. Focusing devotionally on the world-changing entry of God into his own creation in human form also directs our minds to how amazing God's interactions with the world and humanity are. Bringing alive our reason, which is part of the precious image of God in us, we will begin to thirst again for knowledge of this active, present God. Theology, after all, is not the study of God in isolation from the world or humanity in isolation from God; rather, it is the study of the interactions between God and humanity. The incarnation is the flabbergasting fact in the middle of that.

When we appreciate the humanity of humanity and the ways in which Christ is incarnated not only in his own flesh as a first-century Jew from Nazareth but also (though in a different sense) in his church and in all humanity, our sense of the sacredness and dignity of others will be heightened. It will change the ways we treat others in our ordinary lives—in our workplaces, our families, and our societies.

There is an important corollary of this incarnational principle in ethics: incarnational morality is *ordinary morality* of the sort that C. S. Lewis portrayed so winsomely in the household of St. Anne in *That Hideous Strength*. By seeing our ethical lives in the light of our bodily limitations, illuminated further by God's own assumption and elevation of human nature, we are released from the pressure of perfection. We are released not *to* sin but rather *from* aspiring to the impossible: a life lived as if we do not have bodies ourselves—a perfectly godlike life. This is the mistake some make: to expect superhuman, super-spiritual exploits on the part of ourselves and other Christian people. This sort of super-spiritualization leads away from, rather than toward, a healthy and godly attention to the needs of others and the responsibilities of our relationships (a point to which I will return shortly).

There is a kind of moral integrity that comes from (re)uniting our two halves, the spiritual and the material, in reflection of the two natures of the incarnate Christ. People who knew Lewis could see that moral integrity in him. As his last secretary, Walter Hooper, reflects:

> I am sure [Lewis] was aware of his shortcomings, but to me he seemed closer to God than I had ever imagined a man could be. Most Christians seem to have two kinds of lives, their so-called "real" life and their so-called "religious" one. Not Lewis. The barrier so many of us find between the visible and the invisible was not there for Lewis. No one ever had less of a split personality.[4]

It is not, I think, a stretch to say that this quality of seamless integrity that Lewis's friend observed in him was at least greatly aided, if not forged, by Lewis's deep absorption of the wisdom of medieval faith.

### Incarnation and Compassion

A renewed incarnational awareness also gives us a renewed and particular energy toward compassionate ministry, as it did for twelfth- and thirteenth-century Christians in the "charitable revolution" of those centuries—and indeed as it did in the whole long Christian growth and development of the hospital and, more broadly, in all forms of compassionate ministry. The medieval Christian's acute awareness of the incarnation was not a theologically fuzzy, inward-turned "mysticism"; as they began to enter emotionally into the events of the passion—that horrific demonstration of God sharing our embodied suffering—the compassion for Jesus that this stirred in them "enabled them to perceive Jesus in other humans"[5] and to act compassionately for their benefit. The resulting works of mercy helped build a strong, humane center that held together medieval society. We may need something like this again, since one result of a false super-spirituality is to keep us from achieving that incarnational awareness that would impel us to compassionate ministry.

### Incarnation and Creation

Attention to the incarnation can renew our sense not only of our embodiedness but also of the wonder of creation, as the God who created the world has now entered and participated in it, and in the process gave creation a renewed dignity. The incarnation is also, as John of Damascus (ca. 675/76–749) argued during the eighth-century Byzantine iconoclastic controversies (and the church agreed with him and made his position dogma), the warrant for the sacramental use of human-made devotional items such as icons.

First, the incarnation prevents us once and for all from the temptation to talk about creation—or any part of creation—as if it is inherently evil. If it were inherently evil, then God could not have joined himself to it. As Herbert Butterfield says, "It has always been realized in the main tradition of Christianity that if the Word was made flesh, matter can never be regarded as evil in itself."[6] Darrel Amundsen strengthens the connection by observing that "individuals or groups (e.g., Gnostics, Manichaeans, Marcionites) on the periphery of Christianity who conceived of matter as inherently evil also balked at the doctrine of the Incarnation."[7]

Second, this raising up of creation was, in fact, the real and final purpose of the incarnation—as Lewis so profoundly reflects in his imagery of the "great dance" in *Perelandra* (quoted in the previous chapter in this book).

### Incarnation and Affective Devotion

As even a cursory study of medieval devotion amply demonstrates, their mystery plays, earthy Franciscan preaching, and imaginative reflection on the Gospels in an Ignatian or Kempean mode opened their hearts and increased their passion for God.

We have seen how, in the late medieval period, the suffering that Jesus underwent in the flesh drew people to him in a deeply human way and in an emotional way, and how it made people focus on him as a human with human experiences and on his mother as a human mother with human experiences. The *emotional* reality that God is "Immanuel"—he is with us in our very sufferings and will never leave or forsake us (Heb. 13:5; Deut. 31:6)—becomes so much more intense and real for people who take the incarnation seriously. Quite simply, reflection on the humanity of Christ draws us closer to the divinity of Christ as we "work out our salvation in fear and trembling" (Phil. 2:12), while God also works within us. An intensive awareness of this reality accounts for Margery Kempe's prophetic words to the archbishop: "Sir, you shall wish some day that you had wept as sorely as I."[8]

Margery's incarnational, "full boisterous" spirituality was just the opposite of our modern spiritual "flatlining." First, it may suggest that we would benefit from openness to what the eighteenth-century American theologian Jonathan Edwards calls "the religious affections."[9] Second, medieval affective piety, in its rootedness in the incarnation, may draw us back to reflection on the amazing love of Christ, who took on our sufferings as his own. Third, such a renewed, intense sense of the reality of Christ's humanity in the incarnation could lead us back into salutary medieval habits of visible, physical devotion.

## Why We Still Need the Ascetic and Monastic Traditions

As a heightened sense of Christ's humanity leads us to pay more attention to our own humanity, helping us realize the spiritual significance of our humanity and the things we do in the flesh, it will also lead us to a renewed spiritual discipline—perhaps an ascetic discipline such as is preserved in the monastic tradition.

This is not a minor point, though it may be one of the more uncomfortable truths medieval faith bequeaths to us. Living in a place and time more wealthy than any other in world history—deluged with enough inducements to materialism and hedonism to challenge the resolve of even the most frugal and disciplined—we urgently need to acquaint ourselves with the ascetic tradition of our faith. How easy it is to sit in front of a glowing screen, sipping an extra-large, high-fructose corn syrup beverage, after the manner of the bloated inmates on the Buy n Large starliner *Axiom* in the movie *Wall-E*.

To be honest, I don't *want* the ascetic tradition embodied in medieval monasticism to hold any truth for me. I want it to be wrong. And I suspect this is true of many moderns who dismiss this ascetic tradition without examining it, going no further than the Monty Python caricature of monks filing through the streets, intoning the missal passage *Pie Jesu Domine, dona eis requiem* and thwacking themselves on their foreheads with boards.[10]

In this final chapter, it is worth spending a bit of time looking at the *real* nature of the Christian ascetic tradition, especially in its medieval monastic form.

We may recoil, asking, "What makes us think monasticism has any answers to our modern problems?" Seriously, it's all so . . . medieval! Stone cloisters, hard beds, celibacy, voluntary poverty, rising every day at ungodly hours to chant psalms? Really? This is the balm for our ills? What modern person could take these strange disciplines seriously? What the heck is this "asceticism" anyway?

The word *askesis* means "training." Originating with the ancient Greeks, it was picked up by the apostle Paul, who insisted that he had to "beat his body"—endure some pain and deprivation—if he was to use that body to excel (1 Cor. 9:26–27).[11]

The church has always known that if we are to run the race of the Christian life well we must practice certain disciplines to keep our physical, emotional, and intellectual lives in check; some of these disciplines actually involve denying ourselves some of the good, God-given pleasures we might otherwise enjoy in those realms.

This important Christian idea is rooted in the classical philosophical understandings of the Platonists, who saw all of material life in two ways: as a reflection, although dim, of divine reality and also as a distraction used by the enemy of our souls. Picture, for example, a robber climbing over a fence and throwing a piece of meat to a pack of guard dogs to distract them from his own flesh long enough for him to rob the house.

As long as we are occupied by the lesser good, the enemy of our souls has successfully distracted us from the greater good, which is our created purpose. The watchdog's purpose is to clamp his jaws down on robbers. Our purpose is to embrace God—in the words of the Westminster Shorter Catechism (1646), "to glorify God and enjoy him forever." The pleasures of the flesh can distract us from that higher (and ultimately much more fulfilling) purpose. Therefore we need to discipline our fleshly desires. Lewis puts it this way:

> You and I have need of the strongest spell that can be found to wake us from the evil enchantment of worldliness which has been laid upon us for nearly a hundred years. Almost our whole education has been directed to silencing this shy, persistent, inner voice [the desire for something greater than what the material world can offer]; almost all our modern philosophies have been devised to convince us that the good of man is to be found on this earth.[12]

Indeed, one might even say that to be an ascetic is to recognize, affirm, and work with our humanness—to recognize the fact that we desire things that we should not desire or desire good things in wrong ways—not to completely cut off those desires but to redirect them toward God. *Askesis* is the training of our humanity toward God, not a masochistic exercise for the sake of the pain that it causes us or a complete elimination of bodily pleasures. It is the turning of our bodily desires toward the God who also took on a body. This was a central understanding of the medieval monastic tradition.

## Our Situation

The ascetic tradition goes over the heads of most modern Christians in part because we assume that life with God has little to do with life in the body. I've struggled with that myself since becoming a Christian; despite even years of advanced theological study, I have gained little clear sense of how faith should be changing such ordinary, bodily activities as my work, my leisure activities, or how I raise my family.

A friend of mine who is a marriage counselor in a practice known for sympathetically serving Christians tells what for him has become an all-too-familiar story. A couple comes in, and one of them has become so enamored with church that this individual wants to spend all of his or her time basking in the spiritual glow of the experiences they are having there. At home, this spouse is distant, curt, and dismissive of the needs of his or her partner, having become quite literally "so heavenly minded they are no earthly good." The result is a crisis in their marriage. The non-spirit-struck spouse feels abandoned and uncared for because his or her emotional needs are unmet. My friend calls this "super-spiritualizing."

When we ignore our own human, God-created needs and desires—treating them as irrelevant to the life of the spirit—we cannot see how the life of human desire, with all its working and earning and spending, loving and begetting and caring, is itself of value (deriving that value from the Creator God who said "it is good . . . it is good . . . it is very good" when making the material world and our own material bodies). If we believe the biblical doctrine of creation, we must also see the material, desiring life as a sacramental one whose proper effect is to lead us to honor and enjoy the God who made all of these good things.

The sacramental principle says that the embodied life contains much that can, if we are honest and open to our Creator God, lead us to him. But honesty about our humanness also reveals something else too—and this is where the ascetic principle joins the sacramental. Quite simply, it reveals that even for people of good will, who want to acknowledge and serve their Creator, the desires and goods of our embodied lives are *so darn distracting*. They have all the dangerous appeal that the Western tradition links to Homer's Sirens, who lured Odysseus with their song. If we let them—if we don't "lash ourselves to the mast" of some counterbalancing discipline—the pull of our material desires can become so strong that we live as if our real and final fulfillment lies in appeasing those desires rather than in pleasing and enjoying God. This is the obverse of a super-spiritualizing disregard for our material lives (the "gnostic" tendency, per chap. 7). It is the problem of materialism, which is idolatry of the material world.

I believe that an honest and open assessment of the Christian ascetic tradition, especially as embodied in early and medieval monasticism, can lead us away from both quasi-gnostic super-spirituality and hedonistic materialism. The sorts of ascetic discipline practiced by the monastics require a degree of honesty about our "desiring life" that few moderns actually possess.

## Some Clues from C. S. Lewis

C. S. Lewis might seem an unlikely guide to this final theme of asceticism and monasticism. True, he lived and worked for decades within the quasi-monastic culture of Oxford and Cambridge. But he also reveled in the material pleasures of ale, tobacco, and the raucous conviviality of the English pub. Surely he was no ascetic.

From early on though, as he struggled toward conversion, Lewis also appreciated the Christian ascetic tradition. In 1931 he took his famous late-night walk with his close friends J. R. R. Tolkien and Hugo Dyson and then, soon after, made a specific commitment to Christian belief while on his way to the zoo with his brother. Already at that time, and for years leading up to his conversion, Lewis contended mightily with his "flesh." Not surprisingly for a brilliant intellectual, the young Lewis's fleshliness often took the form of pride—which monastic fathers agree tends to beset those pressing in to achieve spiritual progress, and which the tradition agrees is the worst of the capital vices and the fountainhead of many others.

On January 30 of the previous year, Lewis wrote to Greeves, "What I feel like saying . . . is 'Things are going very, very well with me (spiritually).' On the other hand, one knows from bitter experience that he who standeth should take heed lest he fall, and that anything remotely like pride is certain to bring an awful crash."[13] He admitted that there seemed to be "no end" to his spiritual pride. He found in himself "depth under depth of self-love and self-admiration," which prevented him from "making even the faintest approach to giving up my own will: which as everyone has told us is the only thing to do."[14]

The struggle with self-will and pride (the deadliest of the seven deadly sins) drove the monastic ascetic quest for holiness. Lewis knew that, and he made the connection at the critical moment in his own spiritual journey. As God stripped away his pretenses and revealed his consequent need for self-denial, Lewis wrote to Barfield in mock exasperation: "Terrible things are happening to me. The 'Spirit' or 'Real I'[15] is showing an alarming tendency to become much more personal and is taking the offensive, and behaving just like God. You'd better come on Monday at the latest or I may have entered a monastery."[16]

Though of course he never did this, we see how strong this awareness of the importance of ascetic self-denial continued to be for Lewis as he lived out his new life in the Christian faith (and how he connected it, in his mind, to the monastic tradition). The following letter was written by Lewis to Barfield in the fall of 1938, as the storm clouds of World War II gathered overhead: "My dear Barfield," Lewis writes,

> What awful quantities of this sort of thing seem necessary to break us in, or, more correctly, to break us off. One thinks one has made some progress towards detachment . . . and begin[s] to realize, and to acquiesce in, the rightly precarious hold we have on all our natural loves, interests, and comforts: then when they are really shaken, at the very first breath of that wind, it turns out to have been all a sham, a field-day, blank cartridges.[17]

He continues:

> This is how I was thinking that night, about the war danger. I had so often told myself that my friends and books and even brains were not given me to keep: that I must teach myself at bottom to care for something else more . . . and I was horrified to find how *cold* the idea of really losing them struck. An awful symptom is that part of oneself still regards troubles as "interruptions" as if (ludicrous idea) the happy bustle of one[']s personal interests was our real [task or work],[18] instead of the opposite.[19]

He concludes, "Since nothing but these forcible shakings will cure us of our worldliness, we have at bottom reason to be thankful for them. We *force* God to surgical treatment: we won't (mentally) diet."[20]

In other words, God forces "troubles" on us because otherwise we will refuse to engage in the discipline (the *askesis*) that we need if we are to be weaned from our selfish interests.

Lewis derived (or at least strengthened) this insight from his reading of certain medieval devotional books. In particular, he studied closely three manuals of devotion that elaborated on the threefold mystical process of purgation, illumination, and union with God first described by Pseudo-Dionysius the Aeropagite (late fifth or early sixth century). These were Walter Hilton's *The Scale of Perfection* (ca. 1400), the anonymous *Cloud of Unknowing* (late 1300s), and the *Theologia Germanica* (1497), which Lewis had just finished reading for the first time when he wrote to Barfield about the "war danger."[21]

Two years after this letter to Barfield, Lewis wrote *The Problem of Pain*, in which he reflects at length on how suffering and self-denial can become parts of our training in holiness. In May of that year (1940), he wrote an essay for the *Guardian* in which he reflects that we can see the self in two ways. First, we can see it as "God's creature, an occasion of love and rejoicing; now, indeed, hateful in condition, but to be pitied and healed." But we can also see it as "that one self of all others which is called *I* and *me*, and which on that ground puts forward an irrational claim to preference."

This second, truly selfish claim, says Lewis, "is to be not only hated, but simply killed." Our struggle with egotism and self-preference is an "endless war," but even in the midst of that war, the wise Christian "loves and approves selves as such, though not their sins. The very self-love which he has to reject is to him a specimen of how he ought to feel to all selves; and he may hope that when he has truly learned (which will hardly be in this life) to love his neighbor as himself, he may then be able to love himself as his neighbor: that is, with charity instead of partiality."[22]

"The wrong asceticism," Lewis concludes, "torments the self: the right kind kills the selfness."[23] He put this personal understanding of the Christian ascetic vision into practice through regular use of such ascetic disciplines as fasting, meditation, and frequent prayer.[24]

## The Elements of Spiritual Mastery: Passion, Tradition, and Discipline

It may help us to see the value of ascetic self-denial if we take it as one species of a larger phenomenon. Consider the drive to achieve mastery in a human enterprise. How does a person master a skill? First, one needs to be passionately committed to a goal. Second, one needs to study and learn practical knowledge handed down in a tradition. Third, one needs to practice a discipline, both in the sense of foregoing various immediate gratifications in order to dedicate many hours to repetitive practice and in implementing a set of discrete "disciplines" (the particular repeated actions required by the craft).

Think of the progress of a young girl toward becoming a skilled violinist. First comes the passion: one day she hears a piece of music, and it pierces her heart with joy. At the beginning, she just wants to hear it again and again; then she wants to know how to make those beautiful sounds herself. And so she begins years of lessons and practice, giving herself to those two complementary means to mastery. She studies a tradition (musical knowledge) and practices an *askesis* (a life of training or discipline). Daniel Levitin argues that it takes ten thousand hours of practice to achieve elite mastery in any field.[25] Let's say that is so. Then when, as a young adult, the girl finally has poured into her goal those ten thousand hours, she achieves the desired mastery—the fulfillment of that passion that overcame her when she first heard those fateful notes.

### The Surprising First Principle of Asceticism: Passion

Passion is simply a necessary part of mastery in any field. The business world calls it a fire in the belly. Jeremiah locates it deeper; he calls it a "fire shut up in my bones" (20:9). The key thing that the "passion dimension" of Christian asceticism reveals is that this asceticism does not equal the hating of the body, nor is it an end in itself—as if we thought there was inherent virtue in fasting (*that* attitude was in fact one of Jesus's criticisms of the Pharisees): we don't stop with the physical deprivations of celibacy or fasting or voluntary poverty. Rather, asceticism is *for* something—*for* union with God, and the "abundant life" that Jesus talks about in John 10:10.[26]

If we are to proceed to the kind of spiritual discipline that makes us better Christians, we must keep before us the joy that Lewis made the central theme of his public theology. Like the mystical notes heard by the girl who decides to play the violin, only the power and bliss of serving God and experiencing his grace can sustain us in that discipline. There will of course be times when we do not feel that bliss—those "dark nights of the soul." But over the long haul, passion provides the fuel to get us where we need to go; teeth-gritting willpower is simply not enough.

For us it is finally as G. K. Chesterton says it was for Francis of Assisi: a love story, not a theory, that can spur us to heroic discipline.[27] Why have men and women throughout history worked countless hours in difficult, grinding jobs? To provide for their spouses and children whom they love. It is the same in our spiritual relationship with God and others. Without the prior love—the affective dimension (to return to the theme of chap. 8)—we will not and cannot effectively practice any spiritual discipline. Moreover, we will be in danger of becoming practical atheists, decoupling what we say we believe from how we actually live.

### The Third Principle of Spiritual Mastery: Discipline

Skipping over the second element of mastery, tradition (for which I made the case in chap. 3), I now turn to discipline. This talk of passion may make us think that what is required by the principle of asceticism is the single big, heroic action: casting ourselves into harm's way for the sake of our loved one (God). But wise teachers of the spiritual life remind us of something we (especially Protestant evangelicals) seem often to forget: our lives as Christians are not all about single, life-changing crisis experiences. The revivalistic imagery of sawdust-trail conversions and emotional "altar calls" may lead some modern Christians to seek a sudden, emotional experience as the solution to their ills, but that's not how it works.

John Wesley, to take just one example, reminds us that those powerful moments of repentance and coming to faith are just the "porch" or the "door" into the Christian life. The substance of the Christian life, which lasts as long as we live, is *holiness*. Wesley has a favorite phrase to explain holiness. He says it is *"having the mind of Christ and walking as he walked."*[28] Achieving that steady character in ourselves requires, in the motto Eugene Peterson borrows from Friedrich Nietzsche (1844–1900), "a long obedience in the same direction."[29] That is to say, the Christian life is an *askesis*—a life of training and discipline. There is a "longitude" to the concept. It is not a single event.

We need to rediscover a discipline that endures over time. If it takes ten thousand hours to learn mastery and if that rule applies to mastery of Christian discipleship, then we need to be aware that we are always doing more at work and at home—where, together, we spend most of our waking hours—than just creating products or services or running households. We are at the same time being re-created, ourselves, after the image of God. And we must join with God in that process, and that process is going to take much time and much self-conscious effort.

There are much worse guides to this particular kind of work than the medieval monastics. Monasticism was set up to provide all three essential components of mastery. We have seen (in chap. 8) how monastic mystics fostered a passion for Christ. In its constant reading, preparation of manuscripts, learning, and *lectio divina*, it was also soaking itself in the tradition—in particular, the moral sense of Scripture.[30] And the monks' life in community afforded ample opportunities to *practice* the virtues (humility and obedience being two of the most important in Benedict's Rule), doing the hard work required to gain spiritual and moral mastery. The monastics understood the need for passion, tradition, and discipline. Using all three, they trained themselves in a strong communal setting, guided by the development of the virtues through the absorption of Scripture, the reading of which was repeated again and again in community.

## A Potential Objection and the Role of Grace

Some readers may be nervous about the term "mastery" that I'm using here. Surely that's the wrong term for the spiritual life. What we're really after is *being* mastered by God, right? Doesn't this analogy of technical mastery risk making the Christian life a matter of earning salvation by works?

This objection shows that we have drifted into a misunderstanding of Reformation teaching that tags all moral effort as works-righteousness. By these lights, grace is *only* for forgiveness from guilt; it has nothing to do with spiritual growth. Says Dallas Willard, "All you have to do is open the pages of the New Testament and you see that this is far, far from the truth."[31]

From the very beginning, the monastic tradition understood this need for grace. The leaders and thinkers among the monks were not pull-yourself-up-by-the-bootstraps Pelagians. They "saw the whole process of man's perfectibility within the economy of divine grace."[32] The Christian tradition of *askesis* describes a way to work out our salvation in fear and trembling, in full awareness that it is God who works in us both to will and to do his good pleasure (Phil. 2:12–13). Grace is still the engine of our salvation, but it is not a paralyzing grace. It is not, as Dietrich Bonhoeffer insists, a "cheap grace."

When we turn to Bishop Athanasius's biography of the proto-monk Antony of Egypt (251–356), we find the bishop describing the monastic life as animated by twin energies. This double dynamic, learned from the apostles and early martyrs, consists on the one hand of near-heroic self-examination and self-exertion and on the other of God's gracious help from heaven through Christ—a duality that would shape all future monastic movements. The importance of both of these elements to the Christian life is the key theological point of the book, which became the pattern and manual for Christian monasticism East and West, as well as the compass of correction whenever a monastic group or tradition felt itself going off course and wanted to return to the purity of early understandings.

In other words, monasticism has always understood the human ascetic effort as working in synergy with the transformative energy of God's grace, through which the monks are saved from sin into blessedness.

## Why We Need Something like Monasticism

I'm not suggesting that we set up medieval monasteries across our twenty-first-century landscape. But we can take lessons from the monastic tradition, working toward effective modes of "discipline toward mastery" that fit our own contexts. Not everything about monasticism is about asceticism; there is also a strong communal wisdom embedded in the tradition—the emphasis on "life together" that Bonhoeffer picked up and implemented in his own experiment at Finkenwalde.[33]

Space does not allow a full treatment of the communal ascetic shape of medieval monasticism here. I will merely skim. At the heart of its dominant, Benedictine form are the "offices"—a daily round of liturgy that includes psalms and readings at specified hours.[34] The medieval Benedictines also practiced the slow, meditative reading of Scripture called *lectio divina*, the focus of which was "conversion of heart rather than intellectual curiosity."[35] Lacking personal Bibles, they memorized huge swaths of text. They prayed often, both individually and communally. They worked with their hands, mostly to keep their communities afloat economically—there was at least in Benedict's monasticism no real vision of a "spirituality of work" (a real gap, I think). The Benedictines served guests and, in many cases, the sick poor in their infirmaries. All of this was a part of the monk's, or nun's, *askesis* (holiness).

Now let me suggest several ways in which we need something like the monastic path of asceticism still today.

### Our Society Needs People Dedicated to Prayer

Antony's "eremitic" (solitary) style of monasticism did not win the day. Quickly, "coenobitic" (communal) forms sprang up and flourished, allowing people to mix their practice of solitary disciplines with a mutually supportive communal experience. Just as the Egyptians of Antony's day discovered that they needed "holy men" for many social reasons, so also medieval society discovered that it needed communally disciplined Christians. Medieval society came to identify three crucial sectors or groups in society, all valued for different reasons. The first two were "those who work" (farmers and craftsmen) and "those who fight" (knights and nobles). The third group was "those who pray" (monks); this group was so precious and desirable that by the late Middle Ages there was no medieval hamlet of even middling size that did not have three or more monasteries in it, all supported by the people through the church. I would argue that in the West today we have plenty of organized workers and organized fighters, but our number of organized pray-ers—certainly in the classic form of monastic communities—has trickled down to nearly nil, and it is hurting us.

### Community Is Necessary for Growth

After the ninth century, the overwhelmingly dominant form of coenobitic monasticism in the West was the Benedictine form. When I talk with students about Benedict's Rule, they are conflicted. Benedict insists on rules and disciplines, obedience both to a rule and to an abbot, and above all humility—all things that we free, democratic, individualistic Americans find quite difficult to grasp. Benedict structures his monastic Rule in a communal way that builds on the relational wisdom of Antony but feels constricting to us. "For Benedict, as for the whole tradition before him, the key to monastic life was accountability to God and to other people."[36]

Why is Benedict so insistent on a lifelong, obedient communal commitment?

*First, because we hear God through one another, and this requires not just attentiveness but obedience.*

Benedictine scholar Columba Stewart identifies two fundamental insights in the Rule: "the divine presence is everywhere," and "Christ is to be met in other people." These could be called the sacramental and the communal principles.[37] "The best kind of self-awareness," says Stewart, "the kind leading to deeper and deeper awareness of God, occurs in the company of others. For most people, to become truly individual before God requires immersion in the common life."[38]

At the center of this communal vision is the active principle of obedience, with its corresponding virtue of humility. Though Benedict's words on obedience may seem at times harsh and oppressive, everyone, including the abbot, must be obedient. "All alike stand before God and under the authority of the Rule."[39] It is clear that Benedict has in mind not a strictly hierarchical obedience but a mutual respect and service.[40] "'I have come not to do my own will, but the will of him who sent me' (RB 5.13, 7.32)."[41] To do obedience well, "love must be the driving force . . . (RB 5.2, 10). Without love, obedience is impossible."[42]

*Second, because we find Christ in each other.*

For Benedict, the incarnate presence of Christ is not limited to Jesus but may also be found in "the monastic superior, the sick, the guest, the poor"—really, just about everyone we meet. In practice, this took a particularly evocative form: when the monks processed into the church, two by two, for the daily worship service, they would stop at the altar and bow to each other as they would to Christ.[43]

*Third, because mutual obedience (accountability, we might say) mortifies the will and keeps us humble.*

Obedience is also important because it mortifies the will, which as Lewis points out is the crucial task at the heart of our spiritual discipline. Again, the corresponding virtue here is humility, which Benedict, like Francis later, stresses as the central Christian virtue (a sensible proposition, given that the tradition saw humility's obverse, pride, as the worst of sins—the fountainhead of the other six capital vices). Benedict's chapter on humility is the Rule's longest and, as Stewart notes, "in many ways its heart." Though the language is certainly harsh and could be misused by "those intent on oppression," the essence of Benedict's exhortations of humility "promise freedom from the burden of creating and maintaining a (false) public image."[44] Wise words in our Facebook era!

### We Are Physical Beings Who Need a Holistic Spiritual Discipline

Against the stereotypes, Christian asceticism still holds the body to be a good thing. Benedict's Rule demonstrates this, for example, in its close attention to the needs of a sick monk, who should be given more food and more sleep, as well as in its strong insistence on hospitality to the stranger and the guest.

We're talking about spiritual dieting here. And diets that work still allow you to eat things you like, but in a more controlled manner. Healthy Christian asceticism has always been spiritual dieting, not spiritual anorexia. Anorexia is an understanding of food as evil and disgusting; it is an aversion to food. Monks did not believe that marriage and procreation (for example) were evil. They believed that by doing without them, they could train themselves toward a higher good. And this is firmly grounded in Augustine's teaching that evil is not a substance; it is not something that is related to creation in any positive way. There's nothing created that's evil. It is the misuse of created things and the misdirection of affection—wrong degree, wrong object, etc.—that is evil.

Benedict, for instance, tried to pull people back from extremes of self-denial. Monks got fed more when they were sick because the body needs that food in order to be healthy. This shows that bodily health is a positive good for the monks, as we saw in chapter 6.

### We Need to Hold the Contemplative and Active Lives Together

Monasticism also blessed medieval society because the active and contemplative lives must be held together. It's a misunderstanding of medieval monasticism that there was no life of loving action to others involved—that it was all about curling up in a corner with Jesus. The charge that there's no evangelism is incorrect; there's an evangelism of example (or more accurately, in a nearly entirely Christian Europe, a *discipleship* of example). The same impulse that led streams of seekers out to the desert to see what the holy man Antony could teach them also led perhaps tens or hundreds of thousands of medieval laypeople to imitate the spiritual disciplines of the monks.

But the bigger charge that the monks did no active, public work is even more incorrect. The monastic establishment did a huge amount of economic work—farming, fishing, manufacturing of various foodstuffs for sale—that blessed and helped surrounding communities to flourish.[45] The monks engaged in prayer for people in the community. They practiced healing in their infirmaries. They followed Benedict's injunctions that prayer be balanced with work and that the brothers serve one another and outsiders in obedience, giving hospitality to all who asked and thereby hosting Christ in the other. This was the most intensive and loving kind of active service, balancing and feeding the monks' contemplative lives. In all of these spheres of activity, the monks followed the insight of that grand theorist of the mixed life (active and contemplative), Gregory the Great, who came to believe and teach that married, publicly active people could become just as spiritually adept as the cloistered, celibate monastics. As a result, many laypeople in the medieval period grabbed hold of that vision and adapted the monastic disciplines for their own busy lives.

### We Need Help with Virtue and Vice

One genius of monasticism is the way it actualizes Aristotle's description of ethics, which recognizes that without long practice forming our habits, virtue cannot become effective in our lives. Medieval monks read Scripture all the time, and they focused on its moral sense. But a man who reads Scripture and goes away and does not do it is like a man who looks in a mirror and goes away and immediately forgets what he looks like—it's not an effective use of the moral understanding of Christianity.

And so monastic discipline went beyond just reading and became a training ground for the virtues. Whether we adapt monastic ways of practicing virtue or find some other mode, spiritual-ethical discipline is crucial, not optional. This is because our interactions with our desires and with the material world are so fraught and so difficult because we fall to temptation in so many ways.

If they've ever been needed, the moral insights of the monastic implementation of our ascetic heritage are needed today. In Ron Sider's *The Scandal of the Evangelical Conscience*, we see that Protestant evangelicals (to take just one representative Christian group) are morally challenged. There's no real difference in how we live compared with how others live. The divorce rates are similar. Obesity rates are similar. We fall in with the national averages in using our discretionary money for ourselves rather than spending it charitably. All of these are moral and spiritual problems with their roots in our inability, or unwillingness, to discipline our bodies, appetites, and desires.

## A Stalled Attempt: The Modern "Spiritual Disciplines" Movement

One modern pushback on these realities is the movement that Richard Foster, Dallas Willard, Eugene Peterson, and Jim Houston started back in the 1970s. Each of these men realized that this lack of discipline is a serious problem in our church culture and has tried to guide us in reorienting ourselves toward God through "spiritual disciplines."

The movement was certainly popular. Foster's *Celebration of Discipline* sold millions of copies, indicating that we are aware of the problem. We know that we need to attend to ascetic disciplines if we are not to be spiritually flabby and morally weak.

But the movement ran aground even as seminary programs in "spiritual formation" multiplied. It was certainly not a bad thing to have the problem of anemic spiritual formation addressed in the training of pastors and other church-paid ministry workers. But this practical study has never been well integrated with the important work of seminary theological and biblical studies departments. In other words, seminary programs in theology and biblical studies have gone merrily on their way, teaching an orthodoxy ("right belief") separated from the orthopathy ("right feeling" or "right passion") and orthopraxy ("right practice") that students may encounter in the few token spiritual formation classes they take.[46] This leaves students without a strong sense of how that affective and practical formation might be grounded in—and vital to!—the biblical and theological traditions that are placed on the throne of seminary training.[47]

To recap, my argument in this discussion of asceticism and monasticism has been that we will continue to fail to make the effort necessary to practice appropriate ascetic disciplines unless we have (1) something of the passion for Christ that animated the monks and (2) a strong traditional foundation on which to build our practice. I have been trying in this book to describe the foundation the medievals had for this and other kinds of practice: their passion for theological knowledge, their understanding of incarnation and creation, the balance they held between Word and world, their whole-person devotion, and so on. We need both the passion *and* the tradition if we are to do the discipline.

To be blunt: this truth may point the way to a truer, more effective integration of spiritual formation within the curriculum of our theological schools. When we see that many Protestant leaders, like my pastor whose question I could not answer at the beginning of chapter 5, do not know how to put a Christian ethic into practice[48] or how to lead their followers out of, in Willard's phrase, their "grace paralysis," then it is time to make a serious attempt to address our modern misunderstandings of Reformation teachings on grace.

In short, we are being kept from applying the practical insights of medieval monasticism by a vague sense that whatever the Reformation was about, it was about dismantling human effort–based understandings of salvation— and that the very viper's nest of such understandings was monasticism.

But though there is truth in this suspicion, it obscures another precious truth: monasticism, as we have seen, *did* carry with it a robust Augustinian/ Pauline priority of grace, right alongside its essential training (*askesis*) in Christian virtue. With nothing to put in place of that practical monastic wisdom today—though the Pietists tried to replace it with new disciplines, as did the Puritans—we fail both to practice and to teach necessary spiritual disciplines and develop necessary Christian virtues.

Our hyper-theological seminary training is missing the point. In our moral lives we do not, as a rule, understand first and then proceed to act out of that understanding. We are, on the contrary, "trained up" over a long period of time in the midst of a community of practice, with the positives and negatives mixed together. That training becomes deeply embedded in our hearts (our affective lives or "chests," as Lewis puts it in *The Abolition of Man*). We act out of that training automatically and indeed passionately, applying moral reasoning only after the fact to rationalize about what we have done and the reasons we have done it.[49]

Therefore, since no straight line exists between an intellectual understanding of morality and the application of that understanding in making us better people, we must ask: How do we in the church get past "mere orthodoxy" to orthopathy and orthopraxy? What is the training? What are the disciplines? I suggested in chapter 3 that part of the answer must be that we imbue ourselves in the Christian tradition, and no enterprise looms larger in medieval Christian tradition than monasticism.

## Where We Are Now and What's Next

Though so many of us yearn to be deeply rooted in Christ in a way that reflects his holiness and to share this rooted, holy life with a close community, we simply find this hard to do in the modern West. Our culture pushes us to strive for individual fulfillment, to consume more and more, and to spend much of our lives working to pay for that consumption. The result is a world of constant mobility, alienation, and loneliness. Quasi-monastic movements like the Catholic ecclesial communities reveal a deep desire for connectedness, a sense not only that we need to live a regular, disciplined life of devotion to God but also that we can't do it alone.

In Protestant circles, this monastic impulse can be seen especially in the phenomenon of "intentional communities." Among these, the self-described "new monastics" have taken their cue from philosopher Alasdair MacIntyre. In his influential 1981 book *After Virtue*,[50] MacIntyre compares the state of the West to the decadence of the late Roman Empire and calls for "another—doubtless very different—St. Benedict." In 1998, Jonathan R. Wilson picked up MacIntyre's ideas and put them into a more explicitly Christian form in *Living Faithfully in a Fragmented World*.[51] He fleshes out a call for a "new monasticism" that will allow the church to truly be the church in this troubling, fragmented age. In 2015, conservative columnist and author Rod Dreher echoes MacIntyre's twenty-five-year-old call for a "Benedict Option," giving examples of two modern Christian communal experiments that draw from monastic wisdom: a Catholic group in Clear Creek, Oklahoma, and an Antiochian Orthodox group in Eagle River, Alaska.[52]

In a time when it seems (to Wilson and the new monastics) that "many parts of the church are sinking with the culture and doing so without any resistance,"[53] Benedict's wisdom has again become a fount of inspiration and guidance. In *School(s) for Conversion: 12 Marks of a New Monasticism*[54] (which emerged from a 2004 meeting of "new monastic" communities), leaders came to the conclusion that at least *some* Christians must engage in *some* form of separation—not only from the "culture at large" but also from the increasingly compromised church—to model a life of true devotion and obedience to Christ. In this, they imitate

Benedict, who wrote in his Rule, "You should become a stranger to the world's ways."[55]

But as we've seen historically, monastics have not stopped at separation—nor do these "new monastics." Benedict founded a monastic way in which hospitality to the stranger and the needy is a prophetic witness to the world. Thus these new quasi-monastic communities have dedicated themselves not only to contemplative disciplines and submission to a communal rule but also to solidarity with the poor, racial reconciliation, and peacemaking.

## Passing Fad or Promising Future?

Of course, members of new communities, both Catholic and Protestant, are aware that this current love affair with monastic forms of worship and life can amount to another unhelpful fad, with people running after books and retreats. A few candles and a few chanted prayers do not a prophetic community make.

Church of the Servant King's Jon Stock says, "It's awful hard for us Westerners not to approach Benedict as another technique, another consumable, another path to self-actualization."[56] Stock also admits that the new monasticism, focused as it often is on social activism, can lose its connection to the larger church and to worship practices anchored in the church—a concern shared by the Roman Catholic hierarchy. Asbury Seminary's Christine Pohl admits that Benedict's four pillars—"life under a rule, life lived in commitment to a particular people and place, obedience, and ongoing conversion"—present a challenge to modern Western Christians, particularly because of our "wariness of vows and commitments, and our individualistic and mobile lifestyles."[57]

Time will tell whether the "new monastic" communities will survive, whether the traditional Benedictine monasteries will continue to thrive, and what new forms of countercultural, prayerful, prophetic community will arise to inspire Christians and shake the culture. But what is clear is that if we can get beyond our modern hubris—the "chronological snobbery" that assumes we have all the best answers and nothing to learn from those benighted souls who lived ages ago—and humble ourselves to sit at the feet of those strange, robed figures, the monks, we may learn much to our own edification and blessing.

## A Parting Word from C. S. Lewis

My exploration into medieval faith via C. S. Lewis has led us to a central truth: we have forgotten the flabbergasting wonder of an incarnate God—a God who has taken on humanity in Jesus. And because we have not properly valued the precious humanity of Christ, we have also not valued the precious humanity of humanity—of ourselves and also of our neighbors, the work we do, the culture we create through that work, our struggles and suffering, and especially our dignity and worth as unique creations of God.

Lewis once pictured in unforgettable terms what it would mean for our relationship with other human beings (and thus with culture) if we regained this incarnational truth today. In a single sermon he shows us what will happen if we truly see Christ incarnated not only in Jesus but also, following Benedict and the long line of Christian hospital workers, in all people. With this I will close, from the conclusion of Lewis's sermon "The Weight of Glory"—a powerful section that draws so much from the medieval mind-set Lewis inhabited as a native, that he even slips into ecclesiastical Latin in the final sentence:

> It is a serious thing to live in a society of possible gods and goddesses, to remember that the dullest and most uninteresting person you talk to may one day be a creature which, if you saw it now, you would be strongly tempted to worship. . . . There are no *ordinary* people. You have never talked to a mere mortal. . . . It is immortals whom we joke with, work with, marry, snub, and exploit. . . . Next to the Blessed Sacrament itself, your neighbour is the holiest object presented to your senses. If he is your Christian neighbour he is holy in almost the same way, for in him also Christ *vere latitat* [truly hides]—the glorifier and the glorified, Glory Himself, is truly hidden.[58]

# Notes

### Chapter 1 My Angle of Approach

1. I remember also T. H. White and Lloyd Alexander—although those have not impacted my adult faith as have the first three mentioned here.

2. *Patron Saints for Postmoderns: 10 from the Past Who Speak to Our Future* (Downers Grove, IL: InterVarsity, 2009).

3. See Lewis's comments in *The Screwtape Letters* concerning "historicism," which are noted in chap. 3.

4. Ian Boyd, in "Chesterton's Medievalism," *Studies in Medievalism: Inklings and Others and German Medievalism* 3 (Winter/Spring 1991): 243–55, has this to say:

[Chesterton] insists on the paradox that genuine medievalism is closely connected to contemporary . . . issues, declaring roundly that medieval history is useless unless it is also modern history, and mocking both the romantic antiquarian who haunts Melrose by moonlight and the Don Quixote figure who fails to understand his own age. But always Chesterton insists that the sign of genuine medievalism is an ability to see the contemporary world with fresh vision. In Chesterton's view, Cobbett, Carlyle, Hood, Ruskin, and Kenelm Digby are true medievalists, because when they look to a medieval past, whether real or imaginary, they look to it only in order to understand better their own age. The false medievalist is recognized by his blindness to the problems of his own day. (246–47)

5. See the recent admission of Willow Creek leadership that they have failed in the area of discipleship, "Willow Creek Repents?," *Christianity Today*, October 18, 2007. www.christianitytoday.com/le/2007/october-online-only/willow-creek-repents.html. For an analysis of the first two phases I mention, rational apologetics and pragmatic programs, see Robert E. Webber, *The Younger Evangelicals: Facing the Challenges of the New World* (Grand Rapids: Baker Books, 2002).

6. Jaroslav Pelikan, *The Vindication of Tradition* (New Haven: Yale University Press, 1984), 65.

7. Phoebe Palmer, *The Way of Holiness, with notes by the way: being a narrative of religious experience resulting from a determination to be a Bible Christian* (London: Alexander Heylin, 1856), 1.

8. www.merriam-webster.com/dictionary/immediatism.

9. C. S. Lewis, *Surprised by Joy* (New York: Harcourt, 1955), 207.

10. In a talk given by MacIntyre at Harvard in the mid-1990s, attended by the author.

11. George M. Marsden, "Presbyterians and the Truth," chap. 8 in *Fundamentalism and American Culture* (New York: Oxford University Press, 1980).

12. Martin Luther, *Prelude on the Babylonian Captivity of the Church* (October 1520), www.ccel.org/ccel/luther/first_prin.v.iii.html.

13. Jaroslav Pelikan, *The Christian Tradition: A History of the Development of Doctrine* (Chicago: University of Chicago Press, 1971), 1:330.

14. Anne T. Fraker, in her summary of Perry Miller's *The New England Mind: The Seventeenth Century* (New York: Macmillan, 1939), in Fraker, *Religion and American Life: Resources* (Urbana: University of Illinois Press, 1989), 94–95.

15. Nathan Hatch, *The Democratization of American Christianity* (New Haven: Yale University Press, 1989).

16. Perry Miller's term, in *The New England Mind: The Seventeenth Century* (New York: Macmillan, 1939).

17. David W. Bebbington, *Evangelicalism in Modern Britain: A History from the 1730s to the 1980s* (London: Unwin Hyman, 1989), 2–17. Related to this observation is the important secondary point that Bebbington's "crucicentrism" (cross-centeredness) is not currently universal among evangelicals—particularly if one includes Pentecostal groups, which still account for a hefty percentage of members in the National Association of Evangelicals. Among many of these, "pneumocentrism" (Spirit-centeredness) has often replaced crucicentrism to a great degree. Pentecostal (or charismatic) styles of worship have deeply influenced much of modern white evangelicalism since the 1970s, so this is not a minor point.

18. Bruce Hindmarsh, "Is Evangelical Ecclesiology an Oxymoron? A Historical Perspective," in *Evangelical Ecclesiology: Illusion or Reality*, ed. John G. Stackhouse (Grand Rapids: Baker Academic, 2003), 15–38.

19. Ibid., 15.

20. Evangelical Anglican J. I. Packer argues that evangelicals are not as stunted *in theory* in their ecclesiology as they are often portrayed, though they may fail to live up to the theory in practice. See J. I. Packer, "A Stunted Ecclesiology?" in *Ancient and Postmodern Christianity: Paleo-Orthodoxy in the 21st Century—Essays in Honor of Thomas C. Oden*, ed. Kenneth Tanner and Christopher A. Hall (Downers Grove, IL: InterVarsity, 2002), 120–27. An interesting footnote: the Anglican communion shares its centering in worship with Eastern Orthodoxy, constructing a bridge across which a few young evangelicals in the twentieth and twenty-first centuries have felt comfortable walking—right into Orthodoxy. According to some Wesley scholars, this affinity is not without substance or precedent, as Wesley is supposed to have been influenced deeply by certain Eastern fathers.

21. See Chris Armstrong, "The Rise, Frustration, and Revival of Evangelical Spiritual Ressourcement," *Journal of Spiritual Formation & Soul Care* 2, no. 1 (2009): 113–21.

22. Richard Foster, in phone interview (2008) conducted by Chris Armstrong.

23. On this, see, for example, *Christianity Today* editor Mark Galli's *Beyond Smells and Bells: The Wonder and Power of Christian Liturgy* (Brewster, MA: Paraclete, 2008); Robert Webber, *Evangelicals on the Canterbury Trail: Why Evangelicals Are Attracted to the Liturgical Church* (1985; repr., New York: Morehouse, 2012); Robert Webber, "The Convergence Movement," *The Christian Century* 99 (1982), quoted in Robb Redman, *The Great Worship Awakening: Singing a New Song in the Postmodern Church* (San Francisco: Jossey-Bass, 2002), 78–80; Elmer L. Towns and Vernon M. Whaley, *Worship through the Ages: How the Great Awakenings Shape Evangelical Worship* (Nashville: B&H Academic, 2012).

24. Dallas Willard, *The Spirit of the Disciplines: Understanding How God Changes Lives* (New York: HarperOne, 1999), 20 (emphasis in original).

25. Ibid., 24.

26. Adolf Harnack, *The Mission and Expansion of Christianity in the First Three Centuries*, trans. and ed. James Moffatt (Gloucester, MA: Peter Smith, 1972).

27. James K. A. Smith points to the mediated, communal texture of our whole lives in his concept of "secular liturgies" in *Desiring the Kingdom: Worship, Worldview, and Cultural Formation* (Grand Rapids: Baker Academic, 2009).

28. A stance grounded, again, in commonsense realist epistemology.

29. T. S. Eliot, "Tradition and the Individual Talent" (1920), www.poetryfoundation.org/learning/essay/237868.

30. Or to use a now-archaic phrase once hurled at the lively early Methodists, "enthusiasm."

31. Dante Alighieri, *The Inferno*, canto 3, line 18, trans. Robert Hollander and Jean Hollander (New York: Anchor Books, 2002), 47.

32. Lewis posited the importance of this moment of separation from the Great Western Tradition in his 1954 inaugural address as Chair of Medieval and Renaissance Literature at Cambridge University, "*De Descriptione Temporum*" (1954), in *Selected Literary Essays*, ed. Walter Hooper (Cambridge: Cambridge University Press, 1969).

33. Bernard McGinn (*Growth of Mysticism: Gregory the Great through the 12th Century* [New York: Crossroad, 1996]), tells us that, in the Middle Ages, the writings of Gregory the Great were more prominent than those of any other postbiblical author.

34. Carole Straw, *Gregory the Great: Perfection in Imperfection* (Berkeley: University of California Press, 1991), 50.

35. Gerard Manley Hopkins, "God's Grandeur," in *The Major Works: Including All the Poems and Selected Prose*, ed. Catherine Phillips (New York: Oxford University Press, 2002), 128.

36. C. S. Lewis, *The Discarded Image: An Introduction to Medieval and Renaissance Literature*, Canto Classics (Cambridge: Cambridge University Press, 1994), 204.

37. Ibid., 112.

38. Ibid., 115.

39. Lewis makes the following statement in *English Literature in the Sixteenth Century, Excluding Drama*, ed. F. P. Wilson and Bonamy Dobree, Oxford History of English Literature (New York: Oxford University Press, 1954):

> High abstractions and rarified artifices jostled the earthiest particulars. . . . They talked more readily than we about large universals such as death, change, fortune, friendship, or salvation; but also about pigs, loaves, boots, and boats. The mind darted more easily to and fro between that mental heaven and earth: the cloud of middle generalizations, hanging between the two, was then much smaller. Hence, as it seems to us, both the naivety and the energy of their writing. . . . They talk something like angels and something like sailors and stable-boys; never like civil servants or writers of leading articles. (62)

40. Lewis, *Discarded Image*, 216.

41. Thomas Okay, Saint Cardinal Bonaventure, E. Gurney Salter, Brother Leo, and Robert W. Steele, *"The Little Flowers" and The Life of St. Francis with the "Mirror of Perfection"* (London: J. M. Dent & Sons, 1912), 61.

42. Aelred of Rievaulx, *Spiritual Friendship*, trans. Lawrence C. Braceland, ed. Marsha L. Dutton (Collegeville, MN: Liturgical Press, 2010), 73.

43. Margery Kempe, *The Book of Margery Kempe* (New York: Penguin, 1994), passim.

44. Louis Bouyer, quoted by Howard G. Hageman, "Reformed Spirituality," in *Protestant Spiritual Traditions*, ed. Frank C. Senn (Eugene, OR: Wipf & Stock, 1986), 68.

### Chapter 2  C. S. Lewis—A Modern Medieval Man

1. That's a jousting reference, for you romantics. "The 'lists' were barriers which defined the battlefield in a [jousting] tournament," www.medieval-life-and-times.info/medieval-knights/medieval-jousting-terms.htm.

2. C. S. Lewis, "The Alliterative Metre," in *Selected Literary Essays*, ed. Walter Hooper, Canto Classics (Cambridge: Cambridge University Press, 1969), 24.

3. Michael Ward, *Planet Narnia: The Seven Heavens in the Imagination of C. S. Lewis* (New York: Oxford University Press, 2010).

4. C. S. Lewis, *Surprised by Joy: The Shape of My Early Life* (London: Harcourt, 1955), 35.

5. C. S. Lewis, "Shelley, Dryden, and Mr Eliot," in Hooper, *Selected Literary Essays*, 203.

6. Michael Ward, "The Son and Other Stars: Christology and Cosmology in the Imagination of C. S. Lewis" (PhD diss., St. Mary's College, 2005), 70.

7. Dorothy L. Sayers, introduction to *The Divine Comedy 1: Hell*, trans. Dorothy L. Sayers (Harmondsworth, UK: Penguin, 1949), 11.

8. C. S. Lewis, letter to Leo Baker, 28 April 1935, in *The Collected Letters of C. S. Lewis*, vol. 2, *Books, Broadcasts, and War 1931–1949*, ed. Walter Hooper (London: HarperCollins, 2004), 161–62.

9. C. S. Lewis, letter to Arthur Greeves, 1 November 1916, in *The Collected Letters of C. S. Lewis*, vol. 1, *Family Letters, 1905–1931*, ed. Walter Hooper (London: HarperCollins, 2004), 244.

10. "Reason is the natural organ of truth, but imagination is the organ of meaning." C. S. Lewis, "Bluspels and Flalansferes: A Semantic Nightmare," in Hooper, *Selected Literary Essays*, 265.

11. Lewis, *Surprised by Joy*, 225 (emphasis in original).

12. C. S. Lewis, "Meditation in a Toolshed," in *God in the Dock* (1970; repr., Grand Rapids: Eerdmans, 2014), 230–34.

13. C. S. Lewis, *The Discarded Image: An Introduction to Medieval and Renaissance Literature* Canto Classics (Cambridge: Cambridge University Press, 1994), 5.

14. Ibid., 10.

15. Dennis Danielson, "Intellectual Historian," in *Cambridge Companion to C. S. Lewis*, ed. Robert MacSwain and Michael Ward (New York: Cambridge University Press, 2010), 50.

16. Ibid., 43.

17. Ibid.

18. Gilbert Meilaender, "On Moral Knowledge," in *Cambridge Companion to C. S. Lewis*, 124–25.

19. Ibid., 129.

20. Cf. Robert Louis Wilken's understanding of early Christian morality as modified classical (pagan) morality in his *Spirit of Early Christian Thought: Seeking the Face of God* (New Haven: Yale University Press, 2005).

21. Ward, *Planet Narnia*.

22. Marsha Daigle-Williamson, *Reflecting the Eternal: Dante's Divine Comedy in the Novels of C. S. Lewis* (Peabody, MA: Hendrickson, 2015).

23. Lyle W. Dorsett, "C. S. Lewis and the Cowley Fathers," *Cowley* 32 (Winter 2006): 11.

24. Ibid.

25. C. S. Lewis, letter to Rhona Bodle, 3 November 1949, in *Yours, Jack: Spiritual Direction from C S Lewis*, ed. Paul F. Ford (New York: HarperOne, 2008), 146.

26. David Downing, *Into the Region of Awe* (Downers Grove, IL: InterVarsity, 2005), 92.

27. Ibid., 71.

28. C. S. Lewis, letter to Arthur Greeves, 11 December 1944, in *Collected Letters of C. S. Lewis*, vol. 3, *Narnia, Cambridge and Joy*, ed. Walter Hooper (New York: HarperSanFrancisco, 2007), 1555.

29. Downing, *Into the Region of Awe*, 71.

30. Ibid., 72.

31. C. S. Lewis, *Letters to Malcolm: Chiefly on Prayer* (New York: Harcourt, Brace & World, 1964), 82; cited in Downing, *Into the Region of Awe*, 72.

32. Downing, *Into the Region of Awe*, 73–74.

33. Lewis, *Letters to Malcolm*, 108.

34. C. S. Lewis to Sister Penelope, 17 September 1963, in Warren H. Lewis, *Letters of C. S. Lewis* (London: Geoffrey Bles, 1966), 307.

35. Lewis, *Collected Letters*, 1:857.

36. C. S. Lewis, *Commentary on Arthurian Torso by Charles Williams* (Oxford: Oxford University Press, 1948), 116.

37. C. S. Lewis, preface to *The Hierarchy of Heaven and Earth: A New Diagram of Man in the Universe*, by D. E. Harding (New York: Harper & Brothers, 1952), 9.

38. Sister Mary J. Beattie, "The Humane Medievalist: A Study of C. S. Lewis' Criticism of Medieval Literature" (PhD diss., University of Pittsburgh, 1967), 30–31.

## Chapter 3 Getting Rooted: Tradition as Source of Truth

1. This and the following twelve paragraphs are adapted from Chris R. Armstrong, "The Future Lies in the Past," *Christianity Today* (cover article), February 8, 2008, 22–29. Used with permission.

2. Robert E. Webber, preface to *Common Roots: The Original Call to an Ancient-Future Faith*, ePub ed. (Grand Rapids: Zondervan, 2009).

3. Robert E. Webber, *The Younger Evangelicals: Facing the Challenges of the New World* (Grand Rapids: Baker Books, 2002), 82.

4. Daryl Charles, "Evangelical Manifesto," *re:generation quarterly* 7, no. 3 (Fall 2001), a review of Robert E. Webber, *Ancient-Future Faith: Rethinking Evangelicalism for a Postmodern World* (Grand Rapids: Baker, 1999) and D. H. Williams, *Retrieving the Tradition and Renewing Evangelicalism: A Primer for Suspicious Protestants* (Grand Rapids: Eerdmans, 1999); http://www.ctlibrary.com/rq/2001/fall/7337.html.

5. D. H. Williams, "*Similis et Dissimilis:* Gauging Our Expectations of the Early Fathers," in *Ancient Faith for the Church's Future*, ed. Mark Husbands and Jeffrey P. Greenman (Downers Grove, IL: InterVarsity, 2008), 69.

6. This book is a journalistic exploration of why young Christians are returning to traditional forms of religion, especially Catholic, Protestant, and Jewish.

7. Richard Lovelace, "A Call to Historic Roots and Continuity," in *The Orthodox Evangelicals: Who They Are and What They Are Saying*, ed. Robert Webber and Donald G. Bloesch (Nashville: Thomas Nelson, 1978), 43–67, quote at p. 45.

8. J. I. Packer, "A Stunted Ecclesiology?," in *Ancient and Postmodern Christianity: Paleo-Orthodoxy in the 21st Century—Essays in Honor of Thomas C. Oden*, ed. Kenneth Tanner and Christopher A. Hall (Downers Grove, IL: InterVarsity, 2002), 120–27. Packer argues that the ecclesiological *thought* of evangelicals has been sufficient; it is the *practice* that has been stunted. I suspect that Packer's own British evangelical Anglican roots shield him from the sort of sheer ideological antitraditionalism of Hatch's nineteenth-century American revivalists, which is still very much alive in many corners of American evangelicalism today.

9. I will continue to use the term "Great Tradition" to refer to the common inheritance of all orthodox Christians—that is, all Christians in the three confessions: Protestant, Catholic, and Orthodox—who together draw from the same well of teachings handed down from the ancient and medieval church fathers, formulated through councils and their creeds. This common heritage is what C. S. Lewis calls "mere Christianity." For modern ecumenical usage of this term, see, e.g., *Reclaiming the Great Tradition: Evangelicals, Catholics & Orthodox in Dialogue*, ed. James S. Cutsinger (Downers Grove, IL: InterVarsity, 1997); and David S. Dockery and Timothy George, *The Great Tradition of Christian Thinking: A Student's Guide*, Reclaiming the Christian Intellectual Tradition Series (Wheaton: Crossway, 2012).

10. C. S. Lewis, *The Screwtape Letters*, in *The C. S. Lewis Signature Classics* (San Francisco: HarperOne, 2007), 263–65 (emphasis added).

11. C. S. Lewis, *Surprised by Joy* (New York: Harcourt, 1955), 206.

12. C. S. Lewis, *The Discarded Image: An Introduction to Medieval and Renaissance Literature*, Canto Classics (Cambridge: Cambridge University Press, 1994), 200.

13. C. S. Lewis, *Surprised by Joy*, 207–8.

14. C. S. Lewis, "Learning in War-Time," in *The Weight of Glory* (1949; repr., New York: HarperCollins, 2001), 47–63.

15. James Patrick, "The Heart's Desire and the Landlord's Rules: C. S. Lewis as Moral Philosopher," in *The Pilgrim's Guide: C. S. Lewis and the Art of Witness*, ed. David Mills (Grand Rapids: Eerdmans, 1999), 79.

16. Ibid., 83.

17. Ibid., 84, quoting Lewis, "We Have No 'Right to Happiness,'" in *God in the Dock* (1970; repr., Grand Rapids: Eerdmans, 2014), 355.

18. C. S. Lewis, "*De Descriptione Temporum*," in *Selected Literary Essays*, ed. Walter Hooper, Cantos Classics (Cambridge: Cambridge University Press, 1969), 12.

19. C. S. Lewis, "Learning in War-Time," in *Weight of Glory*, 58–59.

20. C. S. Lewis, introduction to *St. Athanasius on the Incarnation*, trans. Sister Penelope Lawson, rev. ed. (1944; repr., London: A. R. Mowbray, 1953), 3.

21. Ibid., 4.

22. Ibid., 5.

23. Ibid.

24. Ibid., 9.

25. Ibid.

26. Lewis, *Discarded Image*, 76.

27. In C. S. Lewis, *The Allegory of Love*, Canto Classics (Cambridge: Cambridge University Press, 2013), 57.

28. Samuel Joeckel, "C. S. Lewis, Public Intellectual," in *Sehnsucht: The C. S. Lewis Journal* 4 (2010): 44.

29. Lewis, "*De Descriptione Temporum*," in Hooper, *Selected Literary Essays*, 13–14.

30. Frederick Buechner, *Wishful Thinking: A Theological ABC* (New York: Harper & Row, 1973), 95.

31. As I point out in chap. 2, this distinction between "enjoying" and "contemplating" was very important to Lewis. He picked it up in 1924 from British philosopher Samuel Alexander's 1920 book *Space, Time, and Deity*. Lewis considered the distinction "an indispensable tool of thought" (*Surprised by Joy* [New York: Harcourt Brace, 1955], 218) and explained it to readers in his "Meditation in a Toolshed," in *God in the Dock*, 230–34.

32. C. S. Lewis, "Bluspels and Flalansferes: A Semantic Nightmare," in Hooper, *Selected Literary Essays*, 265.

33. J. R. R. Tolkien, *On Fairy-Stories*, ed. Verlyn Flieger and Douglas A. Anderson (London: HarperCollins, 2008), 73.

34. J. R. R. Tolkien, letter 163 to W. H. Auden, *Letters of J. R. R. Tolkien* (Boston: Houghton Mifflin, 1981), 212.

35. Paul F. Ford citing Augustine, in *Companion to Narnia: A Complete Guide to the Magical World of C. S. Lewis's* The Chronicles of Narnia, 5th ed. (New York: HarperCollins, 2005), 14–15. The quotation comes from a letter (Letter 130) that Augustine wrote to Proba, a Christian Roman noblewoman, which contains Augustine's only substantial treatment of prayer. This translation of the passage may be found in Milton Walsh, *Witness of the Saints: Patristic Readings in the Liturgy of the Hours* (San Francisco: Ignatius Press, 2012), 662.

36. Lewis, *Discarded Image*, 5.

37. Ibid., 185.

38. Space does not allow a thorough correction of this misunderstanding nor a full demonstration from the sources of the truth that tradition's function was always—at least until the end of the late medieval period—to protect and preserve the gospel and pass it down generation

to generation. Medievals had no desire to take away from or add to the primary revelation of Scripture for they knew perfectly well the biblical warnings against adding or taking away from Scripture (e.g., Rev. 22:18–19). However, two good corrections are Baptist patristics scholar D. H. Williams's *Evangelicals and Tradition* (Grand Rapids: Baker Academic, 2005) and Roman Catholic Robert Louis Wilken's *The Spirit of Early Christian Thought: Seeking the Face of God* (New Haven: Yale University Press, 2005).

39. Jaroslav Pelikan, *The Growth of Medieval Theology (600–1300)* (Chicago: University of Chicago Press, 1978), 9.

40. "For one reference to Wade or Weland we meet fifty to Hector, Aeneas, Alexander, or Caesar" (Lewis, *Discarded Image*, 8).

41. R. L. Wilken's phrase, formulated against arch-liberal nineteenth-century historian Adolf Harnack's accusation that the early church had engaged in a woeful "Hellenization of Christianity," which had obscured the beating heart of the faith—Jesus's message of love.

42. See, e.g., Lamin Sanneh, *Translating the Message,* 2nd ed. (Maryknoll, NY: Orbis, 2009), 94–95; Sanneh, *Whose Religion Is Christianity? The Gospel beyond the West* (Grand Rapids: Eerdmans, 2003); and *Disciples of All Nations: Pillars of World Christianity* (Oxford: Oxford University Press, 2008).

43. C. S. Lewis, letter to Dom Bede Griffiths, 4 April 1934, *The Collected Letters of C. S. Lewis,* vol. 2, *Books, Broadcasts and War 1931–1949,* ed. Walter Hooper (London: HarperCollins, 2004), 133–34 (emphasis in original).

44. Lewis, "Is Theology Poetry?," in *The Weight of Glory,* 119.

45. Michael Ward, *Planet Narnia: The Seven Heavens in the Imagination of C. S. Lewis* (New York: Oxford University Press, 2010), 28.

46. C. S. Lewis, letter to the Revd. Henry Welbon, 18 September 1936, unpublished, held at the Marion E. Wade Center, Wheaton College.

47. Ibid.

48. In a letter to Sister Madeleva dated June 7, 1934 (in *Collected Letters*), Lewis says:
    You will observe [in the lecture notes he had loaned her on backgrounds for reading medieval poetry] that I begin with classical authors. This is a point I would press on anyone dealing with the middle ages, that the first essential is to read the relevant classics over and over: the key to everything—allegory, courtly love etc—is there. After that the two things to know really well are the Divine Comedy and the Romance of the Rose. The student who has really digested these (I don't claim to be such a person myself!), with good commentaries, and who also knows the Classics and the Bible (including the *apocryphal* New Testament) has the game in his hands, and can defeat over and over again those who have simply burrowed in obscure parts of the actual middle ages. (2:142)

49. Ward, *Planet Narnia,* 28.

50. Lewis, *"De Descriptione Temporum,"* in Hooper, *Selected Literary Essays,* 5.

51. Ibid., 10.

52. Lewis, "Is Theology Poetry?," in *The Weight of Glory,* 128.

53. Lewis, "Learning in War-Time," in *The Weight of Glory,* 58.

54. C. S. Lewis, "Christianity and Culture" (1940), in *Christian Reflections,* ed. Walter Hooper (Grand Rapids: Eerdmans, 1967), 23.

55. G. K. Chesterton, *Orthodoxy* (New York: John Lane, 1908), 38.

56. Lewis, "Christianity and Culture," 23.

57. Ibid., 29.

## Chapter 4 Getting Thoughtful: The Medieval Passion for Theological Knowledge

1. To be fair, in that church of my youth most of these errant teachings were confined to the occasional guest speaker or admired TV evangelist and were not promulgated by our own pastors.

2. The early "desert theologian" Evagrius Pontus put it like this: "If you are a theologian, you pray truly, and if you pray truly, then you are a theologian" (*Treatise on Prayer* 60, in Patrologia graeca, ed. J.-P. Migne [Paris: 1857–1886], 79.1180).

3. Adam Barkman, *C. S. Lewis and Philosophy as a Way of Life* (Allentown, PA: Zossima, 2009), 212n241; citing Lewis, *Mere Christianity*, in *C. S. Lewis: Selected Books* [Long Edition] (1952; repr., London: HarperCollins, 1999), 331.

4. The "dinosaur" reference is to Lewis's self-characterization as a "native speaker" of the language of the early and medieval Christian tradition in the West, which he used in his address to Cambridge University upon being installed as the Chair in Medieval and Renaissance Literature in 1954. See "*De Descriptione Temporum*," in *Selected Literary Essays*, ed. Walter Hooper (Cambridge: Cambridge University Press, 1969).

5. Owen Barfield, *Owen Barfield on C. S. Lewis* (Oxford: Barfield Press, 2011), 10.

6. From the introduction to David Baggett, Gary R. Habermas, and Jerry L. Walls, eds., *C. S. Lewis as Philosopher: Truth, Goodness and Beauty* (Downers Grove, IL: IVP Academic, 2008), 15. The entry in Joel Heck's extraordinarily thorough online chronology of Lewis's life for the day of Tuesday, October 14, 1924, reads: "Jack's first lecture at University College, 'The Good, Its Position among Values,' is heard by four people," Heck, "Chronologically Lewis," www.joelheck .com/chronologically-lewis.php. This was a few days shy of Lewis's twenty-sixth birthday.

7. C. S. Lewis, "Autobiographical Note," prepared by the Macmillan Company in Spring, 1946, The Marion E. Wade Center, Wheaton College. MS 157.1, 1.

8. C. S. Lewis, letter to Mr. Young, 20 May 1943, in *The Collected Letters of C. S. Lewis*, vol. 2, *Books, Broadcasts and the War 1931–1949*, ed. Walter Hooper (London: HarperCollins, 2004), 575. Not surprisingly, Lewis's sense of the specialized, technical, intellectual nature of his quest led him to downplay that side of his conversion in *Surprised by Joy*, but those interested in that fuller, philosophical story can refer to his earlier semiautobiographical work, *The Pilgrim's Regress*. In the preface to the third edition of that work, he summarized his journey: "On the intellectual side my own progress had been from 'popular realism' to Philosophical Idealism; from Idealism to Pantheism; from Pantheism to Theism; and from Theism to Christianity." Lewis, *The Pilgrim's Regress*, 3rd ed., in *C. S. Lewis: Selected Books* [Short Edition] (1933; repr., London: HarperCollins, 2002), 12.

9. I note the use of the term "inkling" here—perhaps a foreshadowing, or even a source, of the name Lewis gave to his group of literary compadres at Oxford. This would cast a particularly philosophical light on the activities of that group, who provided for Lewis what he once called "the cut and parry of prolonged, fierce, masculine argument and 'the rigour of the game.'" C. S. Lewis, ed., preface to *Essays Presented to Charles Williams* (New York: Oxford University Press, 1947), x–xi, quote at p. xi.

10. C. S. Lewis, *The Pilgrim's Regress: The Wade Annotated Edition*, ed. David C. Downing (Grand Rapids: Eerdmans, 2014), 5.

11. C. S. Lewis, review of *Boethius: Some Aspects of His Times and Works*, by Helen Barrett, *Medium Aevum* 10, no. 1 (February 1941): 33.

12. C .S. Lewis, *The Discarded Image: An Introduction to Medieval and Renaissance Literature*, Canto Edition (Cambridge: Cambridge University Press, 1994), 75.

13. "Lewis insisted that philosophy is the transformation of life and not merely an academic exercise. In this respect he is in agreement with the philosophers of antiquity, starting with Socrates, who understood philosophy to be 'a method of spiritual progress which demanded a radical conversion and transformation of the individual's way of being.' Moreover, Lewis agreed with such philosophers that the truly philosophical life utilizes not only reason but also the imagination and other faculties of the soul to probe physical, metaphysical and mythological reality for answers as to how one ought to live." Barkman, *C. S. Lewis and Philosophy as a Way of Life*, 5, quoting Pierre Hadot, *Philosophy as a Way of Life: Spiritual Exercises from Socrates*

to *Foucault*, ed. Arnold I. Davidson, trans. Michael Chase (Oxford: Blackwell, 1995), 265. See also Baggett, Habermas, and Walls, *C. S. Lewis as Philosopher*, especially the section on truth.

14. C. S. Lewis, *The Last Battle* (New York: Macmillan, 1956), 179.

15. C. S. Lewis, letter to Arthur Greeves: Hillsboro, 13? January 1930, in *The Collected Letters of C. S. Lewis*, vol. 1, *Family Letters, 1905–1931*, ed. Walter Hooper (London: Harper-Collins, 2004), 857 (emphasis added).

16. In C. S. Lewis, *English Literature in the Sixteenth Century, Excluding Drama*, ed. F. P. Wilson and Bonamy Dobree, Oxford History of English Literature (New York: Oxford University Press, 1954), 29–31. Here is a sample:

> The humanists' revolt against medieval philosophy was not a philosophical revolt. What it really was can best be gauged by the language it used. Your philosophers, says Vives (*De Causis*, I), are straw-splitters, makers of unnecessary difficulties, and if you call their jargon Latin, why then we must find some other name for the speech of Cicero. . . . "Calle ye Thomas Aquinas a doctor?" said Johan Wessel, "He knew no tongue but the Latin and barely that!" We are invited to admire the Utopians because they could never understand the [scholastic idea of] Second Intentions (*Utopia*, II. vi). "Second Intentions," says Rabelais in effect, "ask whether a chimaera buzzing in a void can eat them. There'd be a proper question for a schoolman" (*Pantagruel*, vii).

17. Lewis repeats this defense (and appreciation) of Aquinas's breed in a letter in which he refers to him as "one of the great philosophers." "As I perhaps said before, a great many people think I'm being Thomistic where I'm really being Aristotelian. He's a top form boy, and I a bottom form boy, in the same school: what we share we get from the Teacher. I am certainly not anti-Thomist. He is one of the great philosophers." C. S. Lewis, letter to Corbin Scott Carnell, 10 December 1958, *The Collected Letters of C. S. Lewis*, vol. 2, *Books, Broadcasts, and War 1931–1949*, ed. Walter Hooper (London: HarperCollins, 2004), 995. Note that the Oxford don himself tended to owe his own philosophizing more to two of Aquinas's sources, Aristotle and Plato, than to Aquinas himself.

18. "Perhaps every new learning makes room for itself by creating a new ignorance. In our own age we have seen the sciences beating back the humanities as humanism once beat back metaphysics. Man's power of attention seems to be limited; one nail drives out another." Lewis, *English Literature in the Sixteenth Century*, 29–31.

19. Ibid., 11. Norman Cantor identifies this systematizing bent as one of the three essential aspects of Lewis's useful (as Cantor thought, still unsurpassed) characterization of medieval culture: "A second strand in medieval imaginative culture lay in the vast and complex, often university-based, learned conception of a cosmic and world order that came to fruition in the late 13th and 14th centuries and is expressed both in academic treatises and in Dante's Divine Comedy, which draws heavily upon this systematic learning" (Cantor, in his section on the "Oxford Fantasists," in *Inventing the Middle Ages* [New York: Harper Perennial, 1993], 214). Cantor argues that Lewis, since he emphasized this bookish, systematizing nature of medieval culture, was appealed to "by the neo-Thomists to support their point of view and confirm their program, which was to sustain traditional learned order in the midst of the disturbing variety and instability of modern life." In fact, says Cantor, "Lewis's phenomenal popularity in America in the 1940s and 1950s stemmed partly from the compatibility of his perception of medieval culture with neo-Thomist principles" (*Inventing the Middle Ages*, 215–16).

20. Many modern Protestants compound this caricature of medieval stupidity with a caricature of medieval Christianity. Bluntly put, they believe medieval Christianity was not real Christianity at all because it taught "works righteousness" or some such nonsense. Even a cursory glance at the most influential theologian on that era—Augustine—proves this canard false. When Luther taught "salvation by grace through faith," he was pitting Augustine's own teaching of grace against some of the great North African heirs (a decided minority) who had gotten their heads screwed on wrong and were giving human effort primacy in salvation.

21. I use "genius" here in its older sense, to refer to the movement's unique contribution, its particular and unprecedented "take" on things.

22. David Lindberg, "Christian History Interview: Natural Adversaries?," *Christian History: The Christian Face of the Scientific Revolution*, no. 76 (2002), www.christianitytoday.com/ch/2002/issue76/17.44.html.

23. Ibid.

24. Jaroslav Pelikan, *The Christian Tradition: A History of the Development of Doctrine*, vol. 3, *The Growth of Medieval Theology (600–1300)* (Chicago: University of Chicago Press, 1980), 257.

25. David N. Bell, *Many Mansions: An Introduction to the Development and Diversity of Medieval Theology* (Kalamazoo, MI: Cistercian Publications, 2000), 83.

26. Ibid.

27. For example, a common argument against the fourth-century Arians was that they arrived at the conclusion that Christ the Son was less divine than the Father (and indeed was a creature, not preexistent like the Father) because they treated Christian doctrine like an intellectual game and therefore sought to explain Christ in a consistently and purely rational way.

28. Again, "genius" here denotes not extraordinary intelligence (though an Anselm or an Aquinas fits that bill well enough) but a unique and unparalleled contribution in the history of thought.

29. Eugene R. Fairweather, *A Scholastic Miscellany: Anselm to Ockham* (Philadelphia: Westminster John Knox, 1956), 18.

30. For more on how Western civilization developed under the auspices of the church during the Middle Ages, see Christopher Dawson, *Religion and the Rise of Western Culture* (New York: Image, 1991).

31. For a corrective account of science in the Middle Ages, see James Hannam, *The Genesis of Science: How the Christian Middle Ages Launched the Scientific Revolution* (Washington, DC: Regnery, 2011).

32. See Josef Pieper, *Scholasticism: Personalities and Problems of Medieval Philosophy*, 2nd ed. (South Bend, IN: St. Augustine's Press, 2001), 61.

33. "If a question like the 'problem of universals' plays a large part in the formation of scholasticism, it does so ultimately because the solution affects the philosophical approach to God, the interpretation of the divine law for man's moral life, or the theological treatment of the Trinity, of man's sin, of redemption, of the sacraments." Fairweather, *Scholastic Miscellany*, 31.

34. Philip Schaff, *History of the Christian Church, vol. 5, The Middle Ages 1049–1294*, Christian Classics Ethereal Library, 1.1 edition, June 11, 2009, www.ccel.org/ccel/schaff/hcc5.html, states:

> Thomas made a clearer distinction between philosophy and religion, reason and revelation, than had been made before by any of the Schoolmen. The reason is not competent by its own powers to discover the higher truths pertaining to God, such as the doctrine of the Trinity. The ideas which the natural mind can reach are the *preambula fidei*, that is, the ideas which pertain to the vestibule of faith. Theology utilizes the reason, not—it is true—to prove faith, for such a process would take away the merit of faith, but to throw light on doctrines which are furnished by revelation. Theology is the higher science, both because of the certainty of its data and on account of the superior excellence of its subject-matter. There is no contradiction between philosophy and theology. Both are fountains of knowledge. Both come from the same God. (666–67)

35. Aquinas's idea here, expressed in G. R. Evans's words, *Philosophy and Theology in the Middle Ages* (London: Routledge, 1993), 11.

36. Kenneth Scott Latourette, *Christianity through the Ages* (New York: HarperCollins, 1965), chap. 6.

37. The English bishops of the thirteenth century, for example, made sure the laity had a firm foundation of Christian doctrine. They produced manuals of instruction for parish priests to use in educating their parishioners. One, the *De informatione simplicium* by Archbishop Pecham (1281), laid out the standard syllabus, which was quite detailed. It covered "the Apostles' Creed, the ten commandments of the law, the two commandments of the gospel, the seven works of mercy [see chap. 6], the seven virtues, the seven deadly sins [see chap. 5], and the seven sacraments. These were to be expounded to the laity in the vernacular four times a year." Joan Nuth, *God's Lovers in an Age of Anxiety: The Medieval English Mystic* (Maryknoll, NY: Orbis, 2001), 28–29. That same scholasticism-dominated thirteenth century birthed the Franciscan and Dominican orders—a new breed of monastics who traveled widely to preach and teach. With their focus on education, they not only preached a higher class of sermon than many priests but also built large hall churches designed specifically for preaching. This attention to lay education, though sporadic even in the late medieval period, would continue with the Jesuit movement of the sixteenth century, tasked by the "counter-Reformation" Council of Trent to improve the religious smarts of priesthood and laity alike. In short, the scholastics set the table for an improvement in theological knowledge across the *whole* church—not just for an elite academic few.

38. For the dynamics at work in this kind of "rationalization" (they are not always, or even usually, nefarious or even intentional), see Jonathan Haidt, *The Righteous Mind: Why Good People Are Divided by Politics and Religion* (New York: Pantheon, 2012).

39. James A. Arieti and Patrick A. Wilson, *The Scientific and the Divine* (Lanham, MD: Rowman & Littlefield, 2003), say this about Augustine:

> The difference between the thinking of Aristotle and that of Augustine is particularly striking. The doctrine of mystery seemed perfectly respectable to Augustine, indeed preferable to exaggerated claims of knowledge. The Manichaeans, with whom he had become disenchanted, had claimed knowledge but were shown not to know what they claimed to know. The Catholic Church did not make claims of knowledge about many subjects; instead it asked for faith, a humble admission that it did not have knowledge. (62)

We see Augustine (*Sermons for Christmas and Epiphany* [Mahwah, NJ: Paulist Press, 1978]) celebrating the mysterious paradoxes of the incarnation in a Christmas sermon:

> Maker of the sun, He is made under the sun. . . . Creator of heaven and earth, He was born on earth under heaven. Unspeakably wise, He is wisely speechless; filling the world, He lies in a manger; Ruler of the stars, He nurses at His mother's bosom. He is both great in the nature of God, and small in the form of a servant, but so that His greatness is not diminished by His smallness, nor His smallness overwhelmed by His greatness. (85)

40. Irenaeus, *Against Heresies* 8.2.9, in Philip Schaff, *Ante-Nicene Fathers*, www.ccel.org /ccel/schaff/anf01.ix.ii.ix.html:

> Their manner of acting is just as if one, when a beautiful image of a king has been constructed by some skillful artist out of precious jewels, should then take this likeness of the man all to pieces, should rearrange the gems, and so fit them together as to make them into the form of a dog or of a fox, and even that but poorly executed; and should then maintain and declare that this was the beautiful image of the king which the skillful artist constructed, pointing to the jewels which had been admirably fitted together by the first artist to form the image of the king, but have been with bad effect transferred by the latter one to the shape of a dog, and by thus exhibiting the jewels, should deceive the ignorant who had no conception what a king's form was like, and persuade them that that miserable likeness of the fox was, in fact, the beautiful image of the king.

41. Gregory Nazianzen, "The First Theological Oration—Introductory," section 3, *Christology of the Later Fathers*, ed. Edward Rochie Hardy (Philadelphia: Westminster Press, 1954), 130.

42. Quoted in vol. 4 of *The Nicene and Post-Nicene Fathers*, ed. Philip Schaff and Henry Wace, series 2 (New York: Christian Literature Company, 1892), 320n3.

43. "The Chalcedonian Definition," from §246 in *Creeds, Councils and Controversies*, 3rd ed., trans. C. A. Heurtley (Grand Rapids: Baker Academic, 2012), 405–6 (emphasis mine).

44. The title of Abelard's *Confessions*-esque autobiography gives one a sense of the flavor: *Historia Calamitatum*—that is, "Story of His Misfortunes" or "A History of My Calamities."

45. Jaroslav Pelikan says that in the medieval period it is the work of Christ and the reenactment and commemoration of that work in the sacraments that becomes the focus of theologians' greatest labors. So these two examples of atonement theory and sacramental theology hit the medieval bull's-eye theologically.

46. Contra the modern Bernard-versus-Abelard story described a bit later in this chapter.

47. The scholastics' "commitment to the progressive reasoning out of God's will required them to accept that the Bible is not only or always to be understood literally. This too was the conventional Christian view; since, as Augustine noted, 'divers things may be understood under these words which yet are all true.' In fact, Augustine frankly acknowledged that it is possible for a later reader, with God's help, to grasp a scriptural meaning even though the person who first wrote down the scripture 'understood not this.'" Rodney Stark, *The Victory of Reason* (New York: Random House, 2005), 11; citing Augustine, *Confessions*, book 12, chap. 18.

48. C. S. Lewis, *Mere Christianity* (New York: HarperCollins: 2001), 140–41.

49. Bell, *Many Mansions*.

50. John R. Sommerfeldt, *Bernard of Clairvaux on the Life of the Mind* (New York: Newman Press, 2004).

51. Abelard's most famous book, *Sic et Non*, simply laid out the contradictions between key theologians on a range of issues in order to "start the conversation." He did not resolve the contradictions and certainly did not do so in a heretical fashion, as the "logic-choppers" of the early church did.

52. George Marsden, *The Soul of the American University: From Protestant Establishment to Established Nonbelief* (New York: Oxford University Press, 1996).

## Chapter 5  Getting Moral: The Ethical Fabric of Medieval Faith

1. Interview with the author in late 2008, quoted in Chris R. Armstrong, "The Rise, Frustration, and Revival of Evangelical Spiritual *Ressourcement*," *Journal of Spiritual Formation and Soul Care* 2, no. 1 (Spring 2009): 113–21, quote at p. 115.

2. Carl F. H. Henry, *The Uneasy Conscience of Modern Fundamentalism* (Grand Rapids: Eerdmans, 1947).

3. "There seemed to be a sanctification gap among Protestants, a peculiar conspiracy somehow to mislay the tradition of spiritual growth and to concentrate on side issues. 'Liberals' sought to commend Christianity to its cultured despisers, and to apply its ethics to social concerns. 'Conservatives' specialized in personal witnessing activity, sermons on John 3:16, and theological discussion of eschatological subtleties." Richard Lovelace, "The Sanctification Gap," *Theology Today* 29 (January 1973): 363–69.

4. Christian Smith and Melinda Lundquist Denton, *Soul Searching: The Religious and Spiritual Lives of American Teenagers* (New York: Oxford University Press, 2005).

5. Ronald J. Sider, *The Scandal of the Evangelical Conscience* (Grand Rapids: Baker Books, 2005).

6. As reported in, e.g., Paul Pastor and Skye Jethani, "Willow Creek Repents?," *Parse* (online newsletter by *Leadership Journal* editors), posted October 18, 2007, www.outofur.com /archives/2007/10/willow_creek_re.html.

7. Adam Grant, "What Millennials Really Want Out of Work," LinkedIn, August 1, 2013, www.linkedin.com/today/post/article/20130801172600-69244073-what-millennials-really -want-out-of-work.

8. C. S. Lewis, *The Abolition of Man* (1944; repr., New York: HarperCollins, 2001), 26.

9. James Patrick, "The Heart's Desire and the Landlord's Rules: C. S. Lewis as a Moral Philosopher," in *The Pilgrim's Guide: C. S. Lewis and the Art of Witness*, ed. David Mills (Grand Rapids: Eerdmans, 1998), 78–79.

10. From the introduction to David Baggett, Gary R. Habermas, and Jerry L. Walls, eds., *C. S. Lewis as Philosopher: Truth, Goodness and Beauty* (Downers Grove, IL: IVP Academic, 2008).

11. Patrick, "Heart's Desire," 79.

12. Ibid., 85.

13. Ibid., 83.

14. C. S. Lewis, *The Discarded Image: An Introduction to Medieval and Renaissance Literature*, Canto Classics (Cambridge: Cambridge University Press, 1994), 204.

15. C. S. Lewis, *English Literature in the Sixteenth Century, Excluding Drama*, ed. F. P. Wilson and Bonamy Dobree, Oxford History of English Literature (New York: Oxford University Press, 1954), 62.

16. Walter Hilton, *The Scale of Perfection, modernised from the first printed edition of Wynkyn de Worde, London, 1494 by an Oblate of Solesmes*, introduction from the French of Dom M. Noetinger, Monk of Solesmes (London: Burns, Oates and Washbourne, 1927), 21 (emphasis in original).

17. C. S. Lewis, in the preface to *George MacDonald: An Anthology* (1946; repr., New York: HarperOne, 2001), xxxviii (emphasis added).

18. Robert Wilken, *The Spirit of Early Christian Thought: Seeking the Face of God* (New Haven: Yale University Press, 2005).

19. C. S. Lewis, *Miracles* (1947; repr., New York: HarperOne, 2001), 144.

20. C. S. Lewis, "Bluspels and Flalansferes: A Semantic Nightmare," in *Selected Literary Essays*, ed. Walter Hooper (Cambridge: Cambridge University Press, 1969), 265.

21. C. S. Lewis, "Imagery in the Last Eleven Cantos of Dante's *Comedy*," in *Studies in Medieval and Renaissance Literature*, Canto Classics (1966; repr., Cambridge: Cambridge University Press, 2013), 93.

22. C. S. Lewis, *That Hideous Strength* (New York: Macmillan, 1946), 7.

23. As David Downing, "*That Hideous Strength*," in *C. S. Lewis, Life, Works, and Legacy*, vol. 2, *Fantasist, Mythmaker, and Poet*, ed. Bruce L. Edwards (Westport, CT: Praeger, 2007) says,
> The Divine Comedy was never very far from Lewis's mind. He first read the poem, in Dante's medieval Italian, during his midteens, while studying with Kirkpatrick. He read and reread Dante's masterwork for the rest of his life, often praising it in his letters. According to George Sayer, Lewis considered Dante the most sublime of all poets and judged the "Paradiso" to be the greatest poetic achievement in European literature. [In footnote 11, Downing cites George Sayer, *Jack: C. S. Lewis and His Times* (San Francisco: Harper & Row, 1988), 63.] Lewis borrowed freely from the "Purgatorio" and the "Paradiso" in the closing chapters of *Perelandra*; in *That Hideous Strength*, he drew just as heavily on the "*Inferno*." (57)

For a complete treatment of Dante's influence on Lewis, see Marsha Daigle Williamson, "Dante's Divine Comedy and C. S. Lewis's Fiction" (PhD diss., University of Michigan, 1984).

24. Michael Ward, *Planet Narnia: The Seven Heavens in the Imagination of C. S. Lewis* (New York: Oxford University Press, 2010).

25. Thomas C. Oden, *Care of Souls in the Classic Tradition* (Philadelphia: Fortress, 1984), 28.

26. Lewis, "*De Descriptione Temporum*," in Hooper, ed., *Selected Literary Essays*, 2.

27. Rebecca Konyndyk DeYoung, *Glittering Vices* (Grand Rapids: Brazos, 2009), 61, drawing from Augustine, *Confessions*, 1.18.

28. C. S. Lewis, letter to Arthur Greeves, 30 January 1930, in *The Collected Letters of C. S. Lewis*, vol. 1, *Family Letters, 1905–1931*, ed. Walter Hooper (London: HarperCollins, 2004), 878.

29. Rebecca Konyndyk DeYoung, *Vainglory: The Forgotten Vice* (Grand Rapids: Eerdmans, 2014), 52.

30. C. S. Lewis, letter to Arthur Greeves, 30 January 1930, in *Collected Letters*, 1:879.

31. Though some material on vainglory can be found in the *Summa Theologiae*, I don't advise looking there for the really juicy material. For that, look to his *De Malo*. A good edition, which I had the privilege of using at the Calvin Summer Seminar under DeYoung and Kruschwitz, is *On Evil*, ed. Brian Davies, trans. Richard Regan (New York: Oxford University Press, 2003). For a sparklingly accessible layman's introduction to the whole tradition, with many points of application for modern readers, there is no better source than DeYoung's *Glittering Vices*.

32. Wilken, *Spirit of Early Christian Thought*, 267.

33. Protestant readers should remember that this was 1300: the cries for reform in the church did not arise with Luther, Girolamo Savonarola (1452–98), or Jan Hus (1369–1415). It stands to reason, since moral discernment was part of the culture of the church, that an acute moral critique would be turned back on the church when it was found to be immoral. Indeed, this awareness of corruption in church leadership started much earlier in the Middle Ages. Chris Wickham ("In the Medieval Moment," *History Today* 59 [2009]: 6, 20) notes that medievalists have examined "major developments" of the eleventh and twelfth centuries "that seemed to shift Europe's path decisively," including "a wide-ranging movement of criticism of the cozy relationship between secular and ecclesiastical powers."

34. Ronald B. Herzman, lecture 9: "The Sin of Simony," William R. Cook and Ronald B. Herzman, *Dante's Divine Comedy*, video course (Springfield, VA: Teaching Co. Partnership, 2001).

35. Quoted in Barbara Reynolds, *Dante: The Poet, The Political Thinker, The Man* (New York: I. B. Tauris, 2006), 167.

36. Ibid.

37. The forgery was revealed by Lorenzo Valla in his *De falso credita et ementita Constantini donatione declamatio* (1440, ed. Mainz, 1518).

38. Reynolds's translation from the *Inferno* 19.118–20, in *Dante: The Poet, The Political Thinker, The Man*, 168.

39. Geoffrey F. Nuttall, *The Faith of Dante* (London: SPCK, 1969), 3.

40. Barbara Reynolds, "Dante, Poet of Joy," *Theology* 97, no. 778 (1994): 266.

41. Dorothy L. Sayers, introduction to *The Divine Comedy 1: Hell*, by Dante Alighieri, trans. Dorothy L. Sayers (Harmondsworth, UK: Penguin, 1949), 11.

### Chapter 6  Getting Merciful: Why Medievals Invented the Hospital

1. Thomas Hobbes, *Leviathan*, 1651. Hobbes was of course not referring to the Middle Ages but rather, in the mode of political philosophy, to a lawless state of nature entailing a war of all against all. Nonetheless, the stereotype of lawless medieval brutality and cruelty stuck. However, this is ludicrously far from the reality of any subperiod of the era from AD 500 to 1500, including the time of the early medieval barbarian kings and the quite orderly feudal system that developed under them. Even the belief that the average medieval person lived only into his or her thirties—which comes from statistics heavily skewed by infant mortality—is inaccurate. If a person survived childhood, he or she had a good chance of making it at least to their fifties or sixties. For example, a thirteenth-century Englishman of the aristocratic class, at the age of twenty-one, had an average further life expectancy of forty-three years, bringing his age to sixty-four (or quite possibly older) before death. Of course, a commoner might live a few years less. See H. O. Lancaster, *Expectations of Life: A Study in the Demography, Statistics, and History of World Mortality* (New York: Springer-Verlag, 1990), 8.

2. C. S. Lewis, "Some Thoughts," in *God in the Dock: Essays on Theology and Ethics*, ed. Walter Hooper (Grand Rapids: Eerdmans, 2014), 158.

3. Ibid., 156.

4. Ibid.

5. Ibid., 157.

6. Ibid.

7. Ibid., 158–59.

8. Ibid., 159.

9. Ibid., 158–60.

10. Gary B. Ferngren, *Medicine and Health Care in Early Christianity* (Baltimore: Johns Hopkins University Press, 2009), 114.

11. Gary B. Ferngren, "A New Era in Roman Healthcare: How the Early Church Transformed the Roman Empire's Treatment of Its Sick," *Christian History: Healthcare and Hospitals in the Mission of the Church*, no. 101 (2011), www.christianhistoryinstitute.org/magazine/article /new-era-in-roman-healthcare/.

12. Ibid., 11.

13. Ibid., 12.

14. Timothy S. Miller, "Basil's House of Healing," *Christian History*, no. 101 (2011), www .christianhistoryinstitute.org/magazine/article/basils-house-of-healing/.

15. Ibid., 14.

16. Guenter B. Risse, *Mending Bodies, Saving Souls: A History of Hospitals* (New York: Oxford University Press, 1999), 96.

17. Ibid., 94–95.

18. Ibid., 100.

19. Ibid., 103.

20. Peregrine Horden, *Hospitals and Healing from Antiquity to the Later Middle Ages* (Aldershot: Ashgate Variorum, 2008), 138–39.

21. See chap. 7, "Getting Earthy."

22. C. S. Lewis, *The Problem of Pain* (London: Geoffrey Bles, The Centenary Press, 1946), 81.

23. In general, "sin was certainly regarded by early medieval authors as the cause of sickness in the sense that without sin there would have been no material evil," the linking of a person's sickness to some specific sin in that person's life "is very seldom encountered." Darrel W. Amundsen, *Medicine, Society, and Faith in the Ancient and Medieval Worlds* (Baltimore: Johns Hopkins University Press, 1996), 186–88.

24. Ibid., 187, quoting Jerome Kroll, "A Reappraisal of Psychiatry in the Middle Ages." *Arch. Gen. Psychiatry* 29 (1973): 281.

25. Fulbert of Chartres, quoted in Darrel W. Amundsen, *Medicine, Society, and Faith in the Ancient and Medieval Worlds* (Baltimore: Johns Hopkins University Press, 1996), 186–88.

26. Amundsen, *Medicine, Society, and Faith*, 186.

27. Ibid.

28. Risse, *Mending Bodies, Saving Souls*, 105.

29. Ibid (emphasis added).

30. Ibid.

31. Ibid., 106.

32. This shift was economic and social: "For almost 1,000 years, almshouses and hospitals had been organized and run in accordance with highly successful monastic models of prayer and work. Now, in the face of rapid population growth and urbanization, these establishments became inadequate purveyors of traditional charitable assistance. . . . Just at the time their own incomes started to decline, the monasteries' almonries were overwhelmed by the growing influx of needy individuals, a reflection of new and more complex social and economic conditions affecting the European population." Ibid., 107.

33. Ibid., 106.

34. Ibid., 109.

35. James William Brodman, *Charity and Religion in Medieval Europe* (Washington, DC: Catholic University of America Press, 2009), 2.

36. Carole Rawcliffe, *Medicine for the Soul: The Life, Death and Resurrection of an English Medieval Hospital, St. Giles's, Norwich, c. 1249–1550* (Stroud: Sutton, 1999), 5.

37. Nicholas Orme and Margaret Webster, *The English Hospital: 1070–1570* (New Haven: Yale University Press, 1995), 35.

38. Sheila Sweetinburgh, *The Role of the Hospital in Medieval England: Gift-giving and the Spiritual Economy* (Portland, OR: Four Courts Press, 2004), 21–22.

39. Adam J. Davis, "The Charitable Revolution," *Christian History*, no. 101 (2011), www .christianhistoryinstitute.org/magazine/article/charitable-revolution/.

40. Walter Hilton, quoted in J. A. W. Bennett, *Poetry of the Passion: Studies in Twelve Centuries of English Verse* (Oxford: Clarendon, 1982), 60.

41. Davis, "Charitable Revolution."

42. Ibid., 35.

43. Jennifer Woodruff Tait, "The Hospital Experience," *Christian History*, no. 101 (2011), www.christianhistoryinstitute.org/magazine/article/the-hospital-experience/.

44. Ibid.

45. Lewis, *The Problem of Pain*, 44.

46. Thomas Aquinas, *Summa Theologica*, trans. Fathers of the Dominican Province (New York: Cosimo, 2007), 1314.

47. C. S. Lewis, letter to "Mrs. Ashton," 18 February 1954, in *Letters of C. S. Lewis edited, with a Memoir by W. H. Lewis*, ed. Walter Hooper London: Fount, 1988), 438.

48. Lewis, *The Problem of Pain*, 98.

49. C. S. Lewis, letter to "A Lady," 12 September 1951, in *Letters of C. S. Lewis*, ed. W. H. Lewis (Harcourt Brace & World, 1966), 234.

50. C. S. Lewis, letter to Mary Willis Shelburne, 14 June 1946, *Letters to an American Lady*, ed. Clyde S. Kilby (Grand Rapids: Eerdmans, 1967), 55.

51. Another example is Lewis's legendary financial charity—see the comment, later in this chapter, by his friend Owen Barfield, "He gave two-thirds of his income away altogether and would have bound himself to give the whole of it away if I had let him."

52. Owen Barfield, *Owen Barfield on C. S. Lewis*, ed. G. B. Tennyson, 2nd ed. (San Raphael, CA: Barfield Press, 2006), 15.

53. Lewis, *Mere Christianity* (New York: HarperCollins, 2001), 86.

54. Barfield, *Owen Barfield on C. S. Lewis*, 14.

55. C. S. Lewis to Mary Willis Shelburne, 26 October 1962, in *Letters to an American Lady*, 114.

56. Lewis, "Why I Am Not a Pacifist," in *The Weight of Glory* (New York: HarperCollins, 2001), 79.

57. Ibid.

58. C. S. Lewis, "Answers to Questions on Christianity," in *God in the Dock: Essays on Theology and Ethics*, ed. Walter Hooper (Grand Rapids: Eerdmans, 2014), 38 (emphasis added).

59. Ibid., 109.

60. Ibid., 110.

## Chapter 7 Getting Earthy: God's Second Book—The Natural World

1. Jason Micheli, "Top Ten Heresies and Remedies for Them: #10 (Again)," *Tamed Cynic*, September 8, 2013, tamedcynic.org/top-ten-heresies-and-remedies-for-them-10-again/.

2. Ibid.

3. C. S. Lewis, "The Weight of Glory," in *The Weight of Glory* (New York: HarperCollins, 2001), 30–31.

4. C. S. Lewis, "First and Second Things," in *God in the Dock: Essays on Theology and Ethics*, ed. Walter Hooper (Grand Rapids: Eerdmans, 2014), 310; cited by Hans Boersma in his fascinating book *Heavenly Participation: The Weaving of a Sacramental Tapestry* (Grand Rapids: Eerdmans, 2010), 30.

5. Augustine, *De Doctrina Christiana* 1.4.4, ed. and trans. R. P. H. Green (Oxford: Clarendon, 1993), 15; cited in Boersma, *Heavenly Participation*, 30 (emphasis in original).

6. Boersma, *Heavenly Participation*, 30.

7. C. S. Lewis, "Learning in War-Time," in *The Weight of Glory*, 58.

8. Richard Wilkinson, "Missing Persons: Where Are All the Great Evangelical Artists?" *re:generation quarterly* (Summer 1996), www.ctlibrary.com/rq/1996/summer/2313.html.

9. Iconoclasm also arose in the eighth-century Eastern church, but it was soundly defeated at the Second Council of Nicaea in 787.

10. Bishop Joseph Hall, *Hard Measure* (1647; repr., London: n.p., 1710), 15–16.

11. Paul F. Ford, *Companion to Narnia: A Complete Guide to the Magical World of C. S. Lewis's* The Chronicles of Narnia, 5th ed. (New York: HarperCollins, 2005), 248–49. "All which is not itself the Great Dance was made in order that He might come down into it. In the Fallen World He prepared for Himself a body and was united with the Dust *and made it glorious for ever.* This is the end and final cause of all creating, and the sin whereby it came is called Fortunate and the world where this was enacted is the centre of worlds. Blessed be He!" C. S. Lewis, *Perelandra* (London: Collins, 1983), 199.

12. Boersma, *Heavenly Participation*, 23–24.

13. Lewis, "The Weight of Glory," in *Weight of Glory*, 42.

14. Robert Markus, *The End of Ancient Christianity* (Cambridge: Cambridge University Press, 1991).

15. Bernard McGinn, *The Growth of Mysticism: Gregory the Great through the 12th Century* (New York: Crossroad, 1996), 17.

16. Ibid., 18.

17. Gregory the Great, for all his repetition of Augustine, was "the most widely read of the Western church fathers." Jaroslav Pelikan, *The Christian Tradition: A History of the Development of Doctrine*, vol. 3, *The Growth of Medieval Theology (600–1300)* (Chicago: The University of Chicago Press, 1978), 16; citing Adolph Harnack, *Lehrbuch Der Dogmengeschichte*, 5th ed. (Tübingen: H. C. B. Mohr, 1931), 3:259.

18. See, for example, Jean Leclercq, *The Love of Learning and the Desire for God*, 3rd ed. (New York: Fordham University Press, 1982). Leclercq calls Gregory "the doctor of desire" (ibid., 31).

19. Carole Straw, *Gregory the Great: Perfection in Imperfection* (Berkeley: University of California Press, 1991), 8. See also C. S. Lewis (*The Discarded Image: An Introduction to Medieval and Renaissance Literature*, Canto Classics [Cambridge: Cambridge University Press, 1994], 122–38) on the *longaevi*, intermediate spiritual beings who move along the borders of the material and spiritual worlds.

20. Straw, *Gregory the Great*, 8.

21. Ibid., 9.

22. Ibid., 18n67.

23. Ibid., 9–10, 12 (emphasis added).

24. Ibid., 22, 25–26.

25. This period designation typically refers to AD 1000–1300, a particularly generative and vibrant period of medieval faith and culture—hence the name "high."

26. The following are a few of the propositions of Aristotle deemed heretical and condemned in 1270 by the bishops of Paris: "That there is numerically one and the same intellect for all humans." "That the soul separated [from the body] by death cannot suffer from bodily fire." "That God cannot grant immortality and incorruption to a mortal and corruptible thing." "That God does not know singulars." "That God does not know things other than Himself." "That human acts are not ruled by the providence of God." "That the world is eternal." "That there was never a first human." Ralph M. McInerny, *Aquinas against the Averroists: On There Being Only One Intellect* (West Lafayette, IN: Purdue University Press, 1993), 9.

27. Eugene R. Fairweather, *A Scholastic Miscellany: Anselm to Ockham* (Philadelphia: Westminster John Knox, 1956), 19–20.

28. Yes, I am aware of the "Galileo episode." In many ways this was the exception that proves the rule, though I don't have the space to examine them here. To learn more, see *Christian History: The Christian Face of the Scientific Revolution*, no. 76 (2002), www.christianitytoday.com /ch/2002/issue76/, especially my editor's note ("The Christian Face of the Scientific Revolution") and the interview with David Lindberg. See also James Hannam, *Genesis of Science: How the Christian Middle Ages Launched the Scientific Revolution* (Washington, DC: Regnery, 2011).

29. C. S. Lewis, *English Literature in the Sixteenth Century, Excluding Drama* (Oxford: Oxford University Press, 1973), 4.

30. He recorded these results in his *Convivio* (ca. 1304–7).

31. Kenelm Foster, OP, "The Mind in Love: Dante's Philosophy," in *Dante: A Collection of Critical Essays*, ed. John Freccero (Englewood Cliffs, NJ: Prentice-Hall, 1965), 45.

32. Timothy B. Shutt, "Dante and His Divine Comedy: Course Guide" (which accompanies the Dante audio course published by Recorded Books, LLC, 2005), 16.

33. Dante Alighieri, *Paradiso* 33.140–45, trans. James Finn Cotter, web edition by Charles Franco, www.italianstudies.org/comedy/index.htm.

34. Lewis, *The Discarded Image*, 203.

35. Josef Pieper, *Scholasticism: Personalities and Problems of Medieval Philosophy*, 2nd ed. (South Bend, IN: St Augustine's Press, 2001), 121.

36. Émile Mâle, *The Gothic Image: Religious Art in France of the Thirteenth Century* (New York: Harper, 1958), 15.

37. Ibid., 42, 29.

38. Ibid., 41.

39. Ibid., 40.

40. Ibid., 40–42.

41. Ibid., 14–15.

42. Ibid., 15.

43. Ibid., 14.

44. Ibid., 29.

45. Adam of St. Victor, Sequentiae. Patrol., cxcvi, col. 1433; cited in Mâle, *Gothic Image*, 30.

46. Petrus of Mora, *Rosa alphabetica*, in the *Spicilegium Solesmense*, 3.489; cited in Mâle, *Gothic Image*, 30.

47. Mâle, *Gothic Image*, 31–32.

48. Ibid., 28.

49. Ibid.

50. Pieper, *Scholasticism*, 116.

51. Quoted by David Lindberg in "Natural Adversaries," *Christian History*, no. 76 (2002), www.christianitytoday.com/ch/2002/issue76/17.44.html.

52. Boersma, *Heavenly Participation*, 99.

53. David Livingstone, *Darwin's Forgotten Defenders: The Encounter between Evangelical Theology and Evolutionary Thought* (Vancouver: Regent College Publishing, 1984); *Christian History: Debating Darwin*, no. 107 (2013), www.christianhistoryinstitute.org/magazine/issue /debating-darwin/.

54. That said, Baylor University, in Waco, Texas, is trying to get there. "Evangelicals . . . have nourished millions of believers in the simple verities of the gospel, but have largely abandoned the universities, the arts and other realms of 'high' culture. . . . Evangelicals [do not] sponsor . . . a single research university or a single periodical devoted to in-depth interaction with modern culture." Mark Noll, *The Scandal of the Evangelical Mind* (Grand Rapids: Eerdmans, 1995), 51.

55. Ibid., 253.

56. For more on the roots and fruits of this modern problem of self-discovery, philosophically examined and carefully narrated within the history of human self-discovery and self-definition,

see Charles Taylor, *Sources of the Self: The Making of the Modern Identity* (Cambridge, MA: Harvard University Press, 1992).

57. Lewis, *The Discarded Image*, 200.

58. C. S. Lewis, *Surprised by Joy* (New York: Harcourt, 1955), 199.

59. For example, see his *Abolition of Man*.

60. C. S. Lewis, letter to the "American Lady," 26 November 1962, *Letters to an American Lady*, ed. Clyde S. Kilby (Grand Rapids: Eerdmans, 1967), 110–11.

61. Lewis to Arthur Greeves, 12 September 1933, in *Collected Letters of C. S. Lewis*, vol. 2; cited in David C. Downing, *Into the Region of Awe: Mysticism in C. S. Lewis* (Downers Grove, IL: InterVarsity, 2005), 45.

62. Michael P. Muth, "Beastly Metaphysics: The Beasts of Narnia and Lewis's Reclamation of the Medieval Sacramental Metaphysics," in David Baggett, Gary R. Habermas, and Jerry L. Walls, eds., *C. S. Lewis as Philosopher: Truth, Goodness and Beauty* (Downers Grove, IL: IVP Academic, 2008), 228–44.

63. C. S. Lewis, "Transposition," in *The Weight of Glory: And Other Addresses* (1949; repr., New York: HarperCollins, 2001), 94.

64. C. S. Lewis, *The Last Battle* (New York: Macmillan, 1956), 179.

65. C. S. Lewis, letter to Warren Lewis, 24 October 1931, in *The Collected Letters of C. S. Lewis*, vol. 2, *Books, Broadcasts, and War 1931–1949*, ed. Walter Hooper (London: Harper-Collins, 2004), 7–8.

66. In writing the preface to the third edition of his *The Pilgrim's Regress* (London: Geoffrey Bles, 1943), Lewis makes this explicit: "I knew only too well how easily the longing accepts false objects and through what dark ways the pursuit of them leads us: but I also saw that the Desire itself contains the corrective of all these errors. The only fatal error was to pretend that you had passed from desire to fruition, when, in reality, you had found either nothing, or desire itself, or the satisfaction of some different desire" (10).

## Chapter 8  Getting Passionate: Medieval Faith as a Religion of the Heart

1. Joan Nuth, *God's Lovers in an Age of Anxiety: The Medieval English Mystic* (Maryknoll, NY: Orbis, 2001), 14–15.

2. Augustine, *Confessions*, trans. F. J. Sheed (Indianapolis: Hackett Publishing, 2006), 3.

3. Augustine, *Confessions*, trans. Maria Boulding (New York: Vintage Books, 1998), 5 (emphasis added).

4. C. S. Lewis, "The Weight of Glory," in *The Weight of Glory and Other Addresses*, ed. Walter Hooper (New York: HarperCollins, 2001), 25–26.

5. All three quotations may be found in C. S. Lewis, *The Pilgrim's Regress: The Wade Annotated Edition*, ed. David C. Downing (Grand Rapids: Eerdmans, 2014), 5.

6. Boethius, *Consolation of Philosophy* 1.4, trans. V. E. Watts (Middlesex, UK: Penguin, 1981), 46.

7. Boethius, *Consolation of Philosophy* 3.1, 78.

8. Ibid. (emphasis added).

9. Adam Barkman, *C. S. Lewis and Philosophy as a Way of Life* (Allentown, PA: Zossima, 2009), 245.

10. C. S. Lewis, marginalia in his edition of *King Alfred's Old English Version of Boethius' De Consolatione Philosophiae* 4.3, by Boethius, trans. King Alfred, ed. Walter John Sedgewick (Oxford: Clarendon, 1899), in the rare book collection, The University of North Carolina at Chapel Hill.

11. Barkman, *C. S. Lewis and Philosophy as a Way of Life*, 245. The Lewis quotation about "creaturely participation" is from *The Problem of Pain* (London: Geoffrey Bles, The Centenary Press, 1946), 41.

12. An important corollary of this teaching about human fulfillment (which owes something to Aristotle) is that the *farther* we get from God, the *less* human we become; in fact, we become bestial. Lewis conveys this in the endragoned Eustace—just as George MacDonald does in Curdie's power to feel, at a handshake, the hoof or paw hidden within the hand of decadent persons. This concept of a descent into bestiality also appears in one of Boethius's greatest students, Dante, who paints the principle vividly in the *contrapasso* (punishments fitting, even mirroring, the crimes) of some denizens of the inferno, who appear there in various animal forms appropriate to their earthly sins.

13. Lewis, "Weight of Glory," 26.

14. Clarissa Atkinson, "The Tradition of Affective Piety," in *Mystic and Pilgrim: The Book and the World of Margery Kempe* (Ithaca: Cornell University Press, 1989), 154–55.

15. Ibid., 130–31.

16. Robert Wilken, *The Spirit of Early Christian Thought: Seeking the Face of God* (New Haven: Yale University Press, 2005), xviii. "Theory," says Wilken, "was not an end in itself, and concepts and abstractions were always put at the service of a deeper immersion in . . . the thing itself, the mystery of Christ and of the practice of the Christian life." Wilken says that he has tried "to show the indispensability of love to Christian theology" (ibid., xviii). And indeed he caps the book with a final chapter about this "heart dimension" of Christian thought and life.

17. Gregory, cited in Bernard McGinn, *The Growth of Mysticism: Gregory the Great through the 12th Century* (New York: Crossroad, 1996), 61.

18. Wilken, *Spirit of Early Christian Thought*, 292.

19. McGinn calls this teaching "one of [Gregory's] most important contributions to the later history of Western spirituality." McGinn, *Growth of Mysticism*, 48. He continues: "Closely associated with *metanoia*—that is, 'change of heart' or 'conversion'—compunction has a rich history in both Eastern and Western Christianity. It was Gregory who gave it the most attention, though, and who made it a central value in Latin spirituality."

20. Ibid., 60–61. Gregory's teaching on compunction emerged from his "deeply felt sense of the radical insufficiency of all terrestrial goods in relation to those of the heavenly world" (ibid., 48). (As Augustine says, the fact that we desire something that earthly things cannot satisfy indicates that we are made for a spiritual fulfillment.) Gregorian compunction refers not only to simple sorrow for sin but also to "the whole of the Christian's attitude toward present existence in relation to the underlying desire for the stability and joy of heaven" (ibid., 49).

21. McGinn, *Growth of Mysticism*, 50. Note the parallel here to Lewis's observation that the experience of joy itself is one of longing (*sehnsucht*); there may be some fulfillment in it, but it always points toward further longing.

22. Anselm, cited in Atkinson, "Tradition of Affective Piety," 132.

23. Clarissa Atkinson notes the new subjects that Anselm and his circle brought into people's devotional lives: "episodes in Christian history, in the Gospels and the lives of the saints and the Virgin." Atkinson, "Tradition of Affective Piety," 131. On this "shift of canons," see Joseph Lynch, "Religion with a Human Face," *Christian History: Everyday Faith in the Middle Ages*, no. 49 (1996), www.christianitytoday.com/ch/1996/issue49/4908.html.

24. Anselm's prayers show an "unusual combination of intensity of feeling and clarity of thought and expression." Here is "a new note of personal passion, of elaboration and emotional extravagance" that would change devotional practice, opening the way to the "masterpieces of late medieval piety." R. W. Southern, *Saint Anselm and His Biographer: A Study of Monastic Life and Thought, 1059–c. 1130* (Cambridge: Cambridge University Press, 2009), 47.

25. Cited in Atkinson, "Tradition of Affective Piety," 131–32.

26. Atkinson, "Tradition of Affective Piety," 132.

27. Quoted in ibid., 32–33.

28. Daniel Harrell, "Preaching Bernard of Clairvaux: First Kisses and the Ecstasy of Worship," *Patheos*, January 10, 2011, www.patheos.com/Resources/Additional-Resources/Preaching-Bernard-of-Clairvaux-Daniel-Harrell-01-10-2011.html.

29. Bernard of Clairvaux, *Cantica Canticorum: Eighty-Six Sermons on the Song of Solomon*, sermon 69, section 7, trans. and ed. Samuel J. Eales (London: Elliot Stock, 1895), 425.

30. Bernard of Clairvaux, *Sermons on the Song of Songs*, sermon 20, section 4, trans. Killian Walsh, in *Song of Songs 1*, Cistercian Fathers Series 4 (Kalamazoo, MI: Cistercian Publications, 1971).

31. "I think this is the principal reason why the invisible God willed to be seen in the flesh and to converse with men as a man. He wanted to recapture the affections of carnal men who were unable to love in any other way, by first drawing them to the salutary love of his own humanity, and then gradually to raise them to a spiritual love," ibid., sermon 20, section 6.

32. John R. H. Moorman, *Saint Francis of Assisi* (London: SCM, 1950), 65.

33. Thomas Okey, Saint Cardinal Bonaventure, E. Gurney Salter, Brother Leo, and Robert W. Steele, *"The Little Flowers" and the Life of St. Francis with the "Mirror of Perfection"* (London: J. M. Dent & Sons, 1912), 333.

34. G. K. Chesterton, *St. Francis of Assisi* (New York: Empire Books, 2012), 6.

35. "His life was one riot of rash vows; of rash vows that turned out right." Ibid., 33.

36. Moorman, *Saint Francis of Assisi*, 21. Moorman also notes that Francis would often weep for hours at a time while considering the passion of his Lord.

37. Francis practiced ascetic disciplines to a severe degree; biographers agree their effect on his body shortened his life considerably.

38. G. K. Chesterton, "Christianity and Rationalism," in *Collected Works* (1904; San Francisco: Ignatius Press, 1987), 1:373–80; quote at 1:376.

39. Chesterton, *St. Francis of Assisi*, 376.

40. From the *Earlier Rule* of Francis, available at http://www.vatican.va/spirit/documents/spirit_20020113_francesco_en.html. Chesterton also says:

> Say, if you think so, that he was a lunatic loving an imaginary person; but an imaginary person, not an imaginary idea. And for the modern reader the clue to the asceticism and all the rest can best be found in the stories of lovers when they seemed to be rather like lunatics. Tell it as the tale of one of the Troubadours, and the wild things he would do for his lady, and the whole of the modern puzzle disappears. In such a romance there would be no contradiction between the poet gathering flowers in the sun and enduring a freezing vigil in the snow, between his praising all earthly and bodily beauty and then refusing to eat, between his glorifying gold and purple and perversely going in rags, between his showing pathetically a hunger for a happy life and a thirst for a heroic death. All these riddles would easily be resolved in the simplicity of any noble love; only this was so noble a love that nine men out of ten have hardly even heard of it. (*St. Francis of Assisi*, 7–8)

41. Dante, *Paradiso*; quoted in Wilken, *Spirit of Early Christian Thought*, 193.

42. Robert Wilkin argues that the *early* Christians had seen this too, in *Spirit of Early Christian Thought*, *passim*, especially in the last chapter.

43. "This new feeling toward the humanity and suffering of Christ, linked to a similar devotion to the Mother of God, spread throughout the twelfth century, led by Bernard of Clairvaux and the Cistercians, finding expression in countless meditations, poems, hymns and prayers, all designed to inspire and give voice to an intense, intimate love for the Saviour. The Franciscans brought such devotion out of the monastery into the market-place through their sermons and their advocacy of popular devotions to the infancy and passion of Christ. By the fourteenth century the influence of this movement was everywhere present." Nuth, *God's Lovers in an Age of Anxiety*, 17–18.

44. Atkinson, "Tradition of Affective Piety," 145.

45. Ibid., 146.

46. Ibid.

47. Walter Hilton, *Scale of Perfection* (London: Burns, Oates and Washbourne, 1927), 5–7.

48. Ibid., 318.

49. Julian of Norwich, *Revelations* (New York: Penguin, 1999), 129.

50. David C. Downing, *Into the Region of Awe: Mysticism in C. S. Lewis* (Downers Grove, IL: InterVarsity, 2005), 73–74.

51. Julian of Norwich, *Enfolded in Love*, ed. Robert Llewelyn (London: Darton, Longman, and Todd, 1980), 1.

52. Richard Foster, "People Worth Knowing: Discovering Devotional Masters," *Christian History: Mary in the Imagination of the Church*, no. 83 (2004), www.christianhistoryinstitute .org/magazine/article/people-worth-knowing-mary-issue/.

53. Ibid.

54. Julian of Norwich, *Revelations*, 117, 185, 123.

55. Ibid., 116.

56. Ibid., 86.

57. Ibid., 124.

58. Ibid., 72.

59. Ibid., 129–30.

60. Ibid., 159.

61. Ibid., 114.

62. Ibid., 140.

63. Ibid., 148.

64. Ibid., 104.

65. Ibid., 118.

66. Ibid., 36–37.

67. For a full treatment of this highly eccentric and emotional mystic (another polarizing figure in my classroom), see my chapter on Margery in *Patron Saints for Postmoderns*. In this book, I will only summarize this odd character and a few lessons we may take away from her life.

68. Atkinson, "Tradition of Affective Piety," 155.

69. C. S. Lewis, letter to Arthur Greeves, 30 January 1930, in *The Collected Letters of C. S. Lewis*, vol. 1, *Family Letters, 1905–1931*, ed. Walter Hooper (London: HarperCollins, 2004), 877.

70. Ibid., 878.

71. C. S. Lewis, *The Collected Letters of C. S. Lewis*, vol. 1, *Family Letters, 1905–1931*, ed. Walter Hooper (London: HarperCollins, 2004), 23n23; *Symposium* quotation from 192c, translated by Michael Joyce.

72. J. H. Merle D'Aubigné, *History of the Great Reformation of the Sixteenth Century in Germany, Switzerland, etc.* (Philadelphia: John Ball, 1850), 1:47.

73. Martin Luther, "The Heidelberg Disputation," Theological Thesis 20, in *The Book of Concord*, bookofconcord.org/heidelberg.php.

74. Richard Kieckhefer, *Unquiet Souls: Fourteenth-Century Saints and Their Religious Milieu* (Chicago: University of Chicago Press, 1984), 107.

75. Gerard S. Sloyan, *The Crucifixion of Jesus: History, Myth, Faith* (Minneapolis: Augsburg Fortress, 1995), 216.

76. Staupitz in D'Aubigné and Luther in "The Heidelberg Disputation," as cited in notes 72 and 73 above.

77. Neil Postman, *Amusing Ourselves to Death* (London: Methuen, 1987).

78. Margery Kempe, *The Book of Margery Kempe* 1.52 (New York: Penguin, 1994), 163.

## Chapter 9  Getting Human: How the Incarnation Lifts Up Our Humanness

1. At the time of the publication of this book, *Christian History* is very much alive, at www .christianhistorymagazine.org.

2. Chris Armstrong, "Mary: From the Editor," *Christian History: Mary in the Imagination of the Church*, no. 83 (2004), www.christianhistoryinstitute.org/magazine/article/mary-from -the-editor/.

3. Jaroslav Pelikan (*Mary Through the Centuries: Her Place in the History of Cultures* [New Haven: Yale University Press, 1996], 55) uses this awkward but clarifying formula, with which he replaced the suspiciously exalted modern translation "mother of God," to remind us that nobody who used the term in the early and medieval church actually thought Mary was somehow the progenitor of the eternal, immanent, preexistent Second Person of the Trinity!

4. Armstrong, "Mary: From the Editor."

5. C. S. Lewis, *Letters to Malcolm: Chiefly on Prayer* (New York: Macmillan, 1964), 42–43.

6. Ibid., 43.

7. Ibid., 41.

8. C. S. Lewis, letter to a Lady, 17 July 1953, in *Letters of C. S. Lewis*, ed. W. H. Lewis (New York: Harvest/Harcourt Brace Jovanovich, 1966), 250.

9. C. S. Lewis, letter to Mary Willis Shelburne, 2 April 1955, in *Letters to an American Lady*, ed. Clyde S. Kilby (Grand Rapids: Eerdmans, 1967; London: Hodder and Stoughton, 1969), 41. Steven P. Mueller pointed me to this theme and to these passages in Lewis's letters through his essay "Christology in the Writings of C. S. Lewis," in *C. S. Lewis: Lightbearer in the Shadowlands: The Evangelistic Vision of C. S. Lewis*, ed. Angus J. L. Menuge (Wheaton: Crossway, 1997).

10. C. S. Lewis, *Miracles* (1947; repr., New York: HarperOne, 2001), 173.

11. Dorothy L. Sayers, introduction to *The Divine Comedy 1: Hell*, by Dante Alighieri, trans. Dorothy L. Sayers (Harmondsworth, UK: Penguin, 1949), 11.

12. C. S. Lewis, "Christianity and Culture" (1940), in *Christian Reflections*, ed. Walter Hooper (Grand Rapids: Eerdmans, 1967), 23.

13. C. S. Lewis, *Reflections on the Psalms* (San Diego: Harcourt Brace Jovanovich, 1958), 68.

14. Will Vaus, *Mere Theology* (Downers Grove, IL: InterVarsity, 2004), 81–82; Vaus cites C. S. Lewis, *The Four Loves* (San Diego: Harcourt Brace Jovanovich, 1960), 17.

15. C. S. Lewis, *Preface to Paradise Lost* (New York: Oxford University Press, 1984), 72; cited in Jerry L. Walls, "The Great Divorce," in *The Cambridge Companion to C. S. Lewis*, ed. Robert MacSwain and Michael Ward (New York: Cambridge University Press, 2010), 251.

16. C. S. Lewis, *Mere Christianity* (New York: HarperCollins, 2001), 226.

17. Athanasius, *De incarnatione* 54.3: PG 25, 192B. As Lewis summarizes this famous state-ment of the principle of theosis in the top margin of this section in his copy of *The Incarnation*, "God became Man that men might become gods; He made Himself visible that we might know the Invisible: the Impassible suffered that sufferers might be saved." *Athanasius de Incarnatione: An Edition of the Greek Text*, ed. Frank Leslie Cross (London: SPCK, 1939).

18. Vaus, *Mere Theology*, 83.

19. Lewis, *Miracles*, 178.

20. Ibid.

21. C. S. Lewis, letter to Dorothy L. Sayers, 30? May 1943, *The Collected Letters of C. S. Lewis*, vol. 2, *Books, Broadcasts, and War 1931–1949*, ed. Walter Hooper (London: Harper-Collins, 2004), 577.

22. C. S. Lewis, "Panegyric for Dorothy L. Sayers," in *On Stories and Other Essays on Literature*, ed. Walter Hooper (New York: Harcourt Brace Jovanovich, 1982), 93.

23. Lewis, *Collected Letters*, 2:988–89.

24. Paul S. Fiddes, "On Theology," in *The Cambridge Companion to C. S. Lewis*, 98; citing Lewis, *Miracles* (Glasgow: Collins, 1980), 115.

25. Fiddes, "On Theology," 99; citing Lewis, *Miracles*, 128.

26. C. S. Lewis, *Perelandra* (1944; New York: Scribner, 1996), 184 (emphasis added).

27. Cited in Fiddes, "On Theology," 94; Lewis, *Mere Christianity*, 136.

28. Cited in Fiddes, "On Theology," 94; Lewis, *Mere Christianity*, 150.

29. Fiddes, "On Theology," 94.

30. Lewis, *That Hideous Strength* (New York: Scribner, 1996), 40.

31. C. S. Lewis, *English Literature in the Sixteenth Century, Excluding Drama*, ed. F. P. Wilson and Bonamy Dobree, Oxford History of English Literature (New York: Oxford University Press, 1954), 62.

32. C. S. Lewis, *The Collected Poems of C. S. Lewis*, ed. Walter Hooper (London: Fount, 1994), 49.

33. C. S. Lewis, *Prayer: Letters to Malcolm* (London: Collins, 1983), 121.

34. Fiddes, "On Theology," 96–97.

35. Lewis, "Transposition," in *The Weight of Glory* (New York: HarperCollins, 2001), 109.

36. C. S. Lewis to Mary Willis Shelburne, 26 November 1962, *Letters to an American Lady*, ed. Clyde S. Kilby (Grand Rapids: Eerdmans, 1967), 110–11 (emphasis in original). Lewis's last secretary and literary executor, Walter Hooper, identified the "American Lady" as Mrs. Shelburne, of Washington, DC. See Michael Travers, "C. S. Lewis as Correspondent," in *C. S. Lewis: Life, Works, and Legacy*, vol. 4, *Scholar, Teacher, and Public Intellectual*, ed. Bruce Edwards (Westport, CT: Praeger, 2007), 43n46.

37. Vaus, *Mere Theology*, 81; paraphrasing C. S. Lewis, *Reflections on the Psalms*, 134.

38. Lewis, *Miracles*, 244.

39. C. S. Lewis, letter to Arthur Greeves, 19 August 1947, *The Collected Letters of C. S. Lewis*, vol. 3, *Narnia, Cambridge and Joy*, ed. Walter Hooper (New York: HarperSanFrancisco, 2007), 1573–74 (emphasis in original).

40. Lewis, *Miracles*, 250.

41. Lewis, "Transpositions," in *Weight of Glory*, 113.

42. Paul F. Ford, *Companion to Narnia: A Complete Guide to the Magical World of C. S. Lewis's* The Chronicles of Narnia, 5th ed. (New York: HarperCollins, 2005), 57.

43. Ibid., 57–58 and note 5.

44. C. S. Lewis, letter to Hila Newman, 3 June 1953, *Collected Letters of C. S. Lewis*, 3:334.

45. William Short remarks on Francis's "immersion in the wonder of the incarnation." William J. Short, OFM, *Poverty and Joy: The Franciscan Tradition* (Maryknoll, NY: Orbis, 1999), 40.

46. Short, *Poverty and Joy*, 41.

47. Lewis's incarnational appreciation for the earthiness in medieval literature and drama—including the mystery plays—can be seen in an interview from months before his death. The interviewer asked Lewis about the source of the "light touch" in his writing, even when dealing with "heavy theological themes." Lewis responded, "I was helped in achieving this attitude by my studies of the literary men of the Middle Ages [Chaucer and Dante at least, one would think], and by the writings of G. K. Chesterton[, who] was not afraid to combine serious Christian themes with buffoonery. In the same way, the miracle plays of the Middle Ages would deal with a sacred subject such as the nativity of Christ, yet would combine it with a farce." C. S. Lewis, interview at Magdalene College, Cambridge, by Sherwood E. Wirt of the Billy Graham Evangelistic Association on May 7, 1963, in *God in the Dock*, 286.

48. Bonaventure, chap. 74, *The Life of Christ*, trans. and ed. W. H. Hutchings (London: Rivingtons, 1888), 248.

## Chapter 10  Getting It Together: Responding to Our Medieval Heritage and Reflecting on the Ascetic and Monastic Paths

1. Work with Purpose at Bethel Seminary, St. Paul, MN, and Opus: The Art of Work at Wheaton College, Wheaton, IL.

2. This was a phrase used by social gospel proponents in the nineteenth century; it translated Jesus's teachings on the kingdom of God into "ethical parameters governing human solidarity

and kinship under the universal paternity of God. This laid the basis for translating the gospel into a social program," the basis of America's civil religion. See Dale M. Coulter, "How God Became America's Father: Civil Religion and the Fatherhood of God," *First Things*, June 17, 2014, www.firstthings.com/blogs/firstthoughts/2014/06/the-fatherhood-of-god.

3. Catholic modernist thinker George Tyrell (1861–1909) criticized Adolf von Harnack's liberal Protestant view of Scripture with these words: "The Christ that Harnack sees, looking back through nineteen centuries of 'Catholic darkness', is only the reflection of a Liberal Protestant face, seen at the bottom of a deep well." George Tyrrell, *Christianity at the Crossroads* (London: Longmans, Green, 1913), 44.

4. Walter Hooper, "C. S. Lewis: Oxford's Literary Chameleon of Letters," in *Behind the Veil of Familiarity: C. S. Lewis (1898–1998)*, ed. Margarita Carretero Gonzalez and Encarnacion Hidalgo Tenorio, 23–46 (Bern: Peter Lang, 2001), 25.

5. Ellen M. Ross, *The Grief of God: Images of the Suffering Jesus in Late Medieval England* (Oxford: Oxford University Press, 1997), 7.

6. Herbert Butterfield, quoted in Darrel W. Amundsen, *Medicine, Society, and Faith in the Ancient and Medieval Worlds* (Baltimore: Johns Hopkins University Press, 1996), 332; cited in n23.

7. Amundsen, *Medicine, Society, and Faith*, 332.

8. Margery Kempe, *The Book of Margery Kempe* 1.52 (New York: Penguin, 1994), 163.

9. Jonathan Edwards, *A Treatise Concerning Religious Affections*, 1746. Several modern editions are available; the best introduction for lay readers is the modern summary by Gerald R. McDermott, *Seeing God: Jonathan Edwards and Spiritual Discernment* (Vancouver, BC: Regent College Publishing, 2000).

10. Many moderns make self-flagellation the symbol of monasticism, but it rarely crops up in the sources. Benedict doesn't mention it at all and in general warns against untenable extremes in monastic practice. Francis was certainly capable of it, but he did not impose any ascetic burden besides poverty on his order, wisely understanding that each person's path and disciplines must be tailored to his or her own circumstances and led by one's own sense of the Spirit.

11. "Everyone who competes in the games goes into strict training. They do it to get a crown that will not last, but we do it to get a crown that will last forever. Therefore I do not run like a man running aimlessly; I do not fight like a man beating the air. No, I beat my body and make it my slave so that after I have preached to others, I myself will not be disqualified for the prize."

12. C. S. Lewis, "The Weight of Glory," in *The Weight of Glory* (New York: HarperCollins, 2001), 31.

13. C. S. Lewis, letter to Arthur Greeves, 30 January 1930, in *The Collected Letters of C. S. Lewis*, vol. 1, *Family Letters, 1905–1931*, ed. Walter Hooper (London: HarperCollins, 2004), 877.

14. Ibid.

15. This is a term straight out of the medieval spiritual treatise *Theologia Germanica*, which Lewis read repeatedly and annotated copiously.

16. C. S. Lewis, letter to Owen Barfield, 3? February 1930, *Collected Letters*, 1:882–83.

17. C. S. Lewis, letter to Owen Barfield, 12 September 1938, *The Collected Letters of C. S. Lewis*, vol. 2, *Books, Broadcasts, and War 1931–1949*, ed. Walter Hooper (London: Harper-Collins, 2004), 231.

18. Hooper's note on this Greek term, ibid., 232n26: "'task' or 'work.'"

19. C. S. Lewis, letter to Owen Barfield, 12 September 1938, *Collected Letters*, 2:231–32.

20. Ibid., 232.

21. David Downing, *Into the Region of Awe* (Downers Grove, IL: InterVarsity, 2005), 23. Lewis mentions having just read the *Theologia* in the same 1938 letter to Barfield: "I have a lot more to say on this (I've just read the *Theologia Germanica*) when we meet."

22. C. S. Lewis, *God in the Dock: Essays on Theology and Ethics*, ed. Walter Hooper (Grand Rapids: Eerdmans, 2014), 211. This is very much what Bernard of Clairvaux said centuries before: our ultimate goal vis-á-vis self-love, which is only realized fully in heaven, is to love

ourselves for the sake of God—that is, with the fully self-giving *agape* love of God ("charity" in the biblical phrase) rather than the *eros* love of potentially selfish desire.

23. Ibid., 195.

24. On Lewis's spiritual disciplines see, for example, Wallace A. C. Williams, "C. S. Lewis: Spiritual Disciplines for Mere Christians," *For All the Saints: Evangelical Theology and Christian Spirituality*, ed. Timothy George and Alister E. McGrath (Louisville: Westminster John Knox Press, 2003).

25. Daniel Levitin, *This Is Your Brain on Music: The Science of a Human Obsession* (New York: Penguin, 2006), 197; www.audiology.org/news/musician-neuroscientist-interview-daniel-levitin-phd-author-your-brain-music.

26. "The thief does not come except to steal, and to kill, and to destroy. I have come that they may have life, and that they may have it more abundantly" (John 10:10 NKJV).

27. "A man will not roll in the snow for a stream of tendency by which all things fulfill the law of their being. He will not go without food in the name of something, not ourselves, that makes for righteousness. He will do things like this, or pretty nearly like this, under quite a different impulse. He will do these things when he is in love." G. K. Chesterton's Saint Francis of Assisi (1924; repr., New York: Doubleday, 2001), 6–7.

28. See the United Methodist Church's explanation of its "Distinctive Wesleyan Emphases," under the heading "Sanctification and Perfection," www.umc.org/what-we-believe/distinctive-wesleyan-emphases (emphasis added).

29. Friedrich Nietzsche, *Beyond Good and Evil: Prelude to a Philosophy of the Future*, trans. R. J. Hollingdale (New York, Penguin: 1990), 111.

30. Patrick Henry Reardon, "Scripture Saturation: To Achieve Holiness, Believed the Early Monks, You Must Soak in the Moral Sense of the Word," *Christian History: The First Bible Teachers*, no. 80 (2003), www.christianitytoday.com/ch/2003/issue80/9.30.html.

31. Dallas Willard, interview with author, quoted in Chris Armstrong, "The Rise, Frustration, and Revival of Evangelical Spiritual *Ressourcement.*" *Journal of Spiritual Formation & Soul Care* 2(1), (2009):113–21, quote at p. 115.

32. Christopher Brooke, *The Age of the Cloister: The Story of Monastic Life in the Middle Ages* (Mahwah, NJ: Paulist/Hidden Spring, 2003), 43.

33. Dietrich Bonhoeffer, *Life Together*, trans. John W. Doberstein (Harper & Row, 1954).

34. Columba Stewart, *Prayer and Community: The Benedictine Tradition* (Maryknoll, NY: Orbis, 1998), 32.

35. Ibid., 39.

36. Ibid., 53.

37. Ibid., 27–28.

38. Ibid., 54.

39. Ibid., 55.

40. In his chap. 72, on "Good Zeal," Benedict teaches that "obedience becomes fully mutual as the members of the community act with 'most fervent love,' vying to show their respect for one another, to bear one another's weaknesses of mind and body, to be obedient to one another, to prefer to benefit others rather than oneself." The whole Rule, says Stewart, is epitomized in the chapter's final words: "'let them offer the love of brother or sister selflessly to one another. Let them fear God lovingly, love their superior with sincere and humble love, prefer nothing whatsoever to Christ: and may he bring us together to everlasting life' (RB 72.8–12)." Ibid., 55, 59.

41. Ibid., 55.

42. Ibid.

43. Ibid., 29.

44. Ibid., 58.

45. According to Michael Slattery, "The Catholic Origins of Capitalism: Max Weber Clarified," *Crisis Magazine,* April 1988, www.crisismagazine.com/1988/the-catholic-origins-of-capitalism-max-weber-clarified:

> The monks founded capitalism by producing an agricultural revolution in northwestern Europe, Collins observes, and northwestern Europe, not the Mediterranean cities, was the cradle of our modern capitalist society. The rationality that the monks introduced into their agricultural enterprises was a specific application of a general rationality that they applied to all their activities. Similarly, in *The Dynamo and the Virgin Reconsidered* (MIT Press, 1968), Lynn White, Jr., places the monks among the leaders of technical innovation, in the technological revolution that occurred during the Middle Ages. The innovations of the monks in architecture, in agriculture, and other areas are by now well known.

46. This triad of approaches to teaching and learning the essentials of the faith has a venerable heritage. It corresponds to the three approaches of classical rhetoric: *logos* (an appeal to logic), *pathos* (an appeal to emotion), and *ethos* (an appeal to ethics).

47. This insight comes from the late Dallas Willard, who expressed it in interviews with the author, used in Armstrong, "Rise, Frustration, and Revival."

48. The distinctiveness of a Christian ethic may be understood mostly in the particular ways we discipline ourselves toward the good and the spiritual help we believe we can get in that discipline, not by and large in the shape of the ethic itself, which as C. S. Lewis teaches us in *Abolition* is largely a matter of universally shared understandings: we must not steal or kill; we have a moral imperative to protect the innocent from harm, and so forth. In other words, it is not particular moral injunctions (which are more or less universally shared between cultural and religious groups around the world) but rather the animating "theological virtues"—faith, hope, and love—that distinguish the Christian ethic from other world ethical systems.

49. Jonathan Haidt, *The Righteous Mind: Why Good People Are Divided by Politics and Religion* (New York: Pantheon, 2012).

50. Alasdair MacIntyre, *After Virtue: A Study in Moral Theory* (Notre Dame, IN: University of Notre Dame Press, 1981).

51. Jonathan R. Wilson, *Living Faithfully in a Fragmented World: Lessons for the Church from MacIntyre's "After Virtue"* (Harrisburg, PA: Trinity Press International, 1997).

52. Rod Dreher, "Benedict Option," *American Conservative,* December 12, 2013, www.theamericanconservative.com/articles/benedict-option/.

53. Jonathan R. Wilson, introduction in Rutba House, ed., *School(s) for Conversion: 12 Marks of a New Monasticism* (Wipf & Stock, 2005), 9.

54. Rutba House, ed., *School(s) for Conversion.*

55. Benedict's *Rule,* 4:20, trans. Terrence G. Kardong (Collegeville, MN: Liturgical Press, 1996), 80.

56. Jon Stock, interview with author for "Re-Monking the Church," *Christian History: St. Benedict and Western Monasticism* no. 93 (2007), christianitytoday.com/ch/2007/issue93/8.34.html?start=3.

57. Christine D. Pohl, foreword in *Inhabiting the Church: Biblical Wisdom for a New Monasticism,* ed. Jon R. Stock, Tim Otto, and Jonathan Wilson-Hartgrove (Eugene, OR: Wipf & Stock, 2007), vii.

58. C. S. Lewis, "The Weight of Glory," in *The Weight of Glory,* 46.

# Index

Printed and bound by CPI Group (UK) Ltd, Croydon, CR0 4YY

13/04/2025

14656457-0005